W0036768

Springer
Berlin
Heidelberg
New York
Barcelona
Budapest
Hong Kong
London
Milan
Paris
Santa Clara
Singapore
Tokyo

Piet A. M. Kommers
Alcindo F. Ferreira
Alex W. Kwak

Document Management for Hypermedia Design

With 122 Figures and 5 Tables

Springer

Piet A.M. Kommers
Faculty of Educational Technology
Division of Educational Instrumentation
University of Twente
P.O. Box 217
7500 AE Enschede, The Netherlands
E-mail: kommers@edte.utwente.nl

Alcindo F. Ferreira
Venusstraat 68
7557 XW Hengelo (OV), The Netherlands
E-mail: ferreira@edte.utwente.nl

Alex W. Kwak
Siriusstraat 60
7557 XW Hengelo (OV), The Netherlands

Library of Congress Cataloging-in-Publication Data

Kommers, Piet A. M.
    Document management for hypermedia design/Piet A. M. Kommers, Alcindo F. Ferreira,
Alex W. Kwak
        p. cm.
    Includes index.
    ISBN 3-540-59483-3 (softcover: alk. paper)
    1. Interactive multimedia.   2. Hypertext systems.   I. Ferreira, Alcindo F.
II. Kwak, Alex W. III. Title.
QA76.76.I59K66 1998
006.6-dc21   97-6606
                                                        CIP

ISBN 3-540-59483-3 Springer-Verlag Berlin Heidelberg New York

© Springer-Verlag Berlin Heidelberg 1998
Printed in Germany

Cover Design: Meta-Design, Berlin
Typesetting: perform k + s textdesign GmbH, Heidelberg
SPIN 10504404   45/3142 – 5 4 3 2 1 0 – Printed on acid-free paper

Preface

It all started with the desire to implement different versions of what we now know as hypertext. In addition to the idea of hotspots and inter-linking small fragments of text, we decided to visualize the relational structure in a graph called a 'concept map'. Many options were open at that moment. We decided to explore especially those mapping techniques that were ignored or not even discovered by others.

In the past five years we have designed and developed our own hypertext systems, not because there were no systems yet available earlier but mainly because we were convinced that many user support functions still had to be developed, such as tools for conversion, linking, authoring, orientation and navigation. Concept mapping proved to be crucial for many of these functions. That is why you will meet this approach throughout the different subjects in this book. To some degree we feel we were successful in our attempts to integrate the concept mapping metaphor in hypermedia; some of our systems are now in use as educational tools at various sites. Our latest project, HyPresS (Hypermedia Pre-sentation System), has gone commercial. We decided that it might make sense to produce a book containing what we had learned over the past years. The basic idea of using concept mapping stems from the period 1960–1970. This book mainly covers what has happened during the last five years, which most of the developments took place. What makes this book unique is the fact that each part of it has a different user perspective and sometimes starts from different exploitation views. The main idea suppliers were:

- The software engineers, who developed the different applications and provided us with insights into the problems of creating applications that can display hypertext, hypermedia, and multimedia documents.
- The publishers we worked with provided us with large amounts of material to experiment with. They wanted to keep the material in such a form that it would be platform independent, and still useful for paper-based publications as well.
- The editors, those who needed to import and upgrade the material for use with our and other systems. This was mainly done by us, so that we met the weaknesses of our approaches. Some of our applications were re-engineered to make critical processes more effective and efficient.
- The partners we had in the different DELTA projects (SAFE, COSYS, and COPICAT), educators, publishers, users, and developers.

- Our colleagues, educational and computer scientists working in the Faculty of Educational Science and Technology at Twente University.

The various aspects reflected in five parts including nine appendices are:

- **Hypermedia enterprises.** The types of enterprises involved in hypermedia, the problems and solutions to some of the problems.
- **Producing hypermedia.** Practical solutions to edit, author, import, and convert data. A selection of popular applications and formats that are currently used.
- **Graphs for concept mapping.** A somewhat theoretical part explaining what can be done with concept mapping to provide a hypermedia user with an overview of a database.
- **Navigation in hypermedia systems.** Based upon the formalisms for graph representation, but restricted to its more practical implications.
- **Case-based applications.** Seven demonstrators were made for practical settings in the industrial, educational, and publishing sectors. Quite a number of difficulties were encountered and finally translated into pragmatic solutions. These case descriptions may help you to see similarities between your own hypermedia case and those of our clients.
- **Appendices** contain detailed technical specifications for those who prefer to implement hypermedia tools themselves.

We would like to thank all those who inspired and helped us in the previous period of the European research and development projects and the HyPresS expedition, especially:

- Jan Peter Dijkstra, Hans Kingma, Jacob Sikken, and other colleagues in the Division of Educational Instrumentation and the TO-Laboratory in the Faculty of Educational Technology at Twente University
- Luc Röst and Aysso Reudink who were our sparring partners in the two EC DELTA projects: SAFE-Hyperate and COSYS
- Jef Moonen who stimulated these two projects
- Margriet Simmerling of Helix5 as she shared her expertise on the Copicat and the Euromedia EC projects with us
- Hans Wössner and Andrew Ross of Springer-Verlag and Carin Vrugterman who persevered in annotating and correcting the manuscript.

May this book help you and your colleagues in navigating the long roads between paper-based and interactive documents.

Enschede, October 1997

Piet Kommers
Alcindo Ferreira
Alex Kwak

Goal of this Book

This book will help you in making progressive steps from paper-based documents to electronic media like hypermedia, multimedia, courseware, and systems for on-line help.

Who is the Reader for this Book?

If you find yourself making more and more decisions about how to archive large documents, how to manage retrieval adequately, and how to include existing documents into CD-ROM-based hypermedia and World Wide Web pages, etc., then you are the ideal reader, who needs this book.

How to Use What You Learn in this Book

Of course it is of great benefit to both the 'information warehouses' and commercial and corporate publishers that many common software packages like those now available for UNIX, Windows 95, and Apple Macintosh already have tools for document management. But to do real work you will need practical guidance from successful projects in the past. This book aims to give you that support. It will serve as a pathfinder, announcing what you might meet some weeks later. It may also serve as a first-aid reference manual in case you come across concrete problems, like document conversion, navigation control, indexing, or co- and secondary authoring.

When to Put this Book Aside Definitively

In case you delegate the entire responsibility for your precious documents to another person or company, or in case you fully rely on your software supplier who says his product will do 'all the further document management without any problems', you don't need this book. However, we hope you will never experience this phase of blind trust as it might be quite disappointing to face the costs for document recovery. Our desire is that you gradually get more confidence to plan and decide upon the evolution of your documentary assets, partly by consulting chapters in this book. It might also be honest to say here that we still expect many new eras to come, which will bring ever new approaches to document management. However, in order to appreciate them, and to understand what they are pleading for, this book is in our opinion an essential first step.

Dedicated to our late colleague and friend

Professor Dr. Alexei M. Dovgiallo
December 21, 1937 – November 3, 1997

*Deputy Director of the International Research
and Training Centre at the V. M. Glushkov Institute
of Cybernetics, Ukraine Academy of Sciences, Kiev, Ukraine*

*We commemorate him as a great pioneer and founding father
of computer-based learning in the Eastern European countries.*

Table of Contents

Part I
Hypermedia Enterprises

1 Hypermedia Production Scenarios 3

    1.1 Introduction...3
    1.2 What are Hypermedia?...3
    1.3 Overall Scenario and Definitions...6

2 Market-Driven Scenario Elements...9

    2.1 Production 12
    2.2 Scenario Templates..13
    2.3 Scenario Templates Within the First Stream of Initiative............14
        2.3.1 First Stream, Template One......................................14
        2.3.2 First Stream, Template Two 15
        2.3.3 First Stream, Template Three....................................15
    2.4 Scenario Templates Within the Second Stream of Initiative........16
    2.5 Fourteen Steps in the Development of Hypermedia.....................18
        2.5.1 The Preparatory Steps 1a–1f....................................20
        2.5.2 Entering Multimedia Material 20
        2.5.3 Editing Multimedia...20
        2.5.4 Defining Properties...20
        2.5.5 Entering Properties, Adding Properties 21
        2.5.6 Automatic Linking..21
        2.5.7 Manual Linking, Adding Anchors.............................21
        2.5.8 Testing and Reviewing 22
        2.5.9 Production 22
        2.5.10 Conclusions..22

3 Sales and Royalties...24

    3.1 Rights..24
    3.2 Revising 24
    3.3 Re-using..25

3.4 Procedures 25
3.5 Conclusions 26

4   The Publishing Corporation Case 28

4.1 Public Information Division 28
    4.1.1   Management.. 29
    4.1.2   General Management... 29
    4.1.3   Marketing Department.. 29
    4.1.4   Sales Management.. 30
    4.1.5   Production Management.. 30
    4.1.6   Pick and Mix.. 31
    4.1.7   Administration 33
    4.1.8   Predictions About the Future 35
4.2 Scientific Information Division 36
4.3 Professional Information Division... 36
    4.3.1   The Market 36
    4.3.2   Data Management 37
    4.3.3   Overview of Use 37
    4.3.4   Data Entry.. 40
    4.3.5   Management Reports... 40
4.4 Training Divisions.. 41
    4.4.1   Prospectus 41
    4.4.2   Production.. 41
    4.4.3   Reference Material 42
    4.4.4   Homework Management and Administration 42
4.5 Annex: Text Circulation in the Production Process 42

Part II
Producing Hypermedia

5   Popular Formats 46

5.1 SGML 46
    5.1.1   Using SGML for Multimedia Development................. 46
    5.1.2   SGML Document Structure... 47
    5.1.3   Creating and Editing SGML 50
    5.1.4   Hypertext... 50
5.2 HyTime and SMSL.. 51
5.3 HTML 52
5.4 VRML 54
5.5 MHEG.. 55

5.6 CALS 58
5.7 TEX...58
5.8 Conclusions..60

6 Editing...61

6.1 Introduction...61
6.2 MS Word 63
6.3 WordPerfect..64
6.4 Implementing Your Own System 64

7 Authoring..67

7.1 Processes..67
7.2 The Primary Author 67
7.3 The Secondary Author 71
7.4 Tools for the Secondary Author...72
7.5 Extending Hypermedia to an Educational Tool 75

8 Preparing Textual Material 76

8.1 Introduction...76
8.2 Implicit and Explicit Semantic Information 77
8.3 Paper Text 78
8.4 Unstructured Text...79
8.5 Structured Text...79
8.6 Tagged Text...80
8.7 Automatic References..82
8.8 Converting SGML to RTF 82
     8.8.1 SGML to RTF macro..82
     8.8.2 SGML to RTF Translator application..83
8.9 Converting RTF to SGML 85
     8.9.1 RTF to SGML Translator Application..86
     8.9.2 RTF..86
     8.9.3 From RTF to SGML...87
     8.9.4 Implementation..89

9 Creating Hypertext..91

9.1 Storage: Compiling, Importing, or Indexing..91
     9.1.1 Database Selection 93
     9.1.2 Tagged Information...93

10 Picture, Sound, and Video Resources 95

10.1 Embedded Resources 95
10.2 Linked Resources 96
10.3 Hotspots Within Picture Resources 96
10.4 Conclusions 97

11 Managing Hypermedia Documents 98

11.1 The Management of the Production 98
11.2 Paper for Quick Annotations 99
11.3 Computer Assisted Document Management 99
    11.3.1 Creation 100
    11.3.2 Librarian 100
    11.3.3 Production 100
    11.3.4 Annotation 101
    11.3.5 Versioning 101
11.4 Outlining Tools 105
    11.4.1 Word Processor Outlining Tools 106
    11.4.2 Groupware Outlining Tools 108
    11.4.3 Limitations of Outlining Tools 109
11.5 Author and Editor Plans 109
    11.5.1 ASCII/Word Processor A/E Plans 111
    11.5.2 Groupware A/E Plans 112
    11.5.3 Project Management Tools for A/E Plans 113
    11.5.4 Limitations of A/E Plans 113
11.6 Why Still use Paper? 113
11.7 Conclusion 114
11.8 Enriching Information: From Implicit to Explicit 115
11.9 DIS: Documentary Information Systems 119

12 Popular Multimedia Applications 120

12.1 Microsoft's Multimedia Viewer 120
    12.1.1 Searching 122
    12.1.2 Browsing 124
    12.1.3 From Help to Viewer 124
    12.1.4 Conclusions 126
12.2 DynaText 127
    12.2.1 InStEd 128

13 Recipes 129

13.1 Introduction...129
13.2 Paper Recipes...129
    13.2.1 Figures and Pictures 130
    13.2.2 Computer Applications..130
13.3 Plain Text Recipes..131
    13.3.1 Conclusion 132
13.4 Microsoft Windows Help Recipes 133
    13.4.1 Creating Windows Help Files from Existing Material.................133
    13.4.2 Rich Text Format 134
    13.4.3 RTF and the Help Compiler...134
    13.4.4 Pictures...135
    13.4.5 Typefaces and Fonts 136
    13.4.6 Extending Help...136
    13.4.7 Weaknesses...137
    13.4.8 Examples 137

**Part III
Navigational Support**

14 Graph Computation in Structuring Hypermedia 142

14.1 Formalisms for the Representation of Relational Patterns.......................144
    14.1.1 Unlabeled Directed Graphs for
             Representing Hypermedia Relations 144
    14.1.2 Hypergraphs 145
    14.1.3 The Bipartite, Directed (Conditional) Graph
             or Petri-Net Graph..147
14.2 Unlabeled Directed Graph Reflecting Conceptual Entailments.................149
    14.2.1 The Problem Space of the Hypermedia User and the Need
             for Graph Computation 149
    14.2.2 Problem at the Level of a Complete Hypermedia Network 152
    14.2.3 Computational Approaches of the
             Hypermedia Entailment Complexity 152
    14.2.4 Structural Centrality Based on Direct and Indirect Influence......157
    14.2.5 Adjacency Matrix Representing Hypermedia Relations..............158
    14.2.6 Small Scale Example 158
    14.2.7 Hoede's Status Index 160
    14.2.8 Centrality Computation by Hoede's Status Index......................161
    14.2.9 Alternative Graph Computations for Structural Centrality.........162
    14.2.10 Rush: A Measure to Unify Centrality Based on
             In- and Outdegree..162
14.3 Graph Structures as Concise Conceptual Representations.......................165

15 Graphical Display of Concept Maps 167

15.1 Displaying Two-Dimensional Concept Maps................................. 167
15.2 Displaying Three-Dimensional Concept Maps............................. 171
    15.2.1 Illusions of Depth 171
    15.2.2 Vagueness.. 171
    15.2.3 Radius of the Concepts 172
    15.2.4 Shading Spheres.. 172
    15.2.5 Shadows 172
    15.2.6 Text Size 172
    15.2.7 Inner Sphere.. 173
    15.2.8 Algorithms for Showing 3D Concept Maps.......... 174
    15.2.9 Conclusions 175

16 Rule-Based Navigation in Hypermedia Systems 176

16.1 Coaching Methods.. 176
16.2 Navigation Tools.. 177
16.3 Navigation Rules.. 177
16.4 Implementation of Coaching Methods 180
16.5 Preparing a Path 184

17 Calculating a Path.. 186

17.1 Prolog Clauses.. 190

Part IV
Seven Hypermedia Project Cases

Case I   Publishers' Documentation Support System 194
Case II   Genealogical Research Support.. 197
Case III   Newspaper Archiving and Delivery on CD-ROM........................ 201
Case IV   Document Maintenance via CD-I 201
Case V   Preparing Encyclopedias for CD-ROM.. 202
Case VI   Managing Instructional Material 204
Case VII   Product Catalogues for Delivery on Demand 205

Part V
Appendices

Appendix A.   References 208

SGML.. 208
T$_E$X 208

Graphical Display of Two-Dimensional Concept Maps 208
General..209
Deliverables by the COSYS Project 211

Appendix B. Word Translation Macros 212

Appendix C. Glossary..219

Appendix D. First Demonstrator Case Description..223

Introduction..223
Top View...223
Zooming 224
Browsing...224
Pruning 224
Inside View...224
Example 224

Appendix E. Second Demonstrator Case Description......................................230

Introduction..230
General information 230
Use 232
Opening Texts..232
Opening Pictures..233
Opening an Overview 234
Selecting a Database...234
Opening an Article from a Text...235
Opening an Overview from a Text...235
Icons...235
Hotspots...235
Overviews 236
Overview Windows 236
Selecting and Deselecting Nodes..237
Dragging a Node...237
Opening an Overview from Another Overview 239
Overview Icons 239
Menus...239
Dialogue Change Settings...240

Appendix F. TextVision-3D...243

Adding New Concepts 246
Adding Relations...248

Deleting Relations.. 250
Selecting Concepts and Relations.. 250
Moving Concepts 250
Revising to Indegree... 251
Revising to Outdegree 252
Text Windows 252
Subterm View.. 252
Superterm View 253
Text View 253
Rotating the Network.. 253

Appendix G.   Prolog Interpretation of SGML Documents 256

Appendix H.   SGML ↔ RTF Conversion... 264

CPART.G.. 264
F.G 264
GRAMMAR.G.. 267
TOKENDEF.G 271

Appendix I.   Interesting FTP and WWW Sites.. 274

FTP Sites... 274
WWW Sites... 275

About the Authors... 276

Figures and Tables 279

Index 283

Part I
Hypermedia Enterprises

Hypermedia is a combination of hypertext and multimedia. A hypermedia product will typically contain textual information, audio, stills, and video, with a mechanism to jump from one part of the document to another, or even jump to quite another product like a page on the World Wide Web. The key players in hypermedia productions are:

- Publishers of books, reference and documentation works, magazines and newspapers. The traditional publishers probably have the largest amount of (textual) material available compared to other types of enterprise. Problems with copyright have worried some publishers to the extent that they are not willing to commit themselves to hypermedia at all. Other publishers have committed themselves only to a small extent.
- Music labels. Music and sounds are needed for many types of hypermedia. Given that music labels hold the copyright for a lot of music these are slowly dragged in by the other players.
- Movie and television networks. Both have the copyright for audio and video archives, essential for producing multimedia titles. Most of them have delegated the archiving job to special organizations and see no urgent need to re-exploit earlier recordings.
- New enterprises, dedicated to hypermedia development. Many of these enterprises have the knowledge to create hypermedia titles, but have problems with acquiring material copyrighted by others. These enterprises try to interest and involve publishers, music producers, and movie and television networks to put material at their disposal to be used in hypermedia titles.
- Although they are not hypermedia providers themselves, hardware manufacturers also play a role, as they decide upon the final standards in hypermedia hardware.

It may be clear that the different key players are dependent on each other to a certain extent. A publisher needs support from audio and video providers in order to transform hypertext into real multimedia. Also, most of the key players are not very technology-oriented. They need the knowledge of specialized mul-timedia enterprises to create successful titles. Multimedia are becoming im-portant because the infrastructure for playing multimedia is now becoming available. The introduction of the information highway that gives on-line access to information anywhere in the world is one part of the infrastructure. CD-I players and personal computers with CD-ROM drives are another part. CDs provide enough storage at a reasonable price to store realistic hypermedia applications.

This part is divided into several subparts:

A. Hypermedia production scenarios, market-driven scenario elements, production and scenario templates
B. Sales and royalties, about copyrights, revising, reusing
C. Management at large publishing corporations. An overview of how a publishing corporation is structured and how it functions.

1 Hypermedia Production Scenarios [1]

1.1
Introduction

The development of hypermedia requires new ways of producing. Compared with traditional paper based media, hypermedia offer an extra dimension: interactivity. This interactivity gives the user fascinating possibilities, but it makes producing hypermedia more complex and more expensive. Hypermedia publishers need a way to deal with the greater complexity without increasing the costs as compared with traditional paper-based media. A number of scenarios will be outlined in this chapter, in order to raise awareness of typical situations in the case of hypermedia. One of the most efficient ways to produce hyper-media may be the use of existing material (texts, photographs, drawings, etc.). This means that in fact there will be several times at which authoring activities take place. This chapter gives you an outline of different scenarios and scenario templates for the development of hypermedia, specifically for educational hypermedia. As we believe hypermedia need a specific approach in design and development, it is worth giving a preliminary view of its characteristics before actually going into details of co-operation phases between the three partners involved.

1.2
What are Hypermedia?

Hypermedia are multimedia databases which allow the user to browse through all types of information. Besides that, hypermedia facilitate the processes of association and exploration which are vital to learning and maintaining attention in the user. To be more precise, browsing is the walk through aspects of meaning. Say you face a descriptive text about *combustion engines*, and see the word *ignition* in the explanation. At that time you may leave your general scope to learn all about the generality of combustion engines, and zoom in on the aspect of ignition. By clicking on *ignition* you are brought by the system to

---

[1] This chapter is based on an earlier published article named "Scenarios for the development of educational hypermedia" by P.A.M. Kommers (1993) in the journal ETTI 30 (3), 234–254. Re-use of this article was kindly permitted by Kogan Page Limited.

a new item, which may be text, a picture, a schematic animation, or even a video fragment which ultimately supplies an answer to your interest about ignition. This new item about ignition (in general) may evoke a new reaction from the user, e.g. going back to combustion engines in general, or digressing on a specific part of the ignition system.

It will be clear that the main part of a hypermedia system is the hypermedia database (in short, the hyperbase). In the hyperbase is the collection of information items, but even more crucially the information about the connections between these items. In the DELTA (Development of European Learning through Technological Advance) SAFE-Hyperate Project we focused on scenarios for upgrading existing information resources such as reference manuals, pictures, etc., so that they became effective ingredients for a hyperbase (Hatzopoulos et al., 1990). An important point in our explorations was the definition of a language expressing meta information. The language should allow us to express all types of relations between the modalities of the items. In other words, beside the text resources to be presented to the user, we needed a grammar to define the relations between for instance a video fragment and a text fragment. This chapter will depict the stages in primary and secondary authoring, making use of SGML (Standard Generalized Markup Language, a language used extensively by publishers. SGML is an International Standard, ISO 8879; see also ISO 8879–1986e and ISO/IEC JTC 1/SC 18, 1990). The reasons for using SGML are:

1. It meets the requirements of a syntax based on a formal grammar.
2. It allows the authors at several stages to add new semantic attributes to the hyperbase.
3. It is capable of describing the semantic relations between elements of text or textual labels referring to non-text items. These relations in themselves can also be described at a meta- level.
4. It is the default markup language in many of the larger publishing companies, so it unifies the techniques for new hypermedia projects with traditional publications.

Example of an SGML-based media description (reference from a picture to another item):

```
<title>            =    <open_title><text><Close_title>
<coordinates>      =    x-pos,y-pos,width,height
<picture_ref>      =    <open_ref><text><open_hotspot>
                        <coordinates><close_ref>
<picture_          =    <open_pic><open_filename><text>
definition>             <close_filename>[title]picture_ref,
                        [picture_ref,..]]<close_pic>
```

The example above describes the syntax elements occurring while assigning a hotspot area in a picture image to another article. The co-ordinates indicate the location of the hotspot.

The production of educational hypermedia is not only the solution to a routine request for multimedia computer applications. It is also the answer to technical and commercial questions blocking the way to a more intimate symbiosis between publishers and electronic companies, who will become partners in the near future. Three types of partners will be involved in the production and commercialization of hypermedia:

- Traditional publishing companies;
- Dedicated (small) companies who specialize in developing hypermedia user interfaces and tools for resource preparation, and who in many cases are developing customized courseware for training;
- Electronic industries playing an important role in raising standard(s) for hypermedia players and deliverables like CD-ROM(XA), CD-I, CDTV, DVI, etc., and in actually mastering and reproducing data on optical storage media.

Due to the differences in commercial marketing and technical approaches of publishing companies on one side and electronic industries on the other, several scenarios for cooperation between the three partners may emerge. As long as there is no external demand for hypermedia, these three types of partners need to cooperate in symbiosis and share the commercial risk proportionally. The most feasible scenario in this phase is that a traditional publisher takes the initiative to exploit existent information resources in a hypermedia format, because (s)he is familiar with selling information and because (s)he possesses already large domains of information. The two other partners can contribute by developing hardware and software. The two intriguing questions in this chapter addressing the technology to produce hypermedia are:

- What is the type of cooperation between the first and secondary author, before a first-level hypermedia framework arises? The first author is the creator of new information or new ideas. The secondary author is he or she who upgrades existing information so that it can be encapsulated in a hypermedia system.
- What types of scenario (or scenario templates) may we expect as several fields of expertise come together in hypermedia production?

In the last section of this chapter a scenario template is derived from these questions. This template gives an overview of the different actions that need to be taken, in their most probable order, with some specifications of the tools needed by the actors.

Finally a predictive view is given about the persistence of SGML-based hypermedia resources for a variety of educational media in next future.

1.3
Overall Scenario and Definitions

The development of hypermedia requires new ways of producing. Compared with traditional linear media like paper-based editions or broadcast audio and video, hypermedia offer an extra dimension of interactivity. This interactivity gives the user freedom and above all the feeling of unique adventure, but at the same time it makes producing hypermedia more complex and more expensive.

A number of scenario templates will be outlined in this chapter in order to demonstrate some typical situations in the case of hypermedia. The authoring of hypermedia requires a new approach to deal with both its hypertext and multimedia aspects (Kommers, 1988; Kommers et al., 1989). Consider the traditional publishing process (Figure 1):

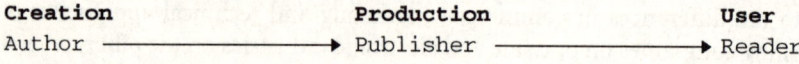

Creation   **Production**   **User**
Author ─────────────────▶ Publisher ──────────────────▶ Reader

Figure 1. The traditional publishing process

The publisher is an intermediate between the author (writers, photographers, artists, etc.) on one side, and readers on the other.

The product is on paper. The process is sequential, so production is straightforward in principle. In practice, the role of the author is split into three separately identifiable steps, as shown in Figure 2. The first author is responsible for the creation of original text, the publisher is responsible for the design of the presentation of the text, and a 'secondary author' or editor revises newly created and existing material for its particular application.

While there is little commercial experience with publishing hypermedia, it is reasonable to extrapolate existing procedures to hypermedia authoring as shown in Figure 2.

Creation   **Design**   **Upgrading**   **Production**   **Product**
1st Author ─▶ Publisher ─▶ 2nd Author ─▶ Publisher   ─▶ Hypermedia User

Figure 2. Extended production process for conventional materials

One of the most efficient ways to produce hypermedia is to make use of existing material (texts, photographs, drawings, etc.) (Frisse, 1988a and 1988b). This means that the extended production process can be used as a general scenario for the production of hypermedia.

In the case of producing hypermedia an extra dimension is added: the interactivity has to be built in. In fact this is quite a specialized activity, for which the original author (from here on called the first author) may not be equipped well enough, especially if the publisher wants to re-use existing material. So we expect that usually a secondary author will upgrade the resources for the hypermedia system. Most of the time this phase of upgrading will be used to interrelate (or link) self-contained information elements (items). Also, when producing hypermedia, the publisher will still be responsible for the overall quality of the authoring and production process.

In cases when hypermedia resources are made from scratch, the functions of first and secondary authors may be combined in one person. The process would be as shown in Figure 3.

Design	Authoring and linking items	Production	Exploration
Publisher → Author	─────────────────────→	Publisher →	Hypermedia user

Figure 3. The hypermedia publishing process, based on new material

One characteristic of hypermedia which complicates the phase of authoring and linking is the widespread expectation about its educational value. Before they are finally ready for educational or training situations a third actor (called the tertiary author) plays a role.

He or she mediates between the generality of published information resources and the more specific learning goals to be met in a particular setting (Waterworth & Chignell, 1989). For some learning situations the third actor is a curriculum designer, in other cases a teacher responsible for a smaller group of students. He or she relieves the publisher from differentiating the learning material for all kinds of specific situations. At the same time, however, the publisher faces the task of facilitating the work of the third actor. One important extra to be supported by the publisher is the specification of relations between the items in the hypermedia resources. After the publisher releases a hypermedia product, two types of users emerge:

- instructional agent(s) and
- learner(s)

In case of entertainment products the publisher will directly address the end user, while educational settings will introduce an instructional agent who installs extra information and didactic arguments in the hypermedia database (see Kibby, 1988, and Kibby et al., 1991). The efforts of secondary authors can be decreased as the instructional agent is prepared to define clear learning goals and minimum requirements for the learner to be met before he or she starts the hypermedia learning session (see Kommers, Grabinger & Dunlap, 1996). In the composition of scenarios we face two unknown variables:

- Generic facilities of hypermedia systems. This means that scenarios for hypermedia production should still be open to a broad potential of multimedia and to new types of mixed-initiative and exploratory learning approaches (Price & Schneider, 1988).

- The impact of secondary authors and instructional agents as they interact with a hypermedia system.

We perceive that authors need additional effort to define more explicit relations between concepts in the information to be delivered. This notion gives some intuition about the necessary milestones to be reached and the difficult decisions to be made in hypermedia production. As there are many different ways to create hypermedia, milestones are ultimately expressed in the content of different scenarios. Publishers are crucial actors in the hypermedia enterprise, first of all because they are responsible for its commercial success, and secondly because they decide upon the production techniques to be used. Their only hope is that the electronic industry is willing to cooperate, in order to create a demand for products like CD-ROM (XA) and CD-I.

2 Market-Driven Scenario Elements

A major feature of the scenario for producing hypermedia is the orientation on the market and sales prospects. This means that instead of the technical procedures for actual design and development, the publisher will usually start with the marketing and selling aspect. The five steps to take, as pictured in Figure 4:

1. Identifying profitable learning resources, on the basis of urgency, uniqueness, the availability of expertise, cost of delivery, etc. Text-based resources are prominent as they can be processed autonomously by hypertext systems (Constanzo, 1989). In case the available resources contain video and/or audio fragments, explicit descriptions of how they allow free browsing should be added to them. For sake of compatibility with other international project approaches, we suggest delivering these external descriptions in SGML. The reasons for delivering the external descriptions in SGML are that this encoding grammar is:

   - Easy to interpret
   - Easy to replace by typesetting codes (important for publisher)
   - Usable for typesetters (also important for publishers)
   - Usable for electronic media, databases, etc.
   - Easy to manipulate (at the level of plain text)
   - Flexible.

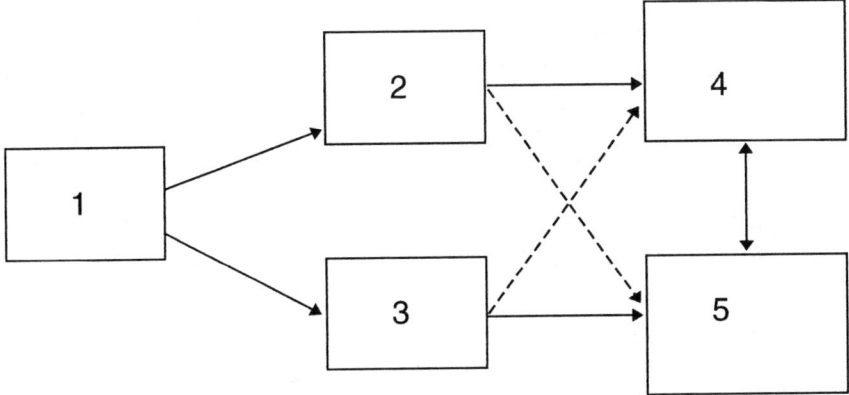

Figure 4. Steps to take

2. Identifying the target group in the market. The group can be assigned to one of the three main markets:

- Consumer market
- Educational market
- Business market.

The unification of the educational and business marketing is promising, as it covers the need for efficient industrial training. The three of them need a different approach in terms of domain definition, marketing, delivery systems, maintenance, and after-sales support. High investments for new educational media can only be paid if the business market accepts high prices for the development phase (return on investment). CD-ROM-based hypermedia allow multiple usability: One disc can be used in a variety of applications, as its information is controlled by a computer program which is external to the CD medium. A reference manual or an encyclopedia on CD-ROM can for instance be addressed by:

- An adventure program (entertainment for the consumer market)
- A courseware module for a specific part in, e.g., a secondary school curriculum
- A diagnostic aid for the St. John's ambulance brigade.

Another example of market-spanning is to reuse industrial information resources by integrating them in commercially available training packages.

3. Identifying adequate advertising, selling and distribution channels. For example, if selling encyclopedias at the front door is forbidden by law (book-hawking) it is necessary to focus on mail order, etc.
4. Defining the information domain, adapting to the interest in the target group. Define the necessary level of appeal. For example, study material may demand a higher level of attention and perseverance from the user than general material for entertainment. The question here is not only what to say, but how to say it. The ratio between textual, graphic, and audio information becomes important. The role of computers in selecting the information domain will become obvious in the near future. At this moment we can only speculate that large publishing companies may start to build databases with their own editions from the last ten years. Databases containing fields of expertise with the associated documents of many publishers are still far away. Good examples of bibliographic (CD-ROM-based) databases are:

- ERIC (Current Index to Journals in Education)
- DIALOG OnDisc (trademark of Dialog Information Services, Inc.)
- UMI periodical abstracts on disc (by Bell & Howell Company), etc.

Bibliographic databases can supply an answer to different types of questions. Important questions to be answered in the context of screening resources for potential hypermedia are: "Who is the owner of the information?" and "How much does the owner ask to reuse a certain resource?"; this information is not present in the available tools as described before. Obtaining copyright licenses is an important phase in the actual acquisition of information resources. The negotiation between publishers about the price of reusing each other's information will be more intense as hypermedia become a popular means of distribution.

5. Choose the actual delivery medium. Beside books and videotapes, broadcasting and telephone channels (dialing 06 numbers) play a role. The media repertoire was substantially enlarged when interactive techniques became available with computer-based media such as interactive video disc, CD-ROM(XA), CD-I, and DV-I.

Check-list for market analysis:

a How to reach the target group
b Needs and/or wishes of target group
c Educational level of target group
d Goals: information/learning/game
e Language needed
f Profitability analysis
g Hardware present at buyers
h Is copy protection necessary?
i Medium: magnetic or optical?
j Competition with other products
k Competition with other media.

The procedure for processing the revealed data by the check-list will be slightly different for the three markets. The factors to be considered in decreasing order of importance per type of market are:

- Consumer market: a, g, h, f, j, e
- Educational market: b, d, j, k, c, i, f
- Business market: f, b, d, c

We may expect the educational market to be the most sensitive regarding the selection of delivery medium and the competition with other products. The reason for this is the fact that regular education is slow in changing and renewing equipment. The consumer market is more flexible as decisions are taken by individual consumers. The business market is relatively free to adjust the purchase of apparatus to application-specific needs.

2.1
Production

The production of hypermedia resources is completely dependent on the tradition and available expertise at the company concerned. This chapter so far emphasized the situation where large text resources are available. Advantages of text-based authoring include:

- It is easier to reuse the resulting resources
- Codes can be used for contents, not for typography.

At a conceptual level, however, there is no reason to accept the primacy of authoring text. Figure 5 displays CD-ROM(XA) or CD-I production as a composition and compilation task. At the level of physical action this is correct; however, it needs many prerequisite steps of design and resource selection before the physical compilation can be done. As we are in the first stage of hypermedia exploitation it is good to be aware of its limitations and constraints. The delivery argument has motivated courseware engineers to explore the potential of CD storage and access.

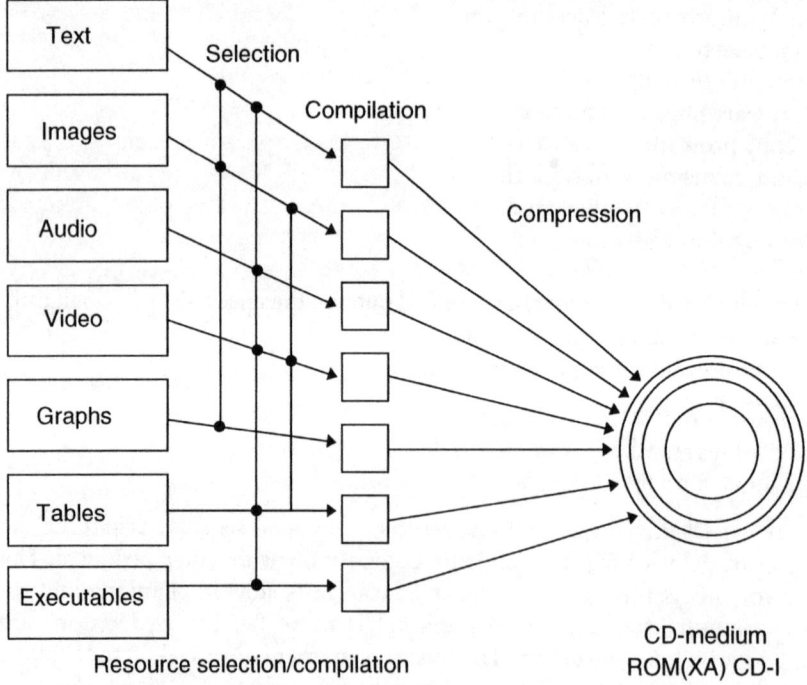

Figure 5. Hypermedia production

Check-list for production:

- Transport the material to a producer or produce in house
- Add copy protection (if necessary)
- Compress the material (if necessary)
- Rearrange material for fast retrieval
- Reproduce the hypermedia system
- Pack it.

Important arguments for using CD media are:

- The delivery medium is cheap, ready for the consumer market, and is the first adequate substrate for storing multimedia data.
- Data reliability, protection, and computability can be guaranteed.

2.2
Scenario Templates

We have seen that there are two competing initiative streams for authoring hypermedia. These streams have opposite directions and are displayed in Figure 6. The first one is an initiative from the technical perspective and is quite familiar in terms of how researchers and developers see it. The second one is initiated by commercial aspiration and may even result in denying or ignoring technological results, because of their unpredictable costs.

From the publisher's point of view, the new media approach is endangering traditional products which are very cost-effective (e.g., text on paper). Seen from the electronic industry, new media are opening new markets, which stimulate a variety of infrastructures like telecommunications, computerized offices, etc.

The first initiative stream is pushed by technological facilities like SGML parsers, multimedia databases, and optical storage devices. In this scenario we meet three coordinated roles which need to cooperate perfectly before a successful hypermedia system comes to life:

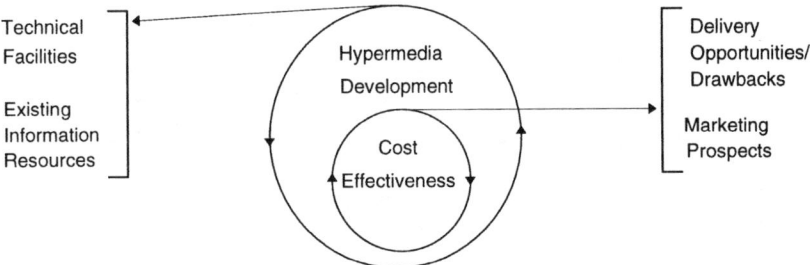

Figure 6. Two initiative streams for authoring hypermedia

A. The publishing company itself which supplies valuable resources like reference manuals, encyclopedias, etc. The publisher will soon take the role of marketer, who knows motives in the buying population.
B. A research/development group. At this moment the hypermedia impulse comes from small cutting-edge companies, which offer their techniques, software tools, and methodology to companies to develop (corporate) hypermedia systems.
C. A partner who represents the electronic industry and who should be equipped to carry out such necessary steps as mastering and pressing the hypermedia data-carrier such as CD-I or CD-ROM(XA) and preparing DV-I.

2.3
Scenario Templates Within the First Stream of Initiative

In the next three templates (Figures 7–9) each of the three partners in the scenario template is represented by a corresponding code (A, B, or C) as indicated above. The horizontal dimension in the figures represents time.

2.3.1
First Stream, Template One

Partner A (publishing company) takes the initiative based on demands in the market, and controls a research/development partner (B) and an electronic products company (C) to do prototyping and CD mastering (Figure 7). Finally the publisher commercializes the hypermedia product and shares the profit with partners B and C. This scenario template is typical for the situation when production techniques are yet unknown and are too risky for A or C to venture by themselves. The strong element in this template is that both B and A stay with their strongest expertise. The weak point is that the actual commercialization is done by the partner who takes the last technical step in the chain of production, which is C in this case. The risk of delegating the commercialization to one of the partners is obvious, for in most cases the hypermedia product is not focused to a particular target group in the market.

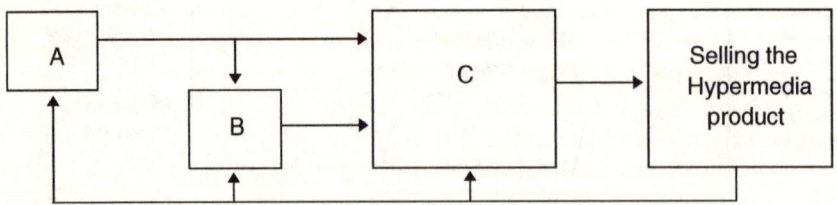

Figure 7. Publisher-driven hypermedia project

2.3.2
First Stream, Template Two

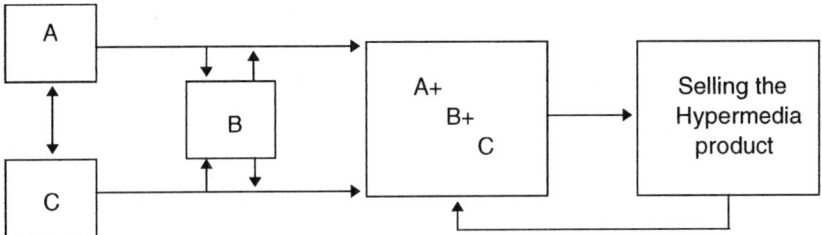

Figure 8. Project initiated by publisher and electronic company

Another scenario template avoids diffuse marketing. In this second scenario template there is a separation between the individual responsibility of the partners in the technical stages of the production phase, and the joint venture of the commercialization (Figure 8). The publisher (A) and electronic company (C) each take a part of the development and innovation activities. The final costs of these activities cannot be predicted in advance. Partner B (research and development group) can be consulted by one or by both of the main initiators A and C. Only after finishing the technical tasks do partners A, B and C make a joint venture for the commercialization phase. The consortium has accepted a superordinate goal to market the hypermedia product. The share of each partner in the final venture should be clear from the start. The weak point is still that expensive technical and human efforts of the three partners are brought in without knowledge of the commercial benefits at the end.

2.3.3
First Stream, Template Three

The most feasible scenario template for producing hypermedia products while guaranteeing commercial benefits and low production overhead seems to be the one which allows the publisher to accept hypermedia gradually (Figure 9). The publisher starts with no experience about hypermedia (A1). By consulting B and C, the publisher will increase his level of expertise and finally come to A2. Once the publisher is at the level of A2 (s)he is in a position to initiate hypermedia development and exploitation independently of B and C.

This scenario template shows that the timing of hypermedia production is of major importance. Early (text-based) hypermedia products were not attractive enough to motivate the consumer market. Early hypermedia including sound, pictures, and video will cause overspending in the production phase, and will lure the public in such a way that it has a negative impact on the selling of books.

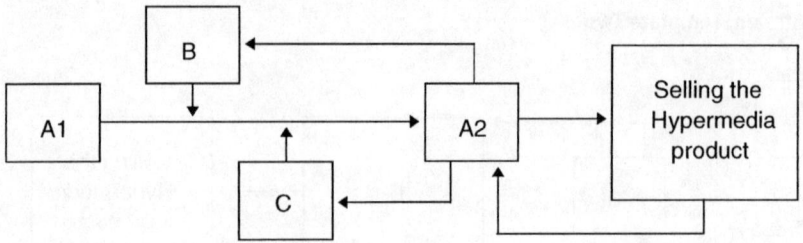

Figure 9. Postponed acceptance model

In other words, the publisher remains the guardian for hypermedia exploitation in the consumer and educational market. Partners B and C should be submissive to the commercial enterprise of the publisher.

2.4
Scenario Templates Within the Second Stream of Initiative

The second stream of initiative is pulled by commercial goals, irrespective of the technological potential of the medium itself. A dominant motive to start hypermedia development in this second stream of initiative is that it may bring down the costs and/or logistics needed for information delivery and updating. In this case the final hypermedia application is aimed at the business community. Examples are hypermedia training programs for car maintenance, airplane repair, etc. The initiative for hypermedia production is clear, and it will be less complicated to define cooperation procedures between partners.

Thus a new partner is introduced, the principal, who wants a hypermedia product to increase the effectiveness of job performance or training sessions. A single scenario template occurs if the necessary information resources are available at the principal's company.

In Figure 10, partner D is a company who possesses considerable amounts of information and wants to optimize its use by implementing it in a hypermedia system. In this situation, the principal is responsible for the dissemination of the hypermedia product in the company. In many cases, however, the intended hypermedia product has a wider bandwidth compared to courseware. The user-controlled interaction in hypermedia allows more flexible usage, and opens the way to reuse a product for other groups in the company as well. For instance, a hypermedia system to train assembly jobs might be useful for maintenance and repair as well. This strategic value of hypermedia products may elicit more complex scenario templates.

Figure 11 shows the migration from a company at level of expertise D to the same company at level D1 and finally level D2. The first transition (D to D1) was enabled by the consultancy of a partner in electronic industry C1. The

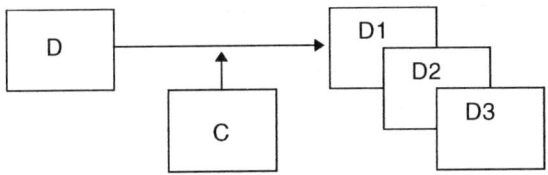

Figure 10. Corporate-driven publishing

second transition only became possible after the same partner C made a consortium with partners A and B who gave input from the publishing and software engineering side.

A second variation of the second stream in scenario templates occurs when the hypermedia resources prove to be useful for other companies as well (Figure 12). After the first transition of D to D1 in which the expertise to embed exis-ting information in a hypermedia system grows, partners A and B are consul-ted in order to increase the scale of hypermedia production (CD-based and adding professional designers for the quality of the product so that it becomes portable to other environments). In all variations on the last template, the principal company (D) stays the guardian of the commercial benefits, and also takes the risks for overspending.

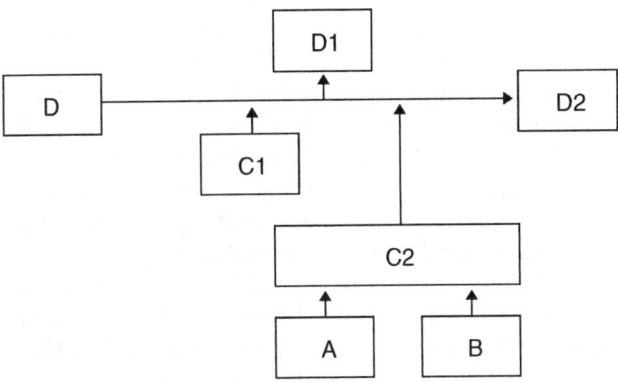

Figure 11. Technology supported migration

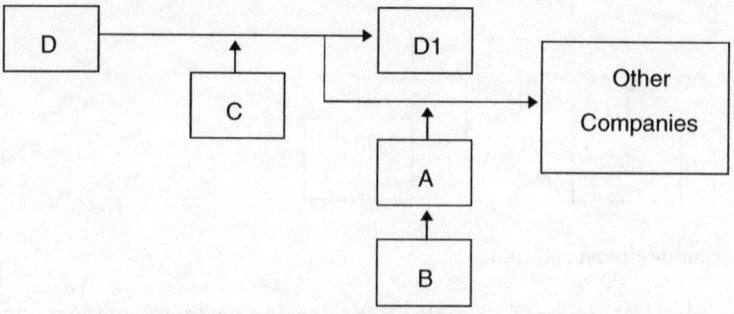

Figure 12. Re-exploitation of corporate information resources

2.5
Fourteen Steps in the Development of Hypermedia

The scenarios mentioned in the previous part of this chapter can be compiled into one overview (see Table 1). This table represents a possible sequence of steps to be taken to create a hypermedia database (hyperbase). Note that this sequences of steps is designed especially for a scenario in which material (not yet in the form of a hypermedia database) is already available. In the case no material is available, Steps 1c, 1f, and 2 will not have to be taken. In case an existing hypermedia database is available, a hypermedia database management system (HMDBMS) should be used from the beginning, in place of a database management system (DBMS) or a multimedia database management system (MMDBMS), to support the information of the already available hypermedia database. If a HMDBMS were not used, linking information would get lost. The hypermedia authoring tools needed by hypermedia authors (see Table 1) are of two different types for each different medium. The first type of tools are the media-editors, such as text editors, etc., and the second type are the hyper-editors. Decision support tools for publishers are omitted, as these tools are not authoring tools in fact. All the tools mentioned could be integrated into one application, but this is neither the easiest nor the best way to do it. If the tools are implemented within operating systems such as GEM, Windows 95, Macintosh, Open-Look, or UNIX-X-windows, some of the tools could be separated and others integrated. The text or pictures could be edited and copied from one of several different editors running within one of these operating systems. This gives the secondary author both a choice of what media-editors to use and the possibility to use the most powerful media-editors at the lowest cost. The hyper-editors should be designed and implemented. The need for integration of these tools should be checked: If the need is small, it could be better to make small separate applications to ensure easier software maintenance. Table 1 lists the different stages of hypermedia preparation. Column 1 mentions the type of activity. Column 2 mentions the numbers of the corres-ponding input for this activity and the stage of operation which produced the necessary resource. The next part of this chapter describes the activities in the sequence of preparatory steps before the hypermedia database can actually be mastered on a CD medium.

Table 1. Fourteen stages in hypermedia production

	Step	Input	Output	Tool	Actor	Meta Inf. Base
1a	Target or domain def.	Checklist data	Target def.	Checklist ed.	Publisher	none
1b	Domain def.	Domain knowledge	Domain def. Domain deci-sion: Continue?	Checklist ed. Network ed. (Expert system)	same	none
1c	Gather meta-inf.	Domain decision (1b) external meta-inf.	Meta inf. base	DBMS ed.	2nd author Publisher	Title, Location, Media, Format, Author(s), Owners, Cost, Other
1d	Mapping of meta-inf. on domain def.	Domain def. 1b Meta inf. base (1c)	List of missing inf.	(Smart inf. com-parator tool)	same	same
1e	Add missing meta-inf.	List of missing inf. (1d) Expertise	Updated meta-inf. base	DBMS ed.	same	same
1f	Collect multi media material	Meta-inf. base (1e)	Inf. on original media		same	same
2	Enter multi media-ma-terial	Meta-inf. base (1e) Inf. on original media (1f)	Mult.M. base	Mult.M. DBMS eds., Scanners , etc.	2nd author	Title Contents
3	Restructure, add, and delete inf. of Mult.M. base	Mult.M. base (2)	Mult.M. base	Mult.M. DBMS Mult.M. ed.s	same	same
4	Define properties	Mult.M. base (3)	List of properties	Mult.M. DBMS Property generator	same	same
5	Enter properties	Mult.M. base (3)	Hyp.M. base	Mult.M. DBMS Property ed.	same	Title Contents Properties
6	Automatic linking	Hyp.M. base (5)	Hyp.M. base	Hyp.M. DBMS Automatic link generator	Computer	Title Contents Properties Links
7	Manual linking	Hyp.M. base (6)	Hyp.M. base	Hyp.M. DBMS link ed.	2nd author	same
8	Testing and reviewing	Hyp.M. base (7)	Hyp.M. base	Mult.M. DBMS Mult.M. ed.s, Logger, Hyp.M. test application	same	same
9	Production	Hyp.M. base (8)	CD	Hyp.M. application	User tools	Users

2.5.1
The Preparatory Steps 1a–1f

The first steps as partially described in Sections 1a–2 may or may not be done by using a computer. If a computer is used, most of the work can be done by using simple checklist, network, and text editors. For Step 1d a smart information tool might be adequate, but it is not clear yet if or how such a tool should be implemented.

2.5.2
Entering Multimedia Material

For entering multimedia material as described in Section 3 into a multi- or hypermedia database a number of tools are needed such as:

- Scanners, with scanning software
- Translator and conversion programs to adapt the multimedia material to the required formats. These programs are needed to convert texts, pictures, drawings, etc., to the internal format of the target hypermedia system.

2.5.3
Editing Multimedia

In this phase different (media-)editing tools are needed, such as:

- Text editors, word processing tools
- Drawing, painting tools
- Audio editing tools
- Video editing tools
- Other editing tools.

2.5.4
Defining Properties

This step will only be necessary if there is a possibility for user definable types of properties. Then there should be a tool for defining the different types of properties. There should always be a number of standard properties (already defined to facilitate the author's work). A number of possible properties for links have been defined, such as:

- "Dependent on"
- "Example of"
- "Causes"
- "Concept"
- "Detail"
- Learner characteristics ("for expert", "for novice", etc.).

2.5.5
Entering Properties, Adding Properties

The addition of anchors was mentioned; the adding of properties was not mentioned yet. A choice should be made whether all anchors will have the same properties or not. Some properties could have something to do with the presentation of the items they refer to, and items could be of different types. This could support the choice to use different types of anchors, depending on what the anchors refer to.

The reason why presentation information will have to be stored in properties is simple: An item is constructed to be presented in a context, and if the context changes, the (presentation of the) item should change. This can only be supported if there are properties to control presentation.

Different properties will be needed to control the presentation: Properties (defined as rules) to control what part of the item referred to is to be presented (part of text, music or picture) and properties to control which of the anchors in the item referred to should be enabled.

2.5.6
Automatic Linking

Automatic linking can be done by scanning for keywords within articles and automatically making references of these. Not all keywords need to become references, criteria for automatic linking can only be done for textual articles. Links to non-textual articles should always be added manually.

2.5.7
Manual Linking, Adding Anchors

Four different hyper-editors for manual linking are defined:

- A hyper-editor for texts
- A hyper-editor for (static) pictures
- A hyper-editor for music
- A hyper-editor for video.

The hyper-editor for text should give the author the possibility to add an anchor (link) manually to a part of the text, which can be a letter or a sequence of letters, such as a word or a sentence or even a paragraph. It should also give the author the possibility to add properties to the anchors.

The hyper-editor for static pictures, such as drawings, should give the author the possibility to add anchors to these and to add properties to the anchors. It should be possible to define the shape of the anchor areas in an easy way, by just dragging around the part of the picture to which the anchor should be defined. The editor should, at least, make it possible to define the shape as a rectangle, but in a better version of the editor should give the possibility to define any shape or even a set of shapes as associated to an anchor. The editor should also prevent the author from defining overlapping anchors.

The hyper-editor for music should give the author the same possibilities as the text editor, but for a note or sequence of notes. The functions the hyper-editor for video (motion pictures) would have to support are difficult to grasp, but it should be possible to define anchors, either static anchors or anchors which change, appear, or disappear after a single frame or after a sequence of frames within the video.

2.5.8
Testing and Reviewing

In this almost final step before putting the hypermedia database on a CD-ROM, the hypermedia database should be checked for errors and omissions. If any are found, the hypermedia database should be edited again (Step 3 and onward). Checking the database should probably be done manually. A tool for calculating centralities may give some indication whether all articles within the hypermedia database are well enough connected. The author should have the possibility of running the same hypermedia presentation program as the users of the finished product, but with the data on a hard disk, not yet on a CD-ROM. In this way errors can be corrected in a less costly way.

2.5.9
Production

Production is sometimes more than copying the master files from a hard disk to CD-ROMs. For the sake of copy protection, it is obvious that publishers stress the need to encrypt the data, so that they can be accessed and used by only one specific application program. Many of the available encryption and decryption methods decrease the access speed. However, in order to boost performance, many CD-ROM products already make use of extra memory or a hard disk to cache the necessary CD information, so that data can be accessed in time for time critical applications such as animations, samples of sounds, etc.

2.5.10
Conclusions

The development of hypermedia requires new scenarios for cooperation between different types of partners like authors, publishers, and electronic and software engineering companies. The merits from their hypermedia investments go beyond the actual products as we meet in CD-ROM(XA) and CD-I based products. During the phase of secondary authoring meta-information and alternative perspectives supplement the original intentions of the primary authors and add new perspectives to the content of the information. The generic prospect of these additions is that they are not only beneficial to new hypermedia products, but can also be used for traditional publications like reference manuals and books for instruction and learning.

The importance of SGML-based hypermedia for courseware design has been researched in the DELTA COSYS project. It explored the so-called "pick-and-mix" procedure, which allows the courseware developer to include multimedia entities in the construction of dialogues. Publishing on demand is another important issue to be realized by SGML hypermedia. It allows an author to compile more specific books by consulting existing resources. Of course, the more specific meta-information is added by the secondary author, the more efficiently can the compilation be assisted by the hypermedia engine.

3 Sales and Royalties

This chapter is specifically meant for companies that produce or buy hypertext or hypermedia documents for use or re-use as building blocks in larger projects. Documents can be either single documents or compound documents. It is assumed that it is possible for a company to get all rights to documents, either by law, after hiring creators, or by contracts. It is also assumed that it may be possible for a creator to still have all rights to (a set of) documents. Rights are copyrights, production rights, selling rights, rights to the royalties, etc.

3.1
Rights

There are a number of different basic rights scenarios:

- All rights are owned by the publishing company, and all royalties have to be paid to this company.
- All rights are owned by another company, and all royalties have to be paid to this company.
- All rights are owned by the creators (i.e., writers), and all royalties have to be paid to the creators.

And then there is the complex scenario:

- A combination of the above.

3.2
Revising

There are a number of basic scenarios for revising information:

- A company revises material they have all rights to, and keeps all rights.
- An individual revises material he or she have all rights to, and keeps all rights.

In the above scenarios no problems arise. The more complex scenarios are:

- A company revises material to which they do not have all rights.
- A creator revises material to which the creator does not have all rights.

The complex scenarios give two problems:

- Who is going to get how much of the income generated by the selling/using of the revised material.
- How to keep track of things.

If an individual or a company wants to revise material to which they do not have all rights they should make up a contract with the creator(s), company, or companies that do have all the rights. This contract should specify what rights are granted to the individual or company that revised the material and when and what royalties should be paid for using the original material (each time or lump sum).

3.3
Re-using

The scenarios for re-using material are essentially the same as with the revising of material. If an individual or company wants to revise material to which they do not have all rights they should make up a contract with the creator(s), company, or companies that do have all the rights. This contract should specify what rights are granted to the individual or company that revised the material and when and what royalties should be paid for using the original material (each time or lump sum).

3.4
Procedures

An important procedure which must be done, either by hand or by machine, is logging what items or documents are sold in what quantity, to whom. It should be possible to derive the following from the log:

- Cost to the customer
- Royalties to authors or owners of the material
- Total quantity of each document, sold in any period
- Material sold to each customer
- Intended use.

If the items above are available, a full administrative system can based on the log file. There are several ways in which the log data can be stored. One of them is storing the log in the document itself. The reasons for wanting to store the transaction and production information with(in) a document are:

- All information relevant to the document can be found with(in) the document.
- Information might be more portable when stored with(in) the document.

There is also a reason for not wanting to do that:

- In most cases there is still the need to store the transaction and production information in a normal accounting system, either because it is faster or because that system is already in use. Thus the information will be stored in a redundant manner. This is considered bad practice for databases.

There are two possible approaches using the log:

- A small application must be written to export the information, in the right format, to another administrative system already available.
- An application must be written to easily retrieve the information in the log and print overviews of sales and bills for the customers.

To make it all possible the publisher should:

- Try to make contracts for reuse and editing of the material with their creators and companies owning the material used. In these contracts you either state a lump sum agreement or an agreement for fixed royalty per copy. It is also important to have an agreement on the possibilities of editing and reusing the material, if possible with the conditions. It makes sense to get a lump sum agreement for material you may want to reuse for other purposes or edit later. If the material is static (no revising) a fixed royalty for each copy may do.
- Add facilities to the pick-and-mix system so it can administer the use of documents. There should be special docinfo fields to administer what royalties have to be paid to whom.

3.5
Conclusions

After searching for work done by others in this field we think it is fair to conclude that not much has been done yet. Electronic publishers have the same problem as software houses that their material can be copied at will. Because of the nature of their material it is often difficult for them to protect it by copy protection as is sometimes done by normal software houses. There are two approaches by electronic publishers at this time:

- They put their material on a normal computer but one that has only a keyboard and a screen connected to it. Sometimes a printer may be attached. All actions of the users are logged. CITED [1] is a prototype example of this.
- The other approach is putting their data on specific platforms, such as the Sony Datadisc or CD-I. On these platforms copying of data is not as easy as

---

[1] CITED is a protocol for the registration and administration of information retrieval. The CITED mechanism has been inherited by the COPICAT project. COPICAT in turn develops a scenario and the technology to protect the copyrights of multimedia resources. Both CITED and COPICAT are ESPRIT projects supported by the EC.

on normal computers. IBM-compatible PCs, Macintoshes, etc., are considered normal computers. Copying is not as easy due to incompatible formats or the sheer amount of data.

Note that many publishers are not going electronic because of the copyright problems associated with it.

Publishers in general do not like the idea that their material can be copied by anyone without their having any control over this. This is for example the case for publishers of music, where CDs can be copied on compact cassettes, and for films and video, which can be recorded on video recorders. This has been solved by having the consumer pay royalties for each empty video tape or compact cassette. Dutch libraries have an arrangement with publishers that the publishers will receive a certain small sum for every copy made on the copiers available in the libraries. The assumption is that these copiers will be used mainly to copy pages from magazines or books available in the libraries.

The main problem with multimedia and hypermedia material is that it has high costs, and is generally targeted to only a small target group. This leads to high prices. In turn this makes it more interesting to the consumer to copy it (illegally).

4 The Publishing Corporation Case

Large publishing corporations are typically divided into several divisions (Figure 13). We expect companies in the non-publishing branch to meet many of the dilemmas that have already appeared in the publishing sector. Therefore in this chapter we take a typical western publishing house as a case study in the strategies and methods of document management. We will mention 'the company' any time we refer to this imaginary case. A typical characteristic of the company is that it is in a permanent state of migration from paper-based document management into a computer-based one. The hard- and software mentioned is appropriate for the period 1992–94 and is only introduced to make the case more realistic. Also, the price indications stem from this period.

4.1
Public Information Division

Let's say the company has a separate division specializing in the publication of encyclopedias, dictionaries, and other reference works. The development of a new product will differ in minor details from that of former products. Calculations of time and cost, in fact, determine what will be made. Therefore, producing a new edition of an existing encyclopedia or dictionary is the safest option.

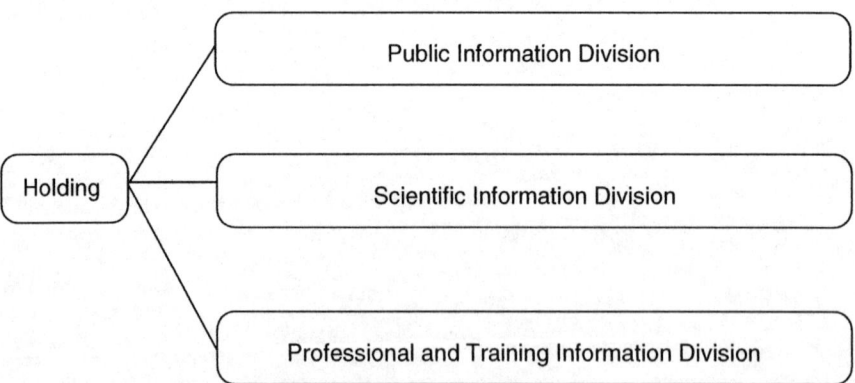

Figure 13. Overview of a large publishing corporation

4.1.1
Management

The company's general management makes the strategic decision about the start of a new project. The decisions are based on information from the marketing division, sales management, and production management. The project initiation has different lines of approach:

- Developing a new concept, starting from the existing databases. The marketing division starts investigating possible markets to find out if the concept fits for a special target group.
- Reaction to a request from the market to develop a product for a special project. The request is recognized by sales management or production management. Calculation about the feasibility of production.
- Production of a new edition of an existing encyclopedia/dictionary. The need for a new edition is detected by sales management.

4.1.2
General Management

The general management (the publisher) decides whether a concept will be published. (S)he decides whether the profit prospects are high enough. (S)he also makes decisions about new developments in the production process.

4.1.3
Marketing Department

The marketing department researches product-market combinations. A new product is initiated by the marketing department. This department tests the product-market combination and makes the market analysis for edition size and price. According to signals from sales management, a market analysis for a new edition of an existing product is made.

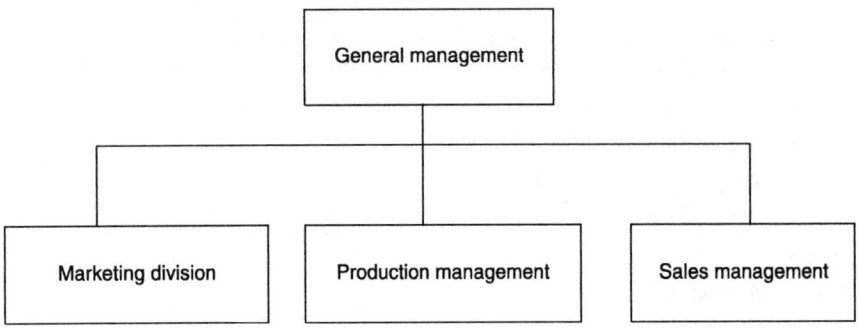

Figure 14. Organization diagram of management structure

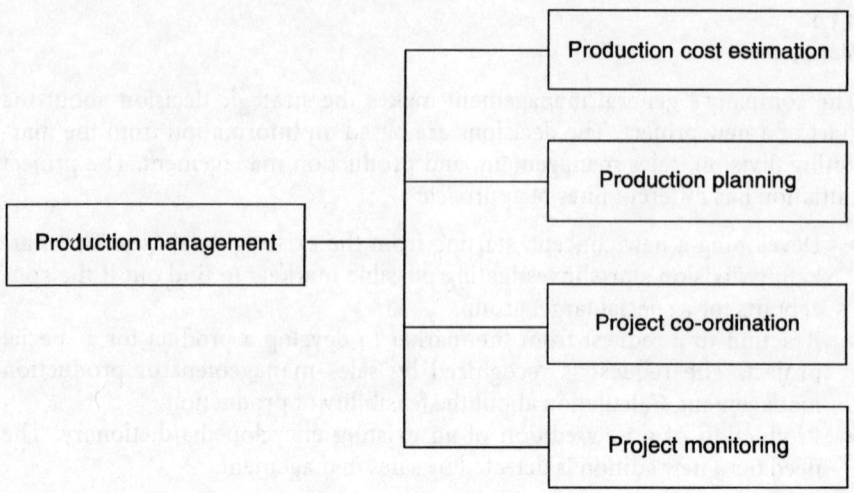

Figure 15. Organization diagram of production management

4.1.4
Sales Management

The sales management makes a calculation of the expected profits based on how many books will be sold in how many years.

4.1.5
Production Management

The production management has four different functions. Sometimes one person is involved in more than one task.

4.1.5.1
Estimation of Production Costs

It is the product producer who makes a calculation of the costs. The cost calculation is based on experience with former publications and depends on:

- Number and length of entries
- Number of pictures, photographs and tables
- Typography
- Number of pages.

4.1.5.2
Production Planning

After the publisher decides to publish a reference work, the producer defines when and where the different elements have to be produced. Time schedules are made at the start of the project for:

- Editors
- Authors
- Typesetters
- Printers
- Binders.

Based on experience, an estimation can be made for the different types of projects. There is knowledge about how long production of one megabyte of new material or one megabyte of recompiled material takes.

4.1.5.3
Project Co-ordination

The editor is responsible for the co-ordination of the whole product. The editor keeps an eye on the time schedule and must take immediate action if, at any point, the project process is delayed.

4.1.5.4
Project Monitoring

In the process of making a new product the editor plays an important role in monitoring the project. He or she is responsible for:

- New topics in the book
- Amount of lines of the text
- The changes made by the author in the text
- The illustrations, photographs, and pictures.

A voluminous product needs more than one editor to deal with the work. Every editor checks his or her own authors, but management receives overall lists (see Route of the Documents).

4.1.6
Pick and Mix

A pick-and-mix system can be used for making new encyclopedias and dictionaries. The editor is the manager of the pick-and-mix system. The editor mixes information from several sources:

- Electronic databases
- Lithograph collection
- Archives and documentation of current articles
- Authors.

The editor gives authors the task of writing/rewriting the text. The result is stored in the electronic database and sent to the production process of printing the new product.

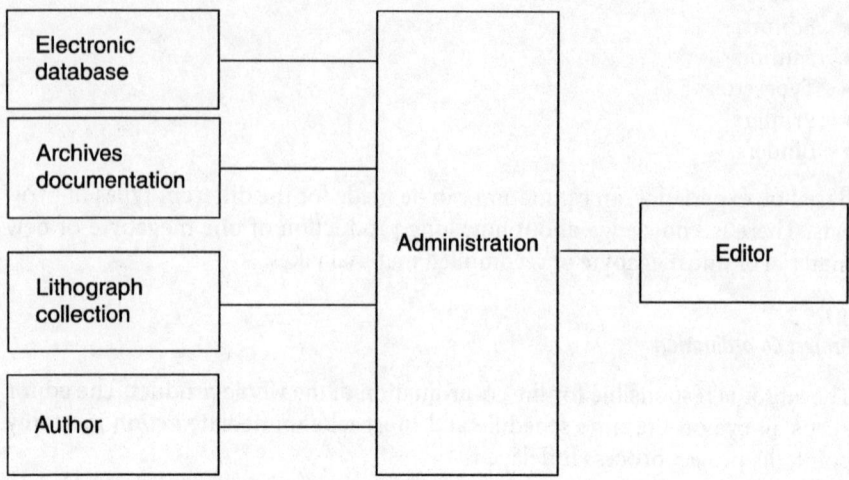

Figure 16. Administration of the pick-and-mix process

The administration administers the outgoing and incoming drafts and takes care of the financial aspect of the copyrights. All texts are printed on paper. The editor picks and mixes using the paper version of the text, authors send their text on paper to the editor. There are several reasons for doing this:

- The quickest way to read for the editor is from paper.
- The alterations are clearly separate from the text.
- The typing corrections are done by a professional typing staff (quicker and fewer mistakes).
- It is a waste of time to introduce the authors to the SGML system used in their electronic text.

This procedure optimizes speed and quality. Figure 16 gives an overview of where in the production process the text on paper is used and where the electronic version of the text is used.

During the pick-and-mix procedure several hard- and software tools may be used:

- IBM PC or clone or Macintosh
- GML sensitive Editor
- IBM Personal Editor
- WordPerfect or MS Word
- Lotus 123 or Excel
- Matrix or laser printers
- The red or blue pen or pencil.

4.1.6.1
Procedures: Text

The marketing division makes a selection of entries for the new publication. The existing information is picked from the electronic database and printed on paper by the database manager. This draft is send to the editor. Now the editor starts the mixing. (S)he uses several sources. The sources are:

- Electronic databases
- Archives and documentation of actual articles
- Information provided by the authors.

The editor has contact with:

- Archives and documentation supplier; the editor buys recent information about the entries
- The author(s) of the entry; who may change the original text or add new text
- The illustration manager: the editor asks for illustrations for certain entries.

The editor makes the decision about the texts:

- Adds new or updated information
- Sends the text to the original author to update the information
- Sends the text to the original author to add new information to the topic.

The author writes new/additional text and sends the draft back to the editor. If there is an electronic version of the text it is sent directly to the typing staff.

4.1.6.2
Pictures

The illustration manager looks for the wanted illustration. If necessary he or she gives the order to make a new one. The illustrations are stored alphabetically. At the end of the procedure, when the editor has finished the pick-and-mix of each entry, the entries are alphabetically sorted and the illustrations are added to the product.

4.1.7
Administration

Each division has its own administrative system for calculation of costs, ordering of production and reproduction, calculation of invoices, and payments to the authors. Concerning the pick-and-mix procedures the administration has two important tasks:

- Administering the route of a document
- Taking care of the financial settlement.

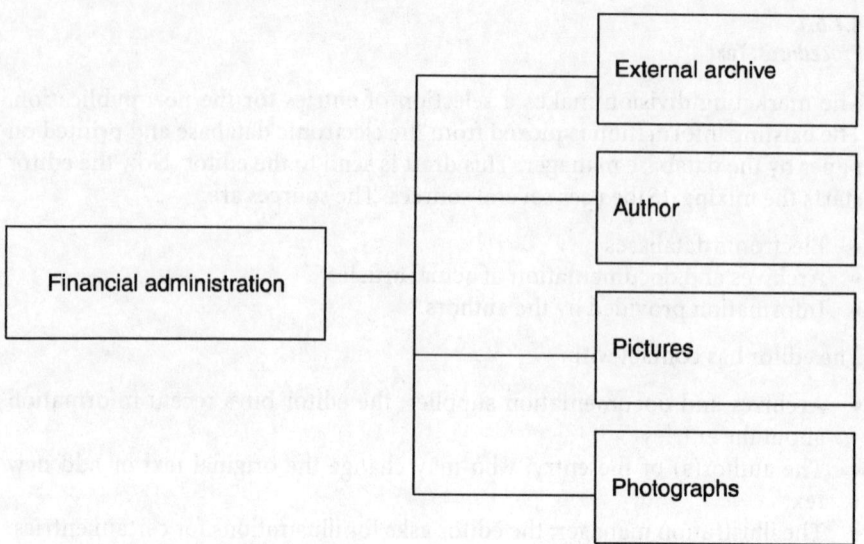

Figure 17. Financial administration

4.1.7.1
Route of the Documents

Every draft that is send from the editor to the author and back is administered by the administration. They have a list with the author's name, discipline, code, editor, and entries. The list gives information about the name of author who wrote the entry the progress of the authors and the editors. Each editor checks his own authors and the management receives the overall list. By sorting on columns the management can get information about the progress of authors or editors.

4.1.7.2
Financial Settlements

The financial aspect is taken care of by the administration. When there are disagreements, the editor is responsible for making a decision.

4.1.7.3
External Archive

The archives and documentation supplier is a sister company. It has an archive of recent articles from newspapers and journals. Most of them are on paper. Some are scanned. From a prestigious newspaper the texts will be electronically available. The sister company charges for its services.

4.1.7.4
Author

The first time the author writes an article he or she is paid per line, a fixed amount of money. The text is then property of the company. When the editor wants to use the text again (s)he sends it to the original author with a specific task, for example, to add ten lines to the text describing the latest development. Then the author will be paid only for those new lines.

When an author isn't available (he or she refuses or is dead) the editor will consult with people the author worked with, and they will advise about a successor.

4.1.7.5
Pictures

The company uses the original lithography of a picture. The production of a lithograph costs about $ 300 (US dollars). A picture editor manages them and is able to find them again for reuse. Customers who want to use a picture from an encyclopedia are charged $ 100. If they use a picture without permission it will cost them about $ 200.

4.1.7.6
Photographs

The photographs stay property of the photographer. The company pays him or her every time the photo is used in a new edition. The costs are $ 200. When a photo is used without permission of the photographer the penalty is $ 600.

4.1.8
Predictions About the Future

4.1.8.1
Internal

The pick-and-mix system used by the company at this moment is satisfactory for the current situation. This means that the pick-and mix-system is only for internal use and uses simple software to keep the expenses and training cost low. However, the company is very interested in facilitating the pick-and-mix system, for example by using a system that uses GML codes. The reason that the company is not already using a SGML code is because of the high costs, and the fact that there is no suitable SGML editor available.

As already described, the editor uses the paper version of an entry for the pick-and-mix process. After the drafts are send to the typing staff and the changes are entered in the electronic database the drafts are kept in the archive and reused for a new edition. When using them again the editor can see at a glance the changes that were made then. In future it will be possible to develop an editor who can substitute this process, but this will not create new possibilities.

Thinking about the future of a pick-and-mix system, one could think of selling information from the electronic database directly to other companies.

At this moment it sometimes happens that the company receives a request from a person or company to use a specific picture or to quote text from one of their works. If there is no objection the company gives permission and the sales administration sends a bill to the customer. Mostly the customer makes his or her own copy (using a color copy machine) or types the text directly from the work, and the customer knows exactly what he or she wants.

When new small-size multimedia publishers start in business, however, we may expect more substantial interest for company material, and a more client-centered pick-and-mix system may be desirable.

4.2
Scientific Information Division

Another division concerns itself with the publishing of scientific journals. Most of the publications published are distributed on paper, some of them on CD-ROM. This division feels a strong need for a new order between functions and processes, as shown in Figure 18 and conceived in the EC CITED project.

4.3
Professional Information Division

Other important divisions are the ones providing education services and training.

One division distributes abstracts of medical articles, more than 300 000 per year. The articles are derived from over 3000 journals and the abstracts are stored electronically in a database. The customer receives the relevant abstracts on CD-ROM, tape, or paper. A database containing data about drugs is also in use. Books, brochures, and leaflets on medical topics are published. The division is part of a collection of semi-autonomous companies and business units. The mission centers on the provision of high-quality sponsored health care communications and information services to the pharmaceuticals industry.

4.3.1
The Market

The principal target market is the international research-based pharmaceuticals industry, especially those companies where a high level of investment drives innovative medicine and high-budget marketing. Compared with earlier, there is a reduced number of companies involved with significantly expanded capabilities and resources. They offer and expect a very high level of medical and marketing support for new products. The products are strategically managed at a global level, yet presented to their markets in localized, tactical packages. The clients wish to deal with communication partners who can both appreciate the need for comprehensive medical communication services and deliver them throughout the product life circle and throughout the world in a coordinated fashion. To prevent the company from delivering confused and conflicting information to the clients, they use a network system.

4.3.2
Data Management

The network system functions as a sales and marketing tool. It is a searchable electronic catalogue of complete projects, current projects, sales activities, and sales prospects on a need-to-know basis. The network system consists of a database and an electronic messaging and information transfer system. It replaces paper-based information such as sales contact reports, project confirmation reports and publication examples.

To enter data, the network system offers prompted menu-driven data entry, controlled by pre-defined glossaries of accepted terms. Local to regional communications is provided in a batch processed, on-line environment (overnight grouping of inquiries, uploads, reports, glossary updates and messages). Communication from regions to host is similar (see Figure 19).

4.3.3
Overview of Use

Categories:

- Each local reporting unit (LRU) employs one or more account managers. These LRU may be consolidated into a business unit, before further consolidation to one or three regional reporting units (RRU).
- Each account manager is responsible for multiple client contacts, each of whom may be responsible for one or more products (note that some client contacts are not responsible for any products).

The client contact belongs to a pharmaceutical company, which in turn is part of a parent corporation. Products are also managed in some cases by a local advertising agency, which assigns certain agency contacts to the account for this purpose.

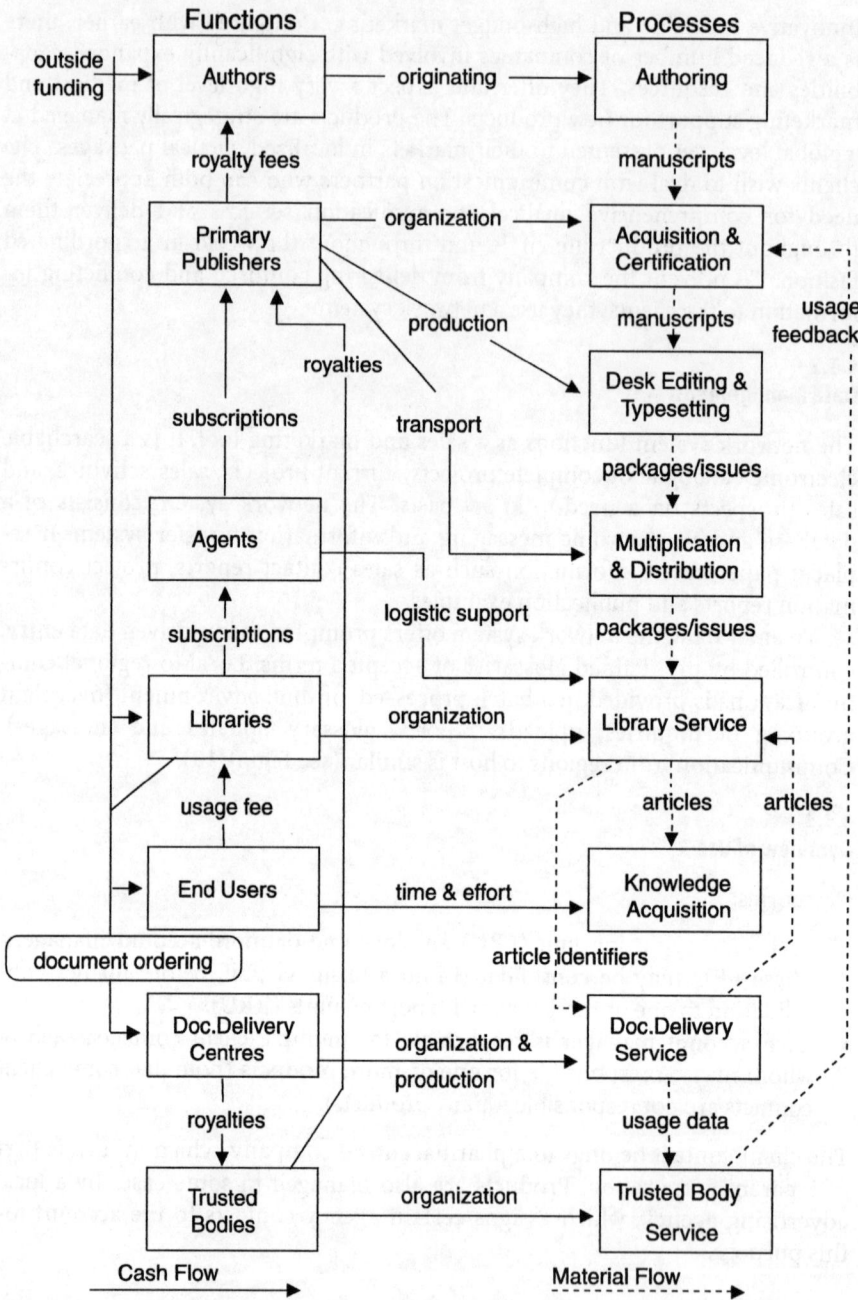

Figure 18. Function and process

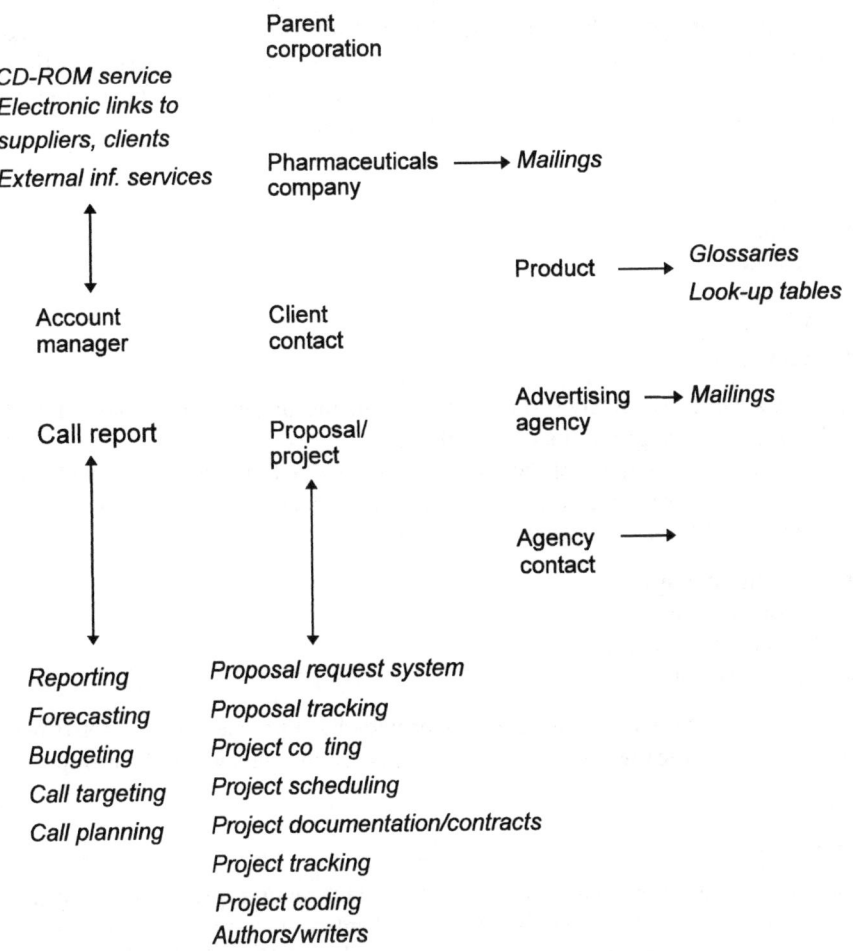

Figure 19. Data exchange

In the course of business, account managers call (in person, by phone, and by letter/fax) on client contacts with the aim of selling projects. A project may consist of a:

- Single advertisement in a journal
- Long term consultancy agreement
- Symposium management program
- Publication
- Computer-based program, etc.

Projects often relate to a single product, or a class of products (the class groups similar products into a standardized sub-category), and are always associated with a specific account manager and client contact.

In the course of selling projects, the account manager may have to make many calls to the client/or agency contact over a considerable period of time, documenting this activity in contact reports and proposals. To operate effectively, the network system requires a set of reference data on:

- Corporations
- Companies
- Contacts
- Products
- Classes
- Agencies
- Agency contacts.

This data will be relatively static once entered, and needs routine maintenance only to reflect changes in the marketplace.

In addition, the network system requires two action-oriented sets of data recording sales contact reports and proposal/project details. These files reflect the actual and forecast business activities per

- account manager
- reporting unit
- business transaction
- market region.

Consolidated at the host level, the files provide both prospective and retrospective analyses of the business at all levels from account manager to the group.

4.3.4
Data Entry

Each month, account managers enter all contact reports, proposal/project updates and any new reference data (i.e., on client contact, products, companies, etc.) into the network system, either directly at their PC/terminal, or by completing forms and passing them on to designated local system administrator for data entry and validation.

4.3.5
Management Reports

When all data are entered, the month is closed and a set of local reports produced and distributed to both the account managers and local management. These reports also form the basis for the monthly narrative reports from the account manager to their local manager, and from local management to the corporate management. The local database is then backed up and summary exports files prepared for transmission (upload) to the host database.

Reports are then generated at the host level (consolidated by business unit and region) for use by corporate management, and subsequent distribution to local management by e-mail. A suite of standard report formats are provided to facilitate this process.

Summary data on sales activities, projects and prospects are also consolidated by the host and sent back to each site, giving all the units access to an overview of group activities. Account managers at the local site can then update themselves on sales and project activities relevant to their personal client/product responsibilities throughout the world.

Facilities for querying the database at any time exist at both the local and the host level to enable the generation of reference lists, address/name details, action/planning aids, etc.

From a data entry, validation, and management perspective, the system must be designed to be operated by personnel with minimal computer or database knowledge. Wherever possible and in all critical data fields, the system must provide default values, identify possible action paths, and prompt for the correct data, selected from an internal glossary by highlighting the desired choice.

4.4
Training Divisions

Another division is a company that develops services for training in the field of technology and information science. The company is an officially recognized education institute. Production and publication of the lessons are a small part of the total product, which includes teacher hours, exams, and study material.

4.4.1
Prospectus

Courses are developed for or on request from the industry. The main goal is to educate their employees in order to support changes in the industry. The company supplies courses in the fields of technical progress, computerization, economics, computer science, communication, new products, new equipment, changing product organization, etc.

In future the company plans to provide the personnel manager of the industries with the possibilities the company can offer on-line or on CD-ROM. The personnel manager can pick-and-mix the study components for a specific employee or group of employees. He or she can have a look at the text of the lessons.

4.4.2
Production

The content matter of the lessons is written by a specialist working in that specific field. The material is delivered as a paper-based document and the text also in one of the standard text processor formats. The department's graphic word-processor makes the layout and edits complicated formulas. The final product is sent to its own printing office.

4.4.3
Reference Material

Sometimes the author recommends the frequent use of technical reference manuals, etc. The company settles an agreement with the publisher of that book and delivers it to the student as part of the package.

4.4.4
Homework Management and Administration

The students combine the study with a full-time job. The company provides them with written material. Students use their spare time to study. Once a month the company sends a study package by post with the work that has to be done according to the agreement. The package contains the subject matter, exercises to check if the topic is understood (the answers are in the package), and homework exercises. The answers for the homework packages are sent to the company. The company sends the answers to the teacher. The teacher marks them and sends them back to the company. The company controls and administers the process, registers the marks, and sends the work back to the student. This takes two weeks.

The company is now developing a bulletin board system as a service for the students. It will fully support the homework activities. This will save time and money (paper, postage stamps). A pilot study took place among computer science students. The students gave a high response. The entry of new students doubled due to this service!

4.5
Annex: Text Circulation in the Production Process

Figure 20 reflects the pick-and-mix method as defined in the DELTA COSYS project. It gives an overview of the circulation of the text during the production process. Normal or bold arrows indicate whether the text is paper-based or electronic. Ellipses and squares indicate persons and departments respectively. How to read Figure 20:

- The starting point is the electronic database. Texts are selected. The editor receives the text on paper.
- The editor receives additional text from archives.
- The editor sends the draft to the administration.
- The administration sends the draft to the author.
- The author writes a new version of the text and sends the text to the administration and to the typing staff.
- The administration sends the text to the editor.
- The editor sends the final version to the administration.
- The administration sends the text to the typing staff.
- The typing staff sends the text to the electronic database.

- From the electronic database the text is sent for proof reading.
- The final text in the database is the source for the product.

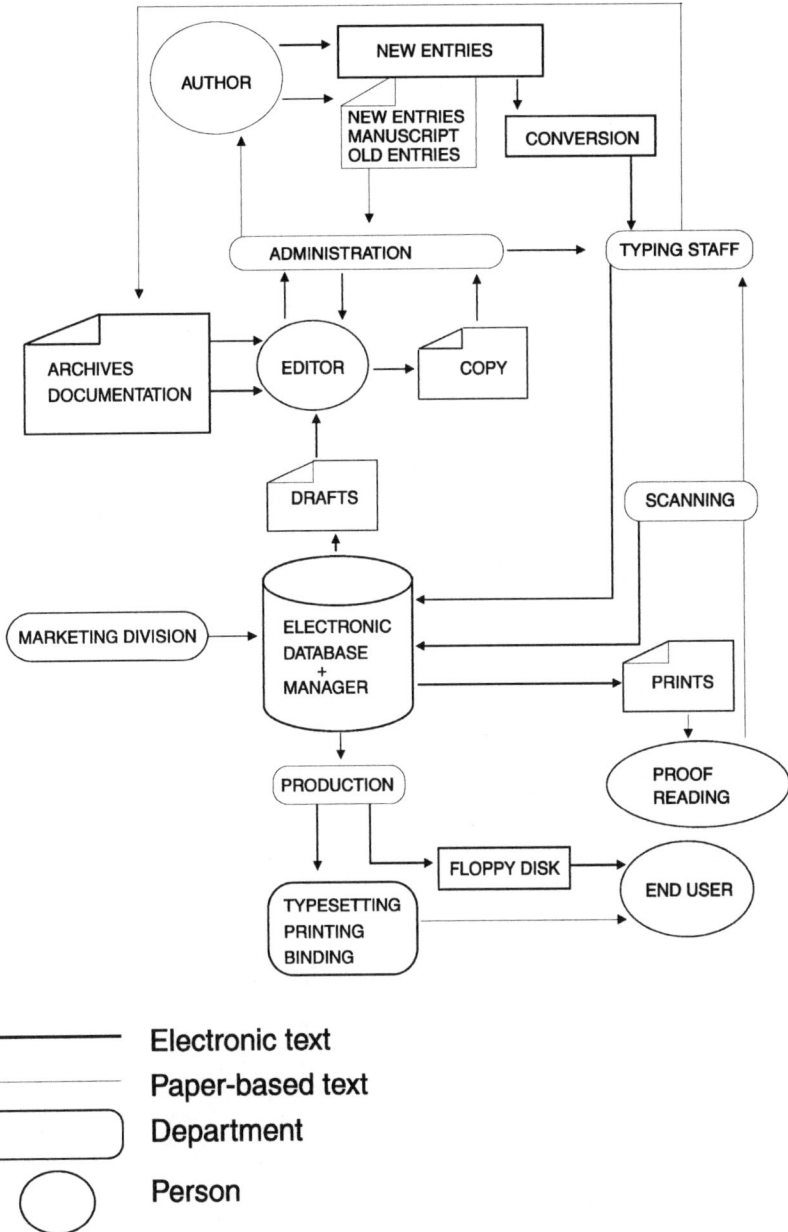

Figure 20. Work flow diagram

Part II
Producing Hypermedia

A number of different abbreviations and acronyms are commonly used in this part of the book. Most of them refer to popular formats (some of them already laid down in ISO standards) which are used in hypertext and hypermedia systems. Some of the formats are popular because much of the data is already in that format and some are popular because they are often used as input for popular hypertext and hypermedia systems. Appendix C gives you a detailed list with acronyms and their explanations.

This part will go into the conceptual background of mark-up languages, how the idea of mark-up can be reconciled with currently available text processing software, and, most of all, how these generic tools can assist us in managing large document domains such as those present in corporate archives.

5 Popular Formats

5.1
SGML

SGML became ISO Standard 8879 in 1986. SGML is a mark-up language (for adding formatting or handling codes to a text) that is now heavily used in the USA and elsewhere. One reason for this has been the Computer-aided Acquisition and Logistics Support or CALS initiative. Many U.S. federal institutions now require textual material to be delivered in SGML format. This is different from Microsoft's RTF (Rich Text Format) because most added information is semantic information. Although typographical information can be added, this is in most cases not necessary until the document has to be printed.

5.1.1
Using SGML for Multimedia Development

There are a number of reasons to use SGML in general and a number of reasons to use it for multimedia development. General reasons are:

- SGML is an ISO standard and supported by the CALS initiative.
- SGML supports semantic information and structure in addition to typographical information. In fact SGML and its derivatives are the only standardized languages explicitly developed for supporting semantic information.
- SGML uses document templates, called document type definitions or DTDs. There are a number of standard DTDs available, which are supported by different SGML applications.
- SGML is supported and used by a number of corporations and institutes.
- SGML supports inclusion of non-SGML data (#PCDATA).

Reasons for using SGML for multimedia development are:

- Documents need to be structured for use in a multimedia title. SGML can be used for this.
- To get the most out of the documents in a multimedia environment, semantic information needs to be added and used. This is supported by SGML.
- A number of multimedia development applications use SGML documents as input.

- SGML documents can be easily translated into any other type of document such as RTF or T$_E$X. In most cases some information will be lost, but as long as the SGML documents stay intact they can always be reused for the same or other purposes.

5.1.2
SGML Document Structure

To clarify the strengths of SGML a description of the SGML document structure and content is necessary. A SGML document consists of two parts:

- The document type definition or DTD which a document may have in common with other documents. The DTD describes the order of items, the tags, and the macros.
- The document data. The data may contain tags and macros.

5.1.2.1
Macros

SGML has been developed as a platform and application independent format. This is why only the basic ASCII set of 128 characters is used. All other special characters or strings are coded with special character macros. The macros are strings starting with an ampersand & character and ending with a semicolon. Because of the different ways special characters are treated on different platforms this makes a lot of sense. The target platform and application need only know what the macro stands for and translate the macro to the wanted character or string. There are already standard lists of special characters in existence. These can be found in the ISO standard.

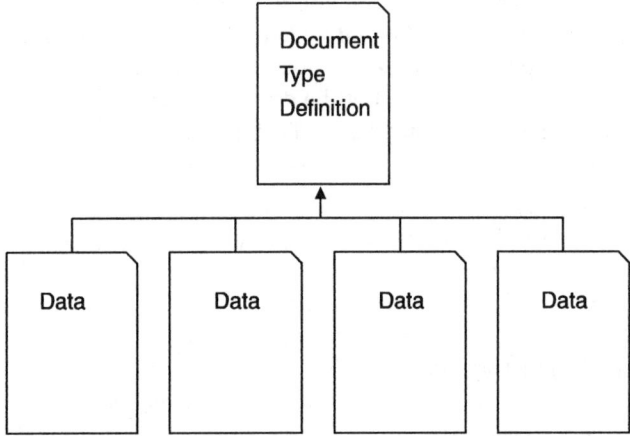

Figure 21. SGML document structure

Examples of standard macros:

```
&amp; gives an ampersand character
&comma; gives a comma
&equals; gives an equals sign
```

It is also possible to define your own lists, but if the characters or strings are already officially defined, it is better not to do so.

5.1.2.2
Tags

Along with macros SGML uses tags. All tags used in SGML start with a < and end with a >. There are two types of tags, open tags and close tags. The close tags are almost the same as the open tags. The close tags have a slash inserted directly after the bracket at the start. An example:

```
<TAG>This text is tagged with tag</TAG>
```

There are some conventions about tags. Examples:

```
<H1>Heading level one, start and end tag<H1>
<P>Paragraph, start and end tag</P>
```

5.1.2.3
DTD

The meaning of the tags is provided by the Document Type Definition. The DTD also provides information about the order and possibilities of nesting of tags. A DTD contains declarations of entities, elements and order of appearance of the elements, and an attribute list. Each line starts with a < bracket. and ends with a > bracket. Comments start after a double dash and end at a double dash. For many applications only one DTD must be made, which can be used over and over for each new document. Most of the documents we worked with were articles in an encyclopedia. An appropriate DTD for an article in an encyclopedia could have been:

```
<!-- DTD for encyclopedia article -->
<!ENTITY % doctype "Article" --document type identi-
fier -->
<!-- ELEMENTS MIN CONTENT (EXCEPTIONS) -->
<!ELEMENT %doctype; - - (Lemma, Body, Close?) >
<!ELEMENT Lemma - 0 (#PCDATA) >
<!ELEMENT Body - 0 (P*) -- zero or more paragraphs -->
<!ELEMENT P - 0 (#PCDATA|ref)* >
<!ELEMENT Pref - 0 EMPTY -- for paragraph references-->
<!ELEMENT Close - 0 (#PCDATA) >
<!-- ELEMENTS NAME VALUE DEFAULT -->
```

```
<!ATTLIST P id ID #implied >
<!ATTLIST Pref refid IDREF #required >
```

The example above is only a simple one. Only lemmas or titles, paragraphs, and references are included in the DTD. The real DTD would have the articles as part of a whole encyclopedia. It would also have elements for tagging names, (birth) dates, and other relevant information. An example of document based on the example DTD:

```
<DOCTYPE ARTICLE SYSTEM "ARTICLE.DTD" [   ]
<Article>
<Lemma>A</Lemma>
<Body>
<P>About the character A...</P>
<P>More about the character A. And could be more than
one line.</P>
</Body>
```

Again a real document could have had references, names, and dates tagged, although none of those existed in this example. A more complete DTD for the encyclopedia:

```
<!-- DTD for encyclopedia -->
<!ENTITY % doctype "Encyclopedia" --document type id -->
<!-- ELEMENTS MIN CONTENT (EXCEPTIONS) -->
<!ELEMENT %doctype; - - (Article+, Close?) >
<!ELEMENT Article - - (Lemma, Body+) >
<!ELEMENT Lemma - 0 (#PCDATA) >
<!ELEMENT Body - 0 (P*) >
<!ELEMENT P - 0 (#PCDATA)*
 +(Reference|Surname|Date|Keyword) >
<!ELEMENT Reference - 0 (#PCDATA)* >
<!ELEMENT Surname - 0 (#PCDATA)* >
<!ELEMENT Date - 0 (#PCDATA)* >
<!ELEMENT Keyword - 0 (#PCDATA)* >
<!ELEMENT Close - 0 (#PCDATA) >
<!-- ELEMENTS NAME VALUE DEFAULT -->
<!ATTLIST P id ID #implied >
```

The encyclopedia DTD now contains one or more articles. Each article starts with a lemma and contains one or more bodies, one body for each possible meaning of the lemma, i.e., one body for each homonym. Each body can be one or more paragraphs, and each paragraph can contain normal text, references, surnames, dates, and keywords.

5.1.3
Creating and Editing SGML

Being ASCII based, SGML can be edited using any editor available. Still, using a WYSIWYG word processor would be nicest and easiest. Using a normal text editor the author needs to have a fair grasp of SGML. Using a special word processor much of the necessary knowledge can stay hidden for the author and handled by the word processor.

The special word processor should be able to generate a DTD or use an already existing one in the same way as most modern word processors use document templates. Work has been done and is being done to adapt or add to some of the currently popular word processors for working with SGML.

WordPerfect Corporation for instance has designed macros to create SGML documents from WordPerfect documents. Microsoft is working on Word document templates for SGML. These document templates contain conversion macros to convert Word documents to SGML documents. Style sheets and typographical information are converted to DTDs and tags.

When DTDs are used transparently by the word processors, a normal user does not need any special knowledge about the codes, macros, or the DTD. The word processor will provide the user with prompts at the right instances.

One of the most daunting problems with creating information in or for SGML applications is the necessity for strict use of tags or styles. Many authors and editors will normally want to add styles or tags to add specific information for that specific document on which they are working. If this is accepted, the validation process will become more difficult due to all those extra tags used only once or twice. Also two authors might decide on different tags for the same information. Thus:

- Authors and editors must decide on one common DTD. If necessary one DTD can be decided upon for each type of document.
- Authors and editors must strictly adhere to the DTD for the type of document they are working on. If real problems occur the common DTD must be adjusted.

5.1.4
Hypertext

Because of all the semantic information in a SGML formatted text, it is very easy to convert it into a hypertext system. Semantic information about references, keywords, titles, headings, etc., as declared in the second example DTD, should be available. If supported by the target hypertext, all this information can be used for hypertext links, searching, navigating, and querying. See Appendix A for some popular books on SGML.

5.2
HyTime and SMSL

The Hypermedia/Time-based Structuring Language (HyTime) is ISO Standard 10744:1992. It is an application of SGML (ISO 8879). HyTime is used as the basis of the ISO Standard Multimedia Scripting Languages or SMSL.

HyTime supports the classic bibliographic model of information representation, whereby it is possible to represent links to anything, anywhere at any time. The extension of this model to the information age, Integrated Open Hypermedia (IOH), is the field of application of HyTime. HyTime based on SGML prompts system developers how to encode and structure hypermedia and time-based data using SGML. It is developed to enable hypermedia and multimedia systems to interchange data.

HyTime has been developed because although SGML can support hypermedia, this had to be done with non-standard solutions. HyTime provides a standard for all to use. HyTime is not widely used yet, but it is expected to be used by a number of future hypermedia applications. It provides facilities for representing static and dynamic information that is processed and interchanged by hypertext and multimedia applications. Normally such information is typically embedded in the processing instructions of hypermedia scripts native to a (hardware or software) platform or application. This makes it harder or impossible to use this information on other platforms or applications. HyTime makes it possible to save the information in a platform and application independent manner. Thus the information can be used on any platform and with any application that supports the HyTime standard.

Which information can be saved in a HyTime-compatible format, and which parts are kept in scripts, is up do the designers and users. What is saved in a HyTime-compatible format and which parts are kept in scripts depends on such questions as:

- How much effort, time and costs there will be in using HyTime, and how much of this is expected to be recouped in the short term, middle term, and long term for this and other projects using the same data.
- How fast the final application will be; HyTime applications may be slower than the scripted counterparts.

Because of these points HyTime is highly modularized to give designers the ability to choose what will be done using HyTime and what will be done using scripting languages.

The architectural forms and attributes of the HyTime language are grouped into six modules, each of which can have both required facilities and options. Support for the modules and their options is indicated by the HyTime support declarations.

1. The base module consists of required and optional facilities. Required are support for SGML hypermedia document management and identification of HyTime properties.
2. The measurement module facilities provide the ability to specify the position and extent of objects in various application defined measurement units.
3. The location address module allows the identification of objects that cannot be addressed by SGML-unique identifiers and objects that are in external documents.
4. The hyperlink module allows connections (hyperlinks) to be made among objects, either within a single document or between multiple documents.
5. The scheduling module allows events to be scheduled in spatial and temporal units.
6. The rendition module, in combination with the scheduling module, can be used to represent parameters governing the rendition process.

5.3
HTML

One of the formats that is rapidly becoming more popular is HTML (Hyper-Text Markup Language). HTML is essentially an SGML derivative with a fixed DTD.

The HTML format is used for documents provided in the WWW or World Wide Web. The WWW project was started by CERN (the European laboratory for particle physics), and now constitutes a distributed hypermedia system. The WWW is a set of hypertext document servers on the Internet that support references and pictures. The references can be within documents or to other documents both on the same or on other servers. The references can be used to jump quickly to a document with more information about the subject referred too. Some servers may support searches on documents on that particular server.

A WWW server can be compared with a Gopher server but a WWW server also supports graphics and hypertext browsing. The WWW can be best described as an advanced browsing system. If the right entry points are known a lot of information can be accessed. If the right entry points are not known a long search will probably be necessary. There are a few ways available to reduce the time searching the WWW:

- Ask someone who is more experienced whether he or she knows a server that might be a good entry point given the question you have.
- If you don't have anyone in the neighborhood a query can be put in an appropriate Internet news group. One such news group is the COMP.INFOSYSTEMS.WWW.USERS.

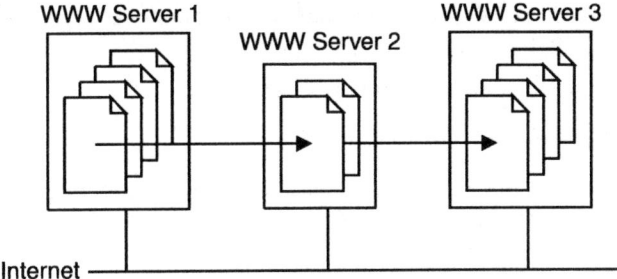

Figure 22. WWW Servers on the Internet

- Get the WWW Beginners Index or the WWW FAQ (Frequently Asked Questions). These pop up once in a while in the previously mentioned news group, but can also be FTP'ed from a number of sites, one of them RTFM.MIT.EDU.

Many educational institutes are starting WWW servers besides the Gopher servers already available. There is also growing interest from businesses in providing services on the WWW. These are customer services in the sense of making documentation about there products available, but also services such as the Encyclopedia Britannica. A number of interesting WWW servers are available:

- WWW tools:
  http://info.cern.ch/hypertext/WWW/Tools/Filters.html
- WWW tools:
  http://oneworld.wa.com/htmldev/devpage/dev-page.html
- NCSA Info Resource Meta-Index:
  http://www.ncsa.uiuc.edu/SDG/Software/ Mosaic/MetaIndex.html
- Hypermedia and the Internet
  http://life.anu.edu.au/education/hypermedia.html
- Game FAQ's:
  http://wcl-rs.bham.ac.uk/~djh/index.html

With applications like Netscape users can browse through the available documents and get binary files. To make it easier return to servers and documents that were previously visited they can leave bookmarks. This is especially important because, while browsing, the path followed might be forgotten.

These applications can also be used to view local documents. In this way a local hypertext system can be created. Compared with more advanced systems such as Hyperwave the WWW lacks advanced search and index capabilities. Index documents can be made, but each time one of the indexed documents changes, the index document must also be changed. This might be possible on a local system, but on a worldwide Internet service an index covering all documents is difficult to maintain, and impossible to keep exactly up to date. However, there is a service called the WWW Worm that is comparable to Veronica for Gopher or Archie for FTP. It can be found at:

http://www.cs.colorado.edu/home/mcbryan/WWWW.htmlsome

HTML documents can be created in several ways:

- Using a dedicated HTML editor. Several of these exists for different platforms. Some are WYSIWYG, others display the HTML tags in the texts.
- Using a SGML editor with the HTML DTD.
- Using a text editor. In this case you need to know exactly which tags to use.
- Using a word processor and a conversion macro. This method is also applicable if you want to convert existing word processor documents to the HTML format. Several macros for use with Microsoft Word for Windows already exist and can be found on FTP sites such as CICA (FTP.CICA. INDIANA.EDU) or one of its mirrors.
- Converters to convert documentation from different formats to HTML. One of those converters is TEX2RTF by Julian Smart (jacs@aiai.edinburgh.ac.uk). It can convert T$_E$X to ordinary RTF, Windows Help hypertext RTF, and HTML.

5.4
VRML

Virtual reality will change both the impact and the production technologies of broadcasting, media-based training, and distance communication. Broadcasting will gradually change into 'narrow casting', and the com-munication in organizations will become more externally oriented, in the sense that part of the organization may be 'virtual', in fact belonging to other companies and freelance individuals. VRML (Virtual Reality Modeling Language) brings the possibility of virtual environments: ("virtual" then recalls a lens that forms a virtual image: what you see is not essentially in conflict with reality, but it provides the illusion that certain information, ideas, or transactions exist closely in space or time, when in fact they are from different contexts; you would not find them together by making use of physical and linear documents). As an extra to static documents, virtual environments offer the user the opportunity to intervene. Any change in the information will bring along further consequences for this user. Also new documents will be aggregated based on the meta-information in the original ones.

VRML has been developed by Silicon Graphics. VRML evangelist Clay Graham has addressed the question how to represent information so that meta-information comes out spontaneously. Database mining, the exploration of information resources in a way that generates more knowledge for the user than actually contained in the information components themselves, thus becomes possible. A good example is the use of data tables and preparation of graphics:

VRML makes it easier for the user to navigate and to recognize his or her searching goal. Like with hypermedia, it is quite unclear to many users what in fact they are searching for. Making this background interest more explicit is an important first step for users in general. More information on VRML can be found at Silicon Graphics:

http://reality.sgi.com/employees/clay/

5.5
MHEG

The possible future international standard for multimedia and hypermedia object is being developed by the Multimedia and Hypermedia Expert Group (MHEG).

This standard defines the representation and encoding of multimedia and hypermedia objects to be interchanged within or across applications or services, by means of interchange including storage devices, telecommunications, or broadcasting networks.

These objects, encoded using ASN.1 (Alternate Standard Notation One) or SGML will provide a common base for other CCITT Recommendations and ISO standards and for many multimedia and hypermedia applications which will be developed in the coming years in a wide rage of domains.

The MHEG standard is designed to meet the requirements of communicating multimedia applications running on heterogeneous workstations and interchanging information in real-time to perform a specific set of services to their users: Computer supported multimedia co-operative work, multimedia messaging systems, electronic publishing and electronic books, audiovisual telematic systems for training and education, simulation and games, sales and advertising, and other new classes of multimedia applications.

These multimedia services will use large quantities of structured multimedia information resident on local hard disks, stored on removable disks, or stored remotely on a local area or wide area network. Acquiring and creating this information may take a considerable investment and thus it is vital that the information remains usable even with changing hardware and software platforms.

User requirements regarding the interchange of multimedia information include: Real-time interactivity through specific interaction structures, real time interchange of multimedia data, composition and synchronization of multimedia data in space and time, linking between elements of composite multimedia objects, reuse of multimedia data by integration in different documents, portability in a multivendor environment, frequent updates of and multimedia data, and manipulation of a set of data elements.

The standard defines the representation and encoding of final-form multimedia and hypermedia information objects for interchange within and across applications, services, and platforms. The standard additionally provides abstractions suited for real-time presentation (through synchronization functionality) and interchange.

The object oriented approach was chosen for the design of the standard because it fits the requirements of active, autonomous, and reusable objects. The standard focuses on the generic structuring aspects of the objects, allowing a wide range of potential multimedia applications to use the objects. The standard defines classes of objects, the design of which relies on the analysis of their common behavior and the commonalties between object categories. The standard provides two representations of objects ASN.1 and an alternate, that is SGML. The main MHEG object classes are:

- Content class. Encoded information itself, plus additional information for identification of the coding method and the formatting of data.

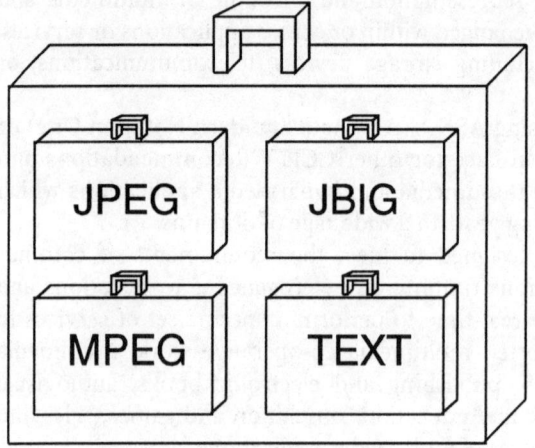

- Action class. This provides information on how and when to show the content (e.g., commands such as Set Volume, Set Visible Size, Show, Kill, etc.).
- Link class. Information about the hyperlink from one object to one or more target objects. Combined with actions it defines the temporal, spatial, and conditional relation between objects.
- Script class. Encapsulation of an external piece of software performing a script in the MHEG formalism.
- Composite class. A container for grouping related objects into a singe object. The composite object includes a set of component objects, a list of links, and an optional list of scripts.
- Selection class and modification class. These provide support for interaction with the user, either by using the facilities of a user interface support system or by allowing an MHEG object to be selectable or modifiable.

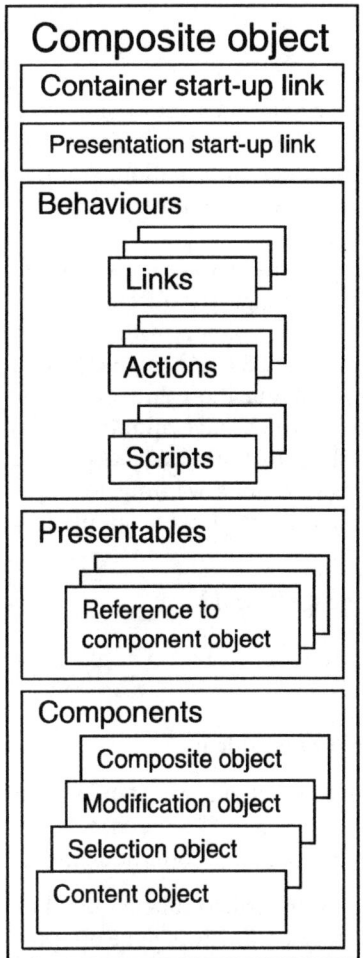

Figure 23. The MHEG composite object can be a MHEG document or a part of it

- Descriptor class. This contains general information about a set of inter-changed objects for presentation resources negotiation.
- Presentable objects. From a single original object several presentable objects can be defined, corresponding to different presentation occurrences.
- Template objects. Any original object may become a template for the generation of copies to be used in different presentation occurrences (as if with macros).

MHEG does not define an Application Programming Interface (API) but a number of mandatory facilities, optional facilities, and application-specific facilities are identified in the standard.

5.6
CALS

During the 1980s the U.S. Department of Defense adopted a set of standards for the transmission of data to and from its suppliers. The transmitted data was mainly in the fields of engineering, maintenance information, training manuals, and logistic support. They named this set of standards Computer-aided Acquisition and Logistics Support or CALS.

The scope of CALS was expanded to all U.S. government agencies embracing concurrent engineering, electronic data interchange (or EDI), and the mutual sharing of engineering and commercial information with industry through common databases. Changing the scope of CALS also had an effect on the acronym: CALS now stands for Continuous Acquisition and Life cycle Support. Currently the U.S. government agencies which have adopted CALS require the organizations that do business with them to adopt CALS. Applying CALS has benefits, but it also requires the organizations wanting to apply CALS to change to be able to apply it. The standards which were adopted by CALS in the first phase are:

- Standardized and Generalized Mark-up Language (SGML)
- Computer Graphics Metafile (CGM)
- Initial Graphics Exchange Specification (IGES)
- CCITT group 4 dither graphics.

In the second phase of CALS some new standards were added:

- Product Data Exchange using STEP (PDES). STEP stands for Standard for The Exchange of Product model data.
- The Open System Interconnection (OSI) environment for communication.

CALS is still evolving so it is expected that more standards will be adopted by CALS. Many larger U.S. companies such as defense contractors have adopted CALS as a result of the U.S. Department of Defense policy. Because of this the use of SGML has been growing in the U.S. Strangely enough, it appears that even though for most European companies there is no such incentive to use SGML, SGML is more widely used in Europe, and support is growing faster than in the U.S.

5.7
TEX

This is a coding language used especially by scientists and mathematicians. Because of TEX's similarity to RTF the similarities and differences are listed first. The impact on creating hypertext from it is stated later. TEX and RTF are alike in many respects, including:

- Both contain typesetting codes,
- They share many of their control characters such as the back slash \ and the curly parenthesis {}.

There are also some differences:

- T$_E$X has more page layout commands.
- T$_E$X has more support for mathematical formulas.
- RTF is specifically paragraph based, whereas T$_E$X is not. In RTF each paragraph has an attached (typographical) style. The paragraph styles can be used to store explicit semantic information.
- T$_E$X supports macros, which are not supported as such in RTF. The macros can be used for expressing explicit semantic information. Because the macros are not paragraph based, explicit semantic information can be attached to any part of the text: character(s), word(s), sentence(s), paragraph(s), or any combination of these. In this respect T$_E$X is more akin to SGML than to RTF.

Some implicit semantic information can be derived from the T$_E$X codes used in a document. Stating that all bold parts of the text are headers is an example of this.

T$_E$X macros can be used to add explicit semantic information to the text. An example:

\def\header{\bf}

The example defines a macro \header as switch to boldface. It is essentially the same as the first example where it was simply stated that all bold parts of the text are headers. But there are two differences:

- Now the typographical information may be changed by changing the macro but without changing the explicit semantic information. The macro itself changes, but its name does not.
- Also the same typographical information can be attached to two macros where only the names of the macros distinguish the semantic information.

For the creation of Windows Help files T$_E$X needs to be converted to RTF. This is possible. When converting T$_E$X to RTF all macros must be converted to typographical commands. This will make the converter somewhat complex. Needless to say, the explicit semantic information will be destroyed in this process, or at best, converted to implicit semantic information. Converting from RTF to T$_E$X is simpler, and this type of converter is available.

If T$_E$X needs to be converted to SGML, this will also be possible. A SGML document type definition (DTD) needs to be generated. Equivalents of all T$_E$X macros must be put in this DTD. Then the content of the document itself must be converted. Because SGML supports explicit semantic information, it can be kept intact. After generating the DTD the translation will be almost as straightforward as converting RTF to SGML.

5.8
Conclusions

- T$_E$X is a good intermediate format for hypertext documents.
- Explicit semantic information can be stored in T$_E$X documents.
- T$_E$X documents can be converted to RTF documents for the creation of Windows Help files. It may be necessary to write your own translator.
- T$_E$X documents can be converted to SGML. Creation of the DTD is an issue. Again, it may be necessary to write your own translator.
- See Appendix A for a popular book on T$_E$X by its inventor Donald Knuth (1984).

6 Editing

6.1
Introduction

While developing tools for presenting hypertext and hypermedia it is necessary to add editing facilities. For this reason we enhanced one of our applications with text editing facilities. Essentially our text and bitmap presentation module was enhanced from a present- only to an editable WYSIWYG (What You See Is What You Get) or presentation module. A number of features were required:

- Inserting text at the cursor position. The text can contain both normal and special characters.
- Inserting bitmaps. Only the references to the bitmaps are inserted in the texts. The presentation module will then automatically make space for the bitmap and present it.
- Selecting text.
- Making selected text bold, italic, underlined, superscript, subscript, or plain.
- Making a reference from the selected text after validating it.
- Selecting a rectangle in a bitmap and creating a reference or hotspot from that rectangle.
- Deleting text at the cursor position with the Backspace and Delete keys.
- Deleting selected text.
- Deleting references.
- Deleting references (hotspots) in the bitmaps.
- Deleting bitmaps, in this case actually deleting references to the bitmaps and the references (hotspots) in the deleted bitmaps.

Implementation of the above gave some problems:

- The manner in which the text was stored in memory had to be changed to support fast insertion of text somewhere in the presentation window. Not changing it would make inserting characters at the start of texts, especially long texts, very slow. Moving all characters from the insertion point once for every character inserted cannot be considered efficient. Thus the text of each presentation window is split into several memory blocks. When characters are inserted, and the block has space at the end, the text is only moved within that block. If the memory block is full, all text from the insertion point to the end is copied into a new memory block. The block will then be empty from the insertion point to the end and characters can be inserted. Some administration has to be done to keep track of the order and number of memory blocks. Compressing the memory blocks regularly can be important to keep the amount of unused space within reasonable limits.

- Determining the exact place in the text where the mouse was clicked proved to be the most illusive problem. This is not really a problem when using a fixed-spaced font, but a real problem when proportional fonts where used. The problem is that the width of a string of characters is different when calculated or when printed. One of the reasons for this is the kerning of characters when printing a string, since the width of a character is not fixed but depen-dent on its neighbors.
- The last problem had to do with updating the database when references were added or deleted. This problem was not solved.

Many modern word processors, such as Microsoft Word, WordPerfect, and Lotus AmiPro have most of the required features and also the following important features for editing hypertext documents:

- They can export and import data to and from different formats.
- They support macros.

Using the import and export features it is possible at times to produce text formatted in such a way that it is immediately usable for creating a hypertext system. The best example of this is using Microsoft Word for Windows to save a document as RTF and compiling it with the Microsoft Help or Viewer compiler. In other cases it is often possible to save it in a format that is easily convertible to the necessary format.

Macros can be used to add (meta-)information necessary for the hypertext documents in an easier manner. An example of this is when marking up a document. Selecting parts of the document to be tagged as something triggers the macro which will either do something without further intervention or prompt the person for some more information. Information prompted can be the kind of tag or in the case of a reference the destination of the reference.

The tags can be added as typographical information or as real tags such as SGML tags. It is possible to create a macro that using a fixed SGML DTD will prompt the user for all relevant information. It can fill in, correctly tagged, what it already knows. Examples of the known information are the name of the user, the company (s)he works for, and the date. These are often already stored somewhere. Then the user can be prompted for the title, the content, etc. Then the user can start selecting parts of the text to tag, and the macro can supply all the correct codes for tagging in right places.

Another possibility with macros is to write one that saves the document in the normal format, then converts the typographical information to the necessary tags and saves the converted document, and then reloads the original document. This can be handy for creating SGML-compatible documents.

6.2
MS Word

Microsoft Word is the word processor most suited for creating RTF files for use with the Microsoft Help and Viewer compilers. Many macros and extensions have already been written by Microsoft and third parties to make it easier to create these RTF files. A good example of an extension is the Viewer Topic Editor included in the Microsoft Viewer Toolkit. It is a tool that interfaces with Word in such a way as to make it easier to tag and insert information in the documents. Other examples are commercial packages such as RoboHelp (Blue Sky Software) and Doc-to-Help (WexTech Systems). Both applications use styles to define topic titles and topic structure. The packages add a number of styles and macros to Word to make it easier to define jumps, popups, topics, etc.

In Appendix B a macro for Microsoft Word (version 6 and 7 for Windows) is given to show how it can be made easier to create a RTF file for use with the Microsoft Viewer compiler. A number of assumptions are made:

- There are no page breaks in the document.
- Each topic has a title formatted with a heading style.
- References are formatted with strike-out/strike-through or double underline.
- References made are literally the same as the topic titles the refer to. Care has to be taken to do this. If a literal topic title is not found, the reference is made to the first topic.
- Sequences of characters that are character-formatted as bold or italic must be put in index and in search fields.
- All indices are in the index and search fields.
- It is assumed that the text to be put in the index (created by the option insert index entry) is identical to a part of the text directly in front of the index.
- The strings XE_ and #=#=#=# may not be used in the document.
- The translated file can be saved with the same name but with the .RTF extension.

The macro works in several steps and does a lot of things:

- Edits all title headings of levels one through three, replacing all by heading one. The assumption is made that each heading is the start of a new topic.
- Inserts page breaks between topics.
- Converts the title headings into topic titles and puts in browsing sequence codes and topic codes.

- Edits all title headings of levels one through three, index, bold and italic text in fields so the compiler will recognize these as different fields and index words.

The macro is slow, as all macros are, but it is still faster then doing it by hand. Also the conversion needs to be done only occasionally. And any document can be easily converted with a minimum of fuss, as long as the assumptions mentioned above are met.

Much time can be saved by using the macros for creating the topics, setting the title, browsing order, and keys. Searching for the keys for the references also can save a lot of time as long as the references are literal.

After this the Viewer compiler must be run using a project file. A sample project file can also be found in Appendix B.

6.3
WordPerfect

This word processor is very similar to Microsoft Word in that text can be entered and edited normally. Again the only requirement is that there is a fixed list of typographical attributes that link. After the documents are ready they can be translated to the necessary format.

Saving WordPerfect documents as RTF is possible, and although they are completely up to the official Microsoft RTF specs, they are not right for use with the Microsoft Help or Viewer compilers. The difference is that the Word-Perfect RTF documents do not have enough accolades in them in the right places for the Help and Viewer compilers. Even the RTF import routine of Word has problems with it at times.

This can be solved by adding the necessary RTF codes into the WordPerfect document and then saving the document as plain ASCII. The codes should contain the necessary accolades in the right places of the document. Given that only a small subset of the RTF specs is used by the Help and Viewer compiler this should be easy to achieve.

6.4
Implementing Your Own System

We needed a WYSIWYG editor that also supported hotspots. No such editor was available that could be easily called from within another application or the other way around. A lot of time went into developing such an editor for Windows. A few problems appeared while developing this editor.

- Memory management was a problem. The 64-kilobyte barrier for each segment was one of our problems. Windows appeared to be very unstable with the way we accessed and used memory. This was solved by writing a memory manager. It worked with 4-kilobyte chunks of memory sub-allocated from large chunks of memory allocated at the start of the application and increased when necessary.

- The width of a character, word or sentence was different while just asking, the width or when actually printing it. This gave all kinds of problems for determining hotspot co-ordinates and the place of the text insertion cursor. The text insertion cursor problem could also be observed in WordPerfect for Windows. This problem was left as it was.
- It was slow because of all the overhead.
- The fact that the editor was an integral part of the application also proved to be a liability. Compiling was slow, and at a certain point became impossible due to the large number of declarations in the source. A new editor would be made as a dynamic link library (DLL), or a separate application controlled and communicating with dynamic data exchange (DDE), or an OLE server. This would reduce the number of lines in the main application by a considerable amount. It might have some performance repercussions and take more disk space.
- Adding and storing hotspots also proved to be a problem. This was mainly in the complex way co-ordinates within scrolling, resizable windows with palettes have to be calculated. The co-ordinates are calculated as what they would have been if the picture had origin 0,0 and was full sized. These co-ordinates can be used to calculate the co-ordinates of the hotspots, even when there is an offset and the window is resized.

Because pictures were stored as separate files in standard windows bitmap format (BMP) they could be edited outside the program with any painting application supporting the BMP format. This reduced the complexity of the application and provided us with the insight that this should be done for all functions in a new version of the application, if possible. A new version of the system would have contained separate DLLs, applications, or OLE servers for each part of the whole system. The parts:

- Database engine for retrieval of text and other information.
- WYSIWYG editor for an editable version.
- Formatted text presentation, for a read-only version.
- Concept map presentation.
- Main application, which controls and calls the other parts when needed.

Splitting the application into a number of parts will have the following effects:

- The whole will be slightly slower, although this might be offset by the ability to better optimize each of the parts.
- The whole will be slightly larger.
- The code will be more maintainable.
- The parts will be easier to debug than the previous single application.
- Because of easier debugging the parts will become more stable in less time than the previous single application.

- Only the parts the user or client is interested in have to be shipped with the product.
- Viewers for new resources can be added without changing other parts.
- Viewers or database parts can be replaced without having to change other parts.

We conclude from this list that splitting into parts is worth the effort.

7 Authoring

Hypermedia may be produced by importing existing material in combination with new material. Usually this will be the most cost-effective way. Organized investigations should be undertaken to find authors and to define the template on which the system will be built. Check-list for research on sources:

- Available software like tools for creation and adaptation, databases, and user interfaces.
- Available material such as texts, pictures, sound.
- Are the formats compatible with the software?
- If not, which actions are to be taken?
- Available authors, including photographers or illustrators.
- What must be totally new?
- What must be added?
- Are there copyrights to be paid?

7.1
Processes

This part describes the different authoring actions which should be undertaken when preparing hypertext systems based on existing material. We distinguish three different steps in the authoring process:

- The first authoring step means conceiving the idea and actually assembling and writing material for different types of media.
- The second authoring step consists of imposing and validating hypermedia structures.
- A tailoring step may occur when a user wants to add his own ideas to the hypertext system.

7.2
The Primary Author

The primary author develops an idea and creates (writes) a publication. He or she may use the following check-list (for writing/recording resources):

- Create new material with a variety of generators, recorders, and editors. In case of text he or she will use a word-processor or text editor. In case of video it will be a camera, animation studio, or computer-based video generator. For audio the first author will record oral conversations, music performances, or on-site happenings such as natural events. Very cost-effective ways to produce audio fragments exist nowadays that make use of MIDI-controlled sequencers, samplers, and synthesizers. (MIDI means Musical Instruments Digital Interface.) Authoring computer animations will make use of dedicated animation tools like Macro Mind Director.

- Combine new material with existing material. Analogue video and audio signals can be mixed and faded by traditional studio equipment. Texts and computer code need in-depth editing and rewriting. As soon as the constituent information sources are prepared, they should be checked against the specifications of the principal or the executive publishers who are responsible for the hypermedia ingredients. It is good to be aware of the quality of the final medium. If we know that the final medium will be a mid-fi set of speakers in a notebook computer, than it needs less resolution in the analogue to digital conversion and mixing stages.

1. Present the new material on traditional monomedia devices.
2. Check its technical quality and test its appeal to the target group.
3. Repair mistakes. In most cases errors occur in the stage of editing, cutting, and mixing. In these cases the master tape must be consulted to repair the mistake. In other cases new recordings must be made.

The author has to keep in mind for whom and for what medium (s)he is writing. His writing process will largely be determined by the criterion of learning effects that should take place in the user. The following questions may help the author to adapt new material to the cognitive processes of the user while assimilating knowledge from the text:

- What is the educational level of my target group?
- What is the age of my target group?
- Which interests does my target group have?
- Which type of publication am I writing? (Types include newspaper article, newsreel item, film-script, book, magazine.)
- How much space do I have?
- Are illustrations available?
- If so, which illustrations?
- Are there tables?
- Which typography/tags do I have to use?

The answers to these questions strongly determine the way the material will look when published. But the consequences to draw from the answers are difficult to prescribe. The answers will give a certain focus to the authors, rather than hard deterministic rules for what to write.

From the educational point of view, the state of the art in techniques for designing instructional texts has developed quickly the last two decades. When we focus on the educational merits of hypermedia, the two major types of design considerations have been formalized in order to improve the readability and learning effects of instructional text:

- Micro considerations, which apply to teaching a single idea (such as the use of examples and practice).
- Macro considerations, which apply to the teaching of many related ideas such as sequencing and systematic review.

Merrill's CDT (Component Display Theory), (Merrill, Reigeluth & Faust, 1977) is an example of the first type. CDT was developed for instructional purposes. It is mainly based on the following seven principles, and reminds the author to anticipate the cognitive processes that may take place in the reader's mind. The principles were defined to improve the structure in text on paper.

- *The three primary presentation forms*: Generality, example, and practice should always be present in texts.
- *Sequencing the primary presentation forms:* The three primary presentation forms should not constantly be presented in a fixed order. Effective texts try to surprise the reader to a certain extent.
- *Freedom to the reader:* Readers are inherently different and have their own idiosyncratic preferences. Authoring text for electronic presentation means anticipating the unknown reader by allowing non-linear structures. Hypertext is the de facto method to create flexible routing.
- *The need for explicit presentation forms:* Primary presentation forms work only in the reader's cognition if they stimulate the reader's awareness. In Part III of this book we will articulate the concept mapping approach. In our view it is the best method nowadays to stimulate the reader's metacognition.
- *Attribute matching.* Both examples and non-examples are essential for understanding the author's theory. They might play an even more important role in the reader's understanding than the expository text itself.
- *Recurring generality:* One of the dominant results of research into reading processes is the persistent need for generality; without generality readers stop integrating their ideas. This means that good texts have many 'conceptual panoramas'.
- *Mathemagenic information.* Mathemagenic information is the total set of typographic attributes that may help the reader to stay focused on the right message. Mathemagenic questions and feedback are even more difficult to arrange. To provide such information the author must know the reader's prior knowledge and misconceptions at the time of reading.

These seven principles are in fact pleas for multi-sequential text and inherently anticipate hypertext presentation. They are the most explicit guidelines for structuring and sequencing an instructional text that we have found in the literature so far. The impact of the CDT principles go beyond assisting first authors as they write for text on paper. In fact they say: If you can, start writing in a hypermedia environment, also if the final presentation to the reader is on paper.

Reigeluth's Elaboration Theory or ET (Reigeluth, Merrill, Wilson & Spiller, 1980) focuses on the integration of knowledge in the reader on the macro level (aspects of instruction that relate to more than one idea). The most fundamental aspect of ET is its prescription of an elaborative sequence at the start of a new text passage. The text should start with the most general or simple ideas that are to be taught and should gradually elaborate on those fundamental ideas by adding layers of detail or complexity, one layer at a time. Each layer should be made up of the same seven strategy components:

- A special type of general-to-detailed sequence for the main structure of the course.
- A learning-prerequisite sequence within individual layers of description.
- A summary at the end of each textual episode.
- A synthesis at the end of each text.
- Analogies where appropriate.
- Cognitive strategy activators where appropriate.
- A learner control format, which guides the reader in to interpreting the information.

Besides the architecture of text in terms of layers and strategy components, ET prescribes dealing with one single type of content relationship (conceptual, procedural, or theoretical). The rationale is that elaborating on a single type of relationship will result in the student's developing more stable cognitive structures, which in turn should cause better long-term retention and transfer.

Reigeluth et al. (1980) compiled the heuristics from CDT and ET into a design and development procedure for writing texts by the first author.

1. Select and sequence the organizing content ideas.
   1.1 Select the kind of organizing content ideas.
   1.2 List all of the important organizing content ideas.
   1.3 Arrange the organizing content ideas into an elaborate sequence and group into chapters.
   1.4 Allocate organizing content to chapters.
2. Select the supporting content for each chapter, and sequence it within each chapter.
   2.1 List all of the important supporting content ideas for each chapter.
   2.2 Sequence both the organizing and supporting content within each chapter.
3. Select strategies for relating new knowledge to prior knowledge of the reader.
   3.1 Decide what within-chapter syntheses to include and where.
   3.2 Decide what cumulative syntheses to include and where.
   3.3 Decide what reader experiences can be used as instances.

   3.4   Decide what analogies to include and where.

   3.5   Decide what motivational components to include and where.

4. Select the review strategies.

   4.1   Decide which content ideas should be included in the within-chapter reviews.

   4.2   Decide where to put cumulative reviews and what to put in them.

5. Select micro strategies for each idea.

   5.1   Select the appropriate micro model for each idea or fact.

   5.2   Decide on the appropriate level of richness for that model.

   5.3   Write the test items and the primary and secondary strategy components for each idea.

6. Write the remaining strategy components.

   6.1   Write the integrative test items.

   6.2   Write the synthesis.

   6.3   Write the reviews.

   6.4   Write the analogies.

   6.5   Write any remaining motivational components.

7. Decide how to format all of the instruction in the text.

   7.1   Separate and label all ideas and strategy components.

   7.2   Format other aspects of the instructional text.

The heuristics compiled above could easily be embedded as a step-by-step procedure in text-and-idea processors. However, it would constrain the versatility of creative writing if it forced the author to do all the expansions any time. Reigeluth therefore recommends taking them as a general agenda for teams of authors, so that they are prompted to consider various aspects of the learning process in the user.

Reusing written material for another presentation medium (even if the target group is the same) needs in-depth adaptation and restructuring. For example, the text base for a reference manual on paper will need extra human efforts to enable a computer medium to exploit implicit references and semantic connotations in the text. This adaptation is the second step in the authoring process. We call the person who takes care of this the secondary author.

7.3
The Secondary Author

The secondary author prepares the existing material for the hypertext system. His or her work consists of the following steps:

- *Search* for out-of-date information and add new information.
- *Split* up existing material into self-contained pieces (items), which can be read and interpreted independently of their context. In some cases the original document already is compartmentalized, like a keyword-oriented

reference manual, thesaurus, or encyclopedia. In other cases the fragments of text are highly interwoven and need to be rewritten so that they become understandable even if they are read in another sequential order. Texts like novels, story-based video, and radio plays which have strong episodic structures are quite fragile in their sequential structure. Changing the order of two fragments may severely destroy the meaning for the user, and/or may create a mystery (in the bad sense).

- Let a specialized editing program *prompt* for possible references between these items and show the relevant items (co-presentation); prompt the secondary author which of the possible references should be validated.
- *Parse* references (including looking up whether references are valid).
- *Compute* centrality of the information nodes in the network, based on graph computation (Kommers 1991, 1992a and 1992b).
- *Match* properties (if necessary).
- *Load* the hypermedia system with all items.
- *Search* for mistakes.
- *Evaluate* the hypermedia system with all items.
- *Repair* the original material and the hypermedia system.

When developing hypertext from existing publications it is a great advantage when typesetting codes are replaced by SGML tags. This work may be done by the secondary author or a specialist. It should take place before the secondary authoring phase starts.

7.4
Tools for the Secondary Author

The computer may help the secondary author in the following ways:

Splitting up the existing material. For the first part of this job a normal text editor of a word processor is sufficient. The author has to identify each item by an identifier (a unique series of characters). The author will need a program that supplies him or her with an overview of all identifiers. If the quality and consistency of the SGML encoding is sufficient, we might think of a dedicated editor, which is sensitive to the markup codes. The results from the first prototype showed us the elegance of hiding the markup codes and presenting the graphical effects as printed on paper in the book. However, the efficiency decreased dramatically as the editing actions could only be performed with mouse clicks and pull-down menu commands instead of, e.g., a macro language.

Creating (or marking) possible links between items. This can be done in various ways:

- The computer analyses which words in a certain item (or description of an item or link) are meaningful. It may do this by comparing a list of meaningful words which is prepared in advance (for instance all substantives in a dictionary or a list of identifiers, if these are characteristic words) with the words in the text of an item. Each word of the list which occurs in an item and occurs in a second item might produce a link between the two items. However, there are some problems:

- Usually references (and thus links) have a direction: From ... to ... Connecting two items merely because the word occurs in both items will lead to a two-way link, which will not always fit the author's view.
- Furthermore, the computer has to cope with synonyms: If the word of the list has a synonym unknown to the computer and this synonym is used in the item, the computer does not make the link.
- Thirdly, homonyms mean different things to the user, but they will not be distinguished by the computer.

As a result, many links without meaning or with a false meaning may be produced. These meaningless or false links may be so numerous that it may take the secondary author more time to restore the inadequacies than to create new links attuned to his or her special purpose and target group. Dictionary help may become important to tackle problems with synonyms and homonyms.

- The computer shows the author which meaningful words have been found in the item, based on a list given by the secondary author or derived from identifiers. The secondary author tells the computer which words in the item have a meaning and which do not. The computer computes the links between the items. This is a better proposition, but will still not solve the problem of the direction of links. The list mentioned may also be a list derived from the index of the publication.
- The computer helps the author to identify words what may refer to other items. (S)he may use the same list as mentioned above. In this case the computer prompts, but the secondary author makes the links. So the hypertext system has been derived by the secondary author and not by the computer.

Hypertext systems usually do not display hierarchic structures. However, to assist the user in approaching the hypermedia database in a top-down mode, it would be useful to provide a network view. It may be possible to develop a secondary, hierarchically constructed system next to the hypertext system itself. Such a system may be derived from the text after adding hierarchic or rubric tags to the various items by the secondary author.

Conceptual mapping as a methodology for modifying/extending/up-dating an existing information resource. Three phases can be distinguished, as shown in Figure 24.

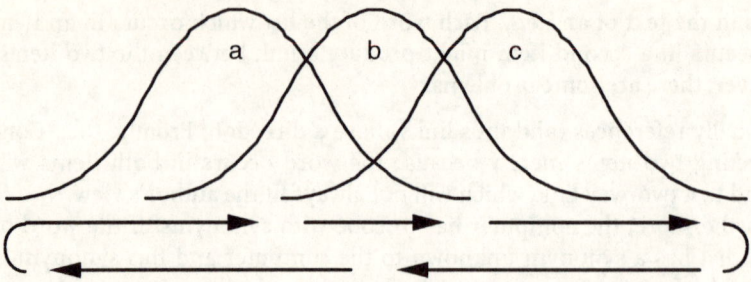

Figure 24. Three phases

1. **Accretioning:** As the author (or the secondary author) starts to describe a new conceptual domain, he or she faces the task of adding new elements. This process of appending can go on until the size of the resulting documents demand for more compact representations like outliners, lists, or network views. Accretioning as typical authoring activity recurs also in later phases of the hypermedia production process, but is then under the control of procedures for consistency checking, or acts as a tuning procedure.

2. **Restructuring:** As existing hypermedia resources have to be integrated in new contexts (typically for embedding printable texts in interactive applications), the perspective of the original documents often has to be changed. The balance between elaborations in the texts may have to be revised, and new contexts may be necessary to make the meaning clear to the reader. This may force the author to rewrite the existing text from scratch. It may also bring the author to revise other parts of the documents. Restructuring in general becomes urgent if the consistency of documents decreases over time, especially if several authors cooperate and the perspective of the text becomes blurred or distorted. Restructuring causes considerable mental load which needs computer assistance. If several persons are occupied with revising the documents, additional meta-information about who changed what and why is needed. If only one person does it, we may generally say that the last version is the definitive one.

3. **Tuning:** Available hypermedia documents need to be updated and tailored to specific educational goals; characteristic for this phase is that the overall outline of the document stays intact:

   • *Assign properties* to the nodes and links by using property-matching tools.
   • *Repair the hypermedia database* by using appropriate tools.

Upgrading information resources by secondary authors can be compared to software engineering. It is an iterative process which will terminate if:

A. The context of the information is covered and represents the key issues to be delivered to the end user; and

B. All inconsistencies between old and new information have been removed; and

C. The internal references between the information elements (items) reaches a certain level of saturation; and

D. Navigating consequences (in terms of reachability and centrality) are optimized to a certain level.

7.5
Extending Hypermedia to an Educational Tool

Hyperbases contain lots of information. The price of the information may be high, especially when many highly qualified people made contributions to it. It is therefore desirable that the use of hyperbases should be very broad. An interesting area of use will be the field of education. There are various ways in which hyperbases can be used.

The first is to extract a small part of the total hyperbase and present it to learners. The learner can browse through the subject matter in his own way, which is known as *exploratory learning*. Another approach is to construct a curriculum where the parts to be learned are already existing parts of the hyperbase. Extra information then has to be stored in order to control the learning process of the learner. Why should this not be done with SGML?

We will not discuss the first presented approach here, because the subject has more to do with educational psychology than with hypermedia databases. The second view is very interesting, because a new concept is added to the stored SGML code: *flow control.*

For the creation of curricula it might be useful to add a curriculum editor beside the SGML editor that is already being developed. This curriculum editor should allow the author to define a sequence of articles to be read and the conditions for all possible sub-sequences based on exercises done by the learner while running the curriculum.

Progress of learner actions might be recorded in special files to inform the teacher about the progress and behavior of the learner. For this approach the hypermedia database application should be extended with a subprogram for the creation of the curriculum. As exercises are not yet coded in SGML, a construction has to be designed for the notation. When that is done, almost the same program can be used for both curriculum design and teaching. Only the entry point to the program will differ.

8 Preparing Textual Material

8.1
Introduction

It makes sense to structure textual material for use in hypertext or hypermedia. This can be done in many different ways. From the beginning we decided to take the approach of structuring the material in a platform and application independent way. Thus the resulting material can be used on any platform and in theory with any application.

- All added information and structure added should also be useful for the paper-based publications.

Many of the hypertext and hypermedia applications in use in the period 1985–1995 made it possible to import and structure material within the applications, but it was practically impossible to export the resulting structured material again. Thus all the added value of the material could only be harvested within the applications. The added value could not be extracted to be used in their paper documents. This is one of the reasons that large companies hesitate to accept hypertext as a document delivery technique.

Because of the heavy use of SGML by publishing houses, we targeted SGML as a focus at the start. We used only one document type definition or DTD, which made things a lot easier.

In 1992 and 1993, we also targeted Microsoft Rich Text Format (RTF). This was mainly because of Microsoft Windows Help files. These are created with especially formatted RTF files. The resulting help files can be regarded as hyper-text applications in their own right. The help files offer a lot of standard hyper-text features, while only needing a computer running MS Windows.

Some of the raw material was converted to RTF. This was easily done from the original SGML material. The resulting RTF files were converted into Windows Help files. It was not a problem to convert them into RTF. But even so, some of the material could not be converted to a help file. This was because of the sheer volume of the material and the number of topics and references within the documents. But with smaller amounts (4 000 topics, 100 000 references) it worked quite well.

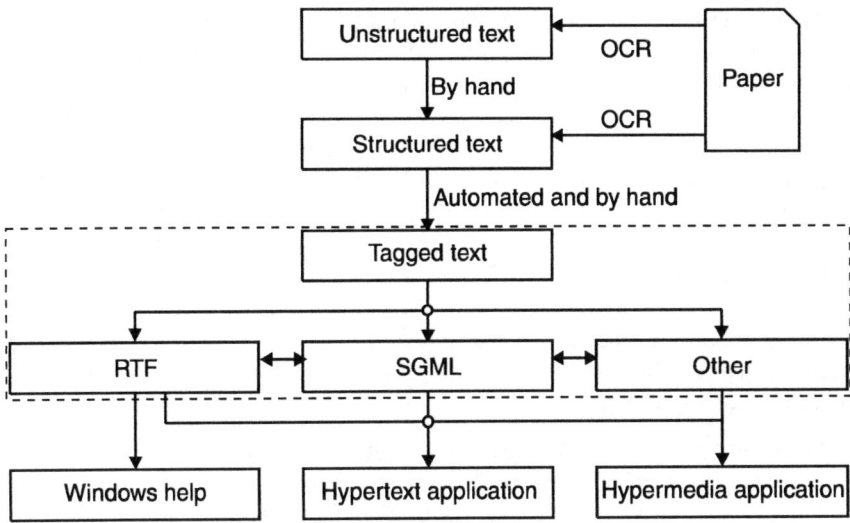

Figure 25. Differential streams for hypertext applications

For the above reasons and for convenience we assume that all textual material will be converted either to SGML-like tagged material or to Microsoft RTF. Using SGML-like tagging has the advantage that you can add more information than only typographic codes. RTF has one advantage, it can easily be converted to a Windows Help file, but it will only contain formatting information.

While we were building our own hypertext applications and trying to fund our research and development many questions were asked by interested parties. For demonstration versions, some of the parties delivered material on different media. The material came on computer disks, paper, parts of books, photographs, etc. The material was processed in many different ways. Figure 25 gives an overview of the paths followed. It also gives an overview of the items in this chapter.

8.2
Implicit and Explicit Semantic Information

Before moving on it is very important to realize the different ways information can be contained in documents. Within textual documents information can be contained as:

- Plain text,
- Typographical information,
- Semantic information.

Depending on the format of the document the semantic information can be implicit or explicit. Implicit semantic information can be derived from keywords used in the text such as Chapter or Paragraph. It can also be derived from the formatting of the text. When typographical codes are used, at times it is possible to derive some semantic information from that. This is only the case when specific information is always coded with the same typographical codes, which are otherwise never used in the same or another context. An example would be a document where all titles are bold and all references are italic.

Explicit semantic information can be found in documents that are marked up with a tagging language, such as SGML, or with other codes that are not specific typographical codes. An example of this would be the use of macros in T_EX or styles in Microsoft Word. Adding explicit semantic information to a document has advantages:

- At any stage a decision can be made about which parts of the documents are needed for the specific needs later in a project. Also searching can be made more powerful. If all names of persons and dates are encoded as such, searches can be made for all persons that lived at a certain time with a certain name, according to the document.
- The typographical effects for each type of semantic information can be chosen at the moment the document has to be presented. Must personal names be presented in normal or italic type?

In many cases the end documents will contain a combination of explicit and implicit semantic information. The old typographical coded document are polished up, and all added semantic information is explicit whilst all old semantic information stays implicit.

8.3
Paper Text

In some cases it may still be that the documents only exist in printed versions. The documents can either be converted by typists or by using optical character recognition or OCR applications. If the documents are well printed, with clear lettering and spacing, using OCR will be very fast and quite accurate. The best accuracy will be obtained when the documents are printed in one language, known to the OCR application. Documents imported into a computer by OCR applications will not be error free. Proof-reading the documents will be necessary.

If the documents are not well printed or have unclear lettering (e.g., gothic type) or spacing, OCR will probably produce many errors. Correcting the errors made by the OCR application might take more time than typing the document into the computer. In many cases the best thing to do is to test the OCR application with a number of representative pages. Checking the number of errors and the time necessary to scan and correct will give an indication of the costs and benefits of using that OCR application. Some OCR applications can even distinguish bold and italic type. It might be possible to derive some structure from the text with this.

8.4
Unstructured Text

Unstructured text-only material is most difficult to convert. Example of unstructured text:

> *An example of unstructured text. It is not clear if the body text starts with this sentence. It is also not clear if the first sentence is a title. If we want to refer to structured text this is also not clear.*

If it has no structure, and in many cases no formatting, it will have to be structured first by hand. This can be done by importing the text(s) into a word processor such as Microsoft Word, WordPerfect, or Lotus AmiPro. Structure can be added by (for example):

- Giving titles a specific typographical code such as bold. If all titles have their own line of text a (bold) style could be connected to that line.
- Making all keywords italic.
- Underlining all references.
- Other information such as authors or literature might also get a style or typographical code connected.
- If the parts of the text should have a certain order, the parts should be moved if necessary.

After the above the text is structured and more of the tedious work can be done by the computer.

8.5
Structured Text

Textual material is considered to be structured if clear distinctions can be made between some or all parts of the text. The parts to be distinguished are titles, body text, keywords, references, etc. Note that if typographical codes are used, there must be a list of unique typographical codes for each type of information. If the codes are not unique, some information will be lost that previously was there while converting. It is also possible to use styles. Styles are associated with different parts of the texts.

Example based on the previous example:

> **An example of structured text.** It is clear that the body text starts with this sentence. It is also clear that the first sentence is a title because it is bold. We refer to <u>unstructured text</u>, which is clear from the use of underlining.

If the texts are structured, a word processor macro can be used to convert the structured texts into tagged texts (a tag is a symbol representing a logical element within an SGML document). The macro tags unique sequences of characters. SGML recognizes two kinds of tags, start tags and end tags, and uses <Code> as a start tag and </Code> as an end tag. RTF uses {/Code as a start tag and } at the end. Both RTF and SGML support nesting. But the support of overlap of formatted text by SGML is better than that of RTF. SGML example:

```
<b>Bold text <u>Bold and underlined text
</b>Underlined only</u>
```

RTF example:

```
RTF:  {/b Bold text {/u Bold and underlined
text }Bold only }{/u Underlined only}
```

The SGML example assumes that <b> has bold typographical style attached and </u> underlined.

Some of the structure of a text may be apparent from the use of carriage returns, linefeeds, and specific words. An example:

Chapter 1
This is a short example with a paragraph in it.
Paragraph 1.1
This is the content of this paragraph. See also: Chapter 2.

In the example the special words that can be used for conversion are printed bold. The rules here are:

- If the word chapter or paragraph is at the start of a new paragraph and followed by a number it indicated the beginning of a new chapter or paragraph.
- "See also" indicates that the next word or words are a reference.

If the texts are written in a consistent manner much work can be left to the com-puter. Still almost always inconsistencies occur or ambiguities exist in the text. All texts have to be proof-read after each conversion stage.

8.6
Tagged Text

A macro or a stand-alone application should check if all references refer to existing titles. If a reference is not correct a warning must be given. A best-match algorithm may be considered. (See also Automatic references). In many cases it is also necessary to check if all titles are unique. Again a warning must be given if this is not the case.

After the tagged text is checked, it can be converted to a standard format or RTF. It should be noted that there is not much difference between a generic tagged text or RTF text. Parts of the RTF text are tagged by typographical codes. Tags in SGML can code more than typographical effects. You can decide what will be shown in what manner at the moment it has to be shown. You can decide to show everything normal, or show only references in italic, etc. RTF example (incomplete):

```
{/b An example of RTF.} It is clear that
the body text starts with this sentence.
It is also clear that the first sentence
is a title because it is bold. We refer to
{/u unstructured text}, which is clear from
the use of underline tag./par
```

SGML example (incomplete):

```
<TITLE>An example of SGML.</TITLE><BODY>
It is clear that the body text starts with
this sentence. It is also clear that the
first sentence is a title because it is
tagged with TITLE. We refer to
<REF>unstructured text</REF>, which is clear
from the use of the REF tag.</BODY>
```

Converting a Microsoft Word for Windows document to RTF is very simple. Just save it as RTF. Converting it to SGML can be done using special macros.

The assumption made in the examples above was that if we refer to something, something is a literal title. Depending on the type of texts this may or may not be normal. Sometimes there will be a visible reference and an invisible link. An example:

```
{/b An example of RTF.} It is clear that the
body text starts with this sentence. It is also
clear that the first sentence is a title
because it is bold. We refer to
{/u unstructured texts} {/h unstructured text},
which is clear from the use of underlining.
Note that you will see a reference to
unstructured texts (plural) while the link is
to unstructured text (singular). The h tag
stands for hidden text./par
```

If an RTF file needs to be prepared for the help compiler, it must have both a reference and a link, even if these are identical. Our own hypertext applications always assumed that a reference is literally the same as the title it refers to. The best way will probably be somewhere in the middle: If there is no link defined, the reference itself should be used.

8.7
Automatic References

In order to perform our experiments at a realistic scale we took a specialized encyclopedia with about 4000 articles. As few references existed in this encyclopedia we tried to enrich it with more references. Given that not all, but most, of the subjects had unique titles, and given that most of the titles were relatively short, we sought to have all occurrences of the titles in the texts automatically made into references to the titles. This gave us a total of about 100 000 references.

Some of these references were wrong, because some abbreviations where also normal words. And all these normal words referred to the abbreviation. This problem could be corrected to some extent with a better case-sensitive comparison scheme. For this test we did not use any case-sensitivity. In our case we could have, because a title only started with an uppercase character when it was a name. Only words at the start of a sentence might produce problems for matching. And acronyms, written in uppercase characters only, would never be a problem. All of this would have spared us many problems with a Dutch word such as met (English: with) or MET (Middle European Time), which appeared quite often in the texts.

Some words should have been references but weren't because of conflicts with plural and singular forms. This could have been corrected by using a best-match algorithm. But beware, best-match algorithms may do more harm than good.

8.8
Converting SGML to RTF

Converting SGML to RTF can be done with simple macros or simple applications when the document type definition or DTD is fixed for all documents. If the DTD is not fixed there are two choices: Either a complex macro or application must be written to understand all DTDs, or the macros or applications must be rewritten for each different DTD.

8.8.1
SGML to RTF macro

Some precautions must be taken because of the stack based nature of RTF, as shown in the examples. SGML example:

```
<b>Bold text <u>Bold and underlined text
</b>Underlined </u>
```

RTF example:

```
{/b Bold text {/u Bold and underlined
text }Bold }{/u Underlined}
```

Thus the translator macro must keep track of the tag fields entered and exited to create a correct translation. A translation table must be made for the macro to use. This table must contain all tags and their translations. When creating this table care must be taken that all necessary tags are translated uniquely. In some cases the SGML text may be too rich with information for your purposes. This information can just be skipped. It should be noted that in this case the SGML texts must be stored if the skipped information is to be used ever again.

8.8.2
SGML to RTF Translator application

An SGML document contains a number of typical parts:

- A header,
- An (optional) extension to the DTD,
- Tags,
- Codes for special characters.

The header consists of: Document type, DTD-type, identifier of the DTD (this is the place where the DTD can be found) or an ISO number. The extension to the DTD is part of the header and is placed between [and].

Tags appear inside the plain text and there are two kinds, start tags and end tags. A start tag alerts the reader that something special should be done to the following text. Some start tags or end tags are optional. In those cases the tag is implied by another tag. The following characters have a special meaning in SGML : <, >, / and &.

Codes are used for special characters like <, which is the first character of a tag. For example when in the plain text a < is needed, it will be represented by < (including semicolon). A literal ampersand is represented by & .

For translating SGML documents to RTF the DTD of Electronic Books Technologies was used. This DTD is called Rainbow DTD and belongs to the RTF-to-SGML translator of EBT, Rainbow. To test the SGML-to-RTF translator a document that was translated by the Rainbow translator was used.

The syntax of Rainbow documents is described in the DTD, so this DTD is very useful as a grammar for the translator. Rainbow documents are not stack-based. When several codes belong to one part of the text, all codes are put in one tag. Example:

```
<PARA PARATYPE FONT-WEIGHT="Bold"
FONT-SLANT="Ital">. The text is closed by
</PARA>. The translation is a one-to-one
translation.
```

8.8.2.1
Errors in Rainbow Documents

Paragraph types have to be enclosed in double quotes. When a <CLF> occurs several times in a row, the number of <CLF> has to be decreased to one.

The Document Instances created by the Rainbow translator are not compliant to the Rainbow DTD itself. The DTD is supposed to be the grammar for the parser/translator. The DTD was expected to be correct, so it was used as the grammar for the parser/translator. Unfortunately, parsing is not correct because the documents are not compliant to the DTD. There are two solutions to correct the parsing problem:

- Edit the SGML document, or
- Change the grammar of the parser.

The first solution is not relevant: Each time a document has to be translated, the document has to be changed by hand. Choosing the latter solution means that not every SGML document has to be changed. The errors that occurred during parsing are not fatal errors: Most errors have to do with missing close-tags, which are implied by another close tag or a new open tag.

The grammar of the parser/translator was changed by parsing a large document (about 6000 lines) and solving generated parsing errors. (There is no other solution than debugging to solve the parsing errors.)

8.8.2.2
Implementation

Writing a parser using the DTD as a grammar is a straightforward job. A DTD contains three kind of rules: Element rules, Attlist rules, and Entity rules. The Element- and Entity rules are the base for the grammar. Attlist rules contain parameters for tags.

An Element rule in the DTD contains data for tag name, for whether an end tag is necessary or not, and for which element may occur between both tags.

An Entity rule does not describe tags, but show which Element or data may occur.

```
<!ELEMENT eqn - O (SYSATTRS?, EQNCONT?)>
<!ATTLIST eqn format CDATA   #REQUIRED
```

meaning:

```
eqn         :    Name of the tag
-           :    Start tag must be used
O           :    End tag may be omitted
SYSATTRS?   :    Element SYSATTRS may occur
                 directly behind start tag.
```

```
EQNCONT?       :    Element EQNCONT may occur
                    directly behind SYSATTRS;
                    if SYSATTRS is not present,
                    EQNCONT may occur directly
                    behind the start tag.
format CDATA        The start tag has the
#REQUIRED :         parameter:
                    format="CDATA", in which CDATA
                    is a text string.
filename CDATA      The start tag may have the
#IMPLIED>   :       parameter:
                    filename="CDATA" in which
                    CDATA is a text string.
```

8.8.2.3
PCCTS

With PCCTS it is very easy to write a translator. First a parser is created. The parser checks whether the document is compliant to the grammar. A large part of the parser is created by converting the DTD to EBNF-code, which is understood by PCCTS (EBNF is Extended Backus–Naur Form.) Functions for translation can be inserted into the parser code. Those functions are pure C-functions. Example of translating DTD to EBNF:

```
<!ELEMENT   eqn   - O
(SYSATTRS?, EQNCONT?)> <!ATTLIST   eqn   format
CDATA #REQUIRED
eqn : "<EQN" format ">" {sysattrs} {eqncont}
      {"</EQN>"};
```

The question mark in DTD is equivalent to "{" and "}" in EBNF. The words "format", "sysattrs", and "eqncont" (called non-terminals) are declared somewhere in the PCCTS file. Words and characters between double quotes are strings which are used literally in an SGML document.

8.9
Converting RTF to SGML

As the structure of RTF texts in stored in the typographical tags, a translation table must be made of the RTF tags and the SGML counterparts. Because the SGML DTD can always be the same a relatively simple, although possible quite long, macro can do the work. The macro should contain a translation table with the RTF codes and the SGML tags. It should also keep track of which codes are active to put in the right close tags. Note that the translation table needs to be adapted when typographical tags give different information in different texts.

Another method is to write a translator that does the job. This translator will be must faster than a macro, but possibly a bit more complex too.

8.9.1
RTF to SGML Translator Application

Both SGML and RTF are mark-up languages. RTF uses fixed codes for special typographies like bold and italics. SGML also uses codes, but the meaning of these codes is defined in an external table called DTD. Most information in a SGML file is semantic information.

8.9.2
RTF

A clear specification of an RTF was obtained from an FTP site:

(FTP.MICROSOFT.COM/developers/drg/RTF-info/RTF_W2.DOC).

This file contained the grammar of an RTF file. RTF is a specification for text and graphic interchange. It can be used on different platforms. RTF contains a big header. The header contains information about colors, fonts, margins, user information, and so on. In RTF a code always has the same meaning. For example:

```
{\b This is boldfaced text }
(\b stands for bold, \i for italic).
```

An RTF code consists of :

- A backslash \,
- Alphabetic string,
- A delimiter.

The delimiter can be:

- A space. The space belongs to the code.
- A digit or minus sign followed by a digit. In this case another (non-numerical) delimiter follows.
- Any character other than a letter or digit. This character does not belong to the code.

An RTF file consists of groups. Each group contains control words or control symbols and text between {and}. The former marks the beginning of a group, the latter the end. There are different kind of control words: These control words mark the beginning of a collection of related text (The end is marked by }), for example character-, paragraph-, section-, and table-formatting codes. What must an RTF reader do ?

- Separate control words and plain text,
- Perform actions that belong to control words.

More precisely, it must:

1. Read the next character.
2. If it is a {, store the current state.
   If it is a }, remove the current state.
   If it is a \, read the control word, search for the control word in a list, perform the action belonging to the control word.
   Else print data, using the current state.
3. If not all the characters have been read, go to 1.

It may perform the following possible actions:

- Change the destination, for example header, footer, color table.
- Change a formatting property.
- Insert a special character.
- Insert a special character and perform action.

An RTF file contains tokens, which are symbols representing logical elements within a RTF document. Those tokens start with a \ and end with a non-alphanumeric sign (in most cases a space or semicolon). This sign is called closure. The code word comes between \ and closure. An RTF file needs to comply with a certain grammar. In general an RTF file contains the following parts:

- Version number,
- Character set,
- Font descriptions,
- Style definitions,
- Color information,
- Document and author information,
- Typographical codes,
- Plain text.

The easiest way to create a RTF file is by using MS Word. This program has an option to save a file as an RTF file.

8.9.3
From RTF to SGML

Each mark-up language has its own characteristics. RTF codes are pre-defined, SGML codes can be chosen by the user or writer. It is advised to choose obvious codes, like <BOLD>. When a user creates an RTF file and makes conventions about the meaning of compound codes, it is possible to translate the compound codes to a special SGML code. For example: \b\i (bold and italics) could be translated with <REDIRECTION>.

RTF does not have a DTD file, but contains a big header. The header contains information about colors, fonts, margins, user information, and so on. For translating RTF to SGML two files have to be created: a DTD file containing tag definitions and grammar, and the DI (document instance), containing the plain text and a reference to the DTD. A DTD file can be used for a lot of files. Unfortunately, there is no standard DTD file which can be used for all kind of files.

There is no default DTD for all documents, but there are a number of DTDs for one kind of a document, for example for encyclopedias, books, or articles. It is possible to use one of those DTDs. Another possibility is to take all codes used in the RTF file and put these in a DTD file. It is quite impossible to create a DTD file from scratch. A complete grammar should be created. The RTF-to-SGML translator from the firm Electronic Book Technologies uses one default DTD, the Rainbow DTD. This DTD is public-domain and can be used without charges. EBT is well known for its program DynaText.

There is a lot of information in an RTF file which is not relevant for SGML translation. This information will not be destroyed, but will be included as hidden text. When it is necessary to translate the SGML file (back) to RTF, this information can easily be included.

In RTF there is no absolute separation between header and document as in SGML: <DOC> (in SGML) says that the document starts at that point. The use of RTF is of a different kind than the use of SGML. In RTF there are a lot of codes concerning page-layout, fonts, margins. In SGML this kind of code is rarely used. Translating RTF to SGML is almost as simple as translating each RTF token to its equivalent SGML tag, but unfortunately not quite that simple. Tokens can be nested. This means that states have to kept in memory. For example:

```
{\b This part is boldfaced
{\ul and now also underlined}
* and back to bold again }
```

At the position of * (which does not belong to the RTF file!) the previous state needs to be restored: The text following the * has to be bold again (and no longer underlined). So RTF is stack-based, SGML not.

By the way, it is also possible to write the example above as non-stack-based; Word for Windows (version 6 and 7) uses this notation:

```
{\b This part is boldfaced }
{\b\ul and now also underlined}
{\b and back to bold again }
```

Tokens, used in RTF and which have no SGML equivalent, could be inserted as hidden text. The translator consists of an integrated scanner and translator part. The scanner scans control tokens and plain text. There are two kind of token: those belonging to a certain group (like style group, info group) and those affecting text following them. When a token of the latter kind is read, a new state becomes active. This state will be stored on top of all other, still active states. As soon as a } is read, the last (or top) state can be removed.

8.9.4
Implementation

First a scanner was written to recognize RTF files. This scanner was created with PCCTS. PCCTS (Purdue Compiler Construction Tool Set) looks a lot like Lex and Yacc, which are UNIX tools for creating a scanner. PCCTS has several significant advantages over Lex and Yacc. Precedence is forced by the grammar, not by pseudo-instructions like %left and %right. The grammar needs to be in EBNF. Another advantage of PCCTS is the possibility to insert C-code at any place in the grammar. It is possible (and allowed!) to influence the parsing process. Inheritance of variables is very easy with PCCTS.

While scanning the RTF file, the tokens will be translated to SGML files. The user has to create an external table, which will be used as a dictionary. In RTF there are about 350 known tokens, of which one third can have a parameter. These tokens can be separated into several groups (not every token can be used in some places). Tokens which may occur at a certain place have to be put in memory (PCCTS). Unfortunately, the stack-size of DOS is too small for a lot of tokens, so we had to install Linux, which does not have a 64 K segment boundary. Linux is a freeware UNIX clone, compatible with System V UNIX. The current version of the RTF scanner recognizes version-number, character set, font group, color group, and information group.

An integer variable is used to keep track of the bracket level. The brackets tell when to change to another state. The bracket variable can be seen as a stack address. When a { is read, a new situation has to be placed onto the stack. This can be done by incrementing the bracket variable, creating a space, and copying the new state to that space. When a } is read, the space is freed and the bracket variable is decremented. The bracket variable now points to the new current state. Only tokens are allowed on the stack. Each token is represented by a number, so a state can be pushed on the stack as a number. (A number takes less space than a token string). The number zero is not used to represent a token, so this value can be used to initialize.

As soon as a token is recognized, space has to be reserved on top of the stack for it. On each bracket level more than one token can appear. All tokens on one bracket level need to be pushed on one level of the stack. A solution is to see the top of the stack as a (smaller) stack in situ. An example (Figure 26):

```
{\level1 {\level2 {\level3a\level3b\level3c }}}
```

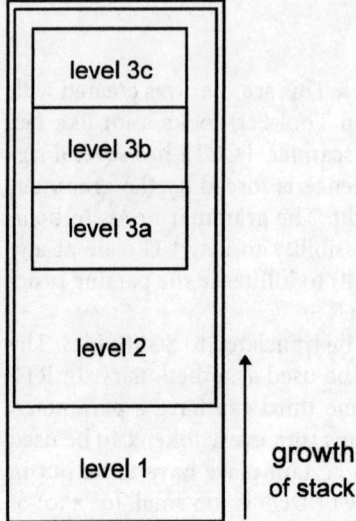

Figure 26. The stack as a mechanism for nested brackets

9 Creating Hypertext

Depending on the target hypertext application, RTF, SGML, or some other format may be most appropriate. Remember that throwing information out is always easier than putting it in later. Many applications such as DynaText, etc., now accept SGML or a subset of SGML as an external format. For small hypertext applications, Microsoft Windows Help files may be appropriate. The Windows Help compiler is available with any compiler able to create Window applications. The Help files may be distributed without paying any fees. As the Microsoft Help Compiler only accepts RTF, material must either be made using RTF or converted to it.

9.1
Storage: Compiling, Importing, or Indexing

Data can be stored for use in a hypertext or hypermedia system in a number of ways:

- *Direct storage*. Data can be stored as is with no other processing. The data must be structured in a manner that can be interpreted by the hypertext or hypermedia presentation application. The main drawback of direct storage is that it becomes slower when the amount of data grows, so it is not normally used. An advantage is that the data remains very portable.
- *Indexing*. The data can be stored as it is, and an index can be created that contains some or all (semantic) information contained in the data. Occurrences of references and where they refer to, titles, etc., can be stored in a small database. Presentation of the data can be slow as the original data has to be interpreted for presentation. The advantages of this method are speed, easy reuse of the data, and that the data stays portable. Previewing is also possible, although incremental indexing must be supported to make previewing of alterations or additions to the data a viable option. The easy reuse of data may also be interpreted as a drawback when possible un-authorized reproduction of the data is an issue. Another drawback is that some of the data may have to be stored in multiple copies to keep the system fast.
- *Compiling*. The data can be compiled so that the original data cannot be reconstructed from the compiled data. For presentation the original data is not necessary. The data is stored in an internal format that can be easily presented. Advantages are speed and the difficulty of unauthorized repro-

ductions of the data by others. The drawbacks are that previewing is impossible without recompiling unless another product is used, the compiled data is not portable, the original data must be stored for new products, additions, and editing. Often the compiled data is internally stored in a com-pressed format.

• *Importing.* All the data may be imported into a (generic) database. Thereafter the original data is no longer necessary. The data can be presented from that available in the database. The original data can be reconstructed from the information in the database, but reconstruction can be difficult, although less than after compiling. Thus the data may not really be portable. The advantages are that access is fast and the data can be previewed and used in a client-server database scheme.

The difference between importing and compiling is not a very clear-cut one. Here importing is done using a generic database engine such as Microsoft Access or Borland Paradox, that is used for storing and retrieving data. Compiling is done using a compiler that imports the data into a database that is an integral part of the hypermedia presentation engine. The Microsoft Help and Microsoft Multimedia Viewer compilers are good examples of compilers. A good example of 'direct storage' is the WWW document.

The different ways that data can be stored for use in a hypertext or hypermedia system, excluding direct storage, can be visualized as the square shown in Figure 27. Note that hybrid systems are also possible. Some systems compile or import parts of the data, and only index (references or filenames of) other parts. Especially audio and video are often stored separately, and even on different mediums such as laser video disks, video tapes, or audio compact disk or audio tapes.

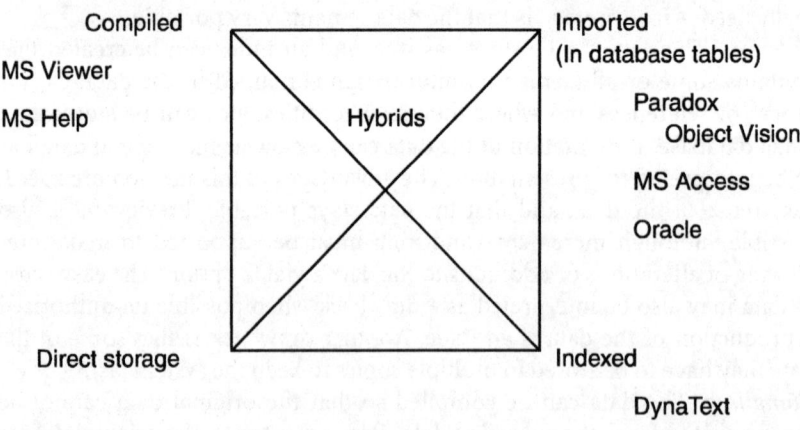

Figure 27. Compiling, importing, indexing, direct storage

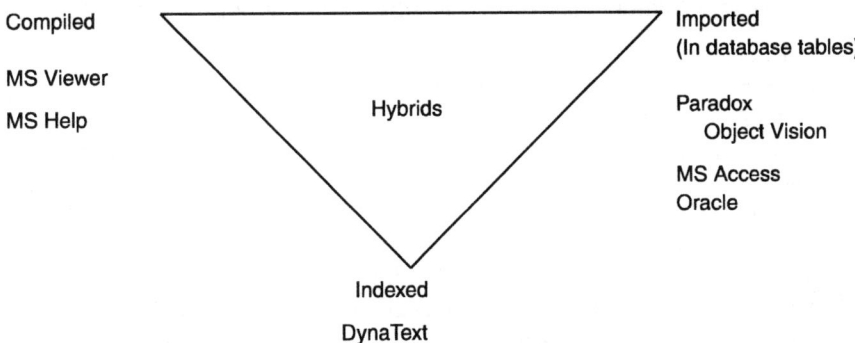

Figure 28. Entry roads for DynaText resources

9.1.1
Database Selection

Selecting a database system depends on the products to be used and what the database needs to do, as well as how much development one wants to do, and how much tailoring of the presentation application is necessary or needs to be possible. For some systems, databases supporting client-server schemes may be needed. In other cases the database is part of the product such as when using the Microsoft Multimedia viewer.

The next part is directed at those who feel the need to develop their own multimedia presentation platform using available database engines and other available tools such as text, bitmap, vector drawing, and video and audio presentation modules.

9.1.2
Tagged Information

Before selecting a database system some thought has to be given to the information types in a document. A number of information types can be distinguished in documents. Examples of information types:

- Normal text
- Titles or headings of different levels
- Synonyms
- Exact references to titles or headings
- Inexact references to titles or headings
- Cross-references to a specific word, sentence, or paragraph in a document
- Rubrics or clusters
- Surnames
- Dates, of birth, death, establishment, and annulment
- Keywords
- Footnotes

The above information types can be classified in four groups:

- Normal text.
- Many-to-one references to headings. These can be exact matching, matching to synonyms, partial matching such as plurals or singulars, etc.
- Many-to-one references to normal text. Some references are made not to a heading but to a specific part somewhere in the document. These are not absolutely necessary if the chunks with a heading are small enough. Then references can be made to the heading just before the part referred to.
- One-to-many attributes. What kind of information is contained in a part of the text. There are different types of attributes: keywords, rubrics or clusters, surnames, and dates of birth, death, establishment, and annulment are all examples. The database needs to contain lists of the different attributes and lists of headings containing specific instances of attributes.
- Expansions. An *in situ* explanation of an abbreviation, word(s), acronym, or sentence(s). Most often these will be in the form of footnotes, endnotes, or yellow notes.

Some database systems such as the Microsoft Windows Help system basically only support keywords, headings, aliases of headings, and references to headings. Other systems support headings, references, and a few alternate keyword lists

If there is a need for many different attributes and different instances of each attribute, a database system which supports it must be selected. In the database system we developed we made a distinction between keywords, rubrics, and the other attributes. This was partially due to the fact that the first version of database system only contained keywords, the second version rubrics, and the third version other attributes too. It also had to do with speed. The retrieval speed could be optimized for separate systems, but the complexity was also greater. With hindsight we can say we should have gone for a more generic approach. It might have been a bit slower to work with, but it would have been less complex and it would have yielded faster development with fewer bugs.

10 Picture, Sound, and Video Resources

There are two ways to include resources into a (hypertext) document:

- Embedded; the resources are included in the document.
- Linked; the filenames (and paths) of the resources are included in the document.

Both of these methods have specific advantages and disadvantages. Most of the following is based on experience with picture resources. However, with products such as Microsoft Video for Windows and Apple Quick Time for Windows and Macintosh the handling of video resources has become as simple as adding a picture to a text. As these products even support sounds, sounds can also be added, either in addition to, or without the video.

10.1
Embedded Resources

Embedded resources are included in the document. In most cases special codes are used to indicate starts and ends of the embedded resource. When the documents are stored as ASCII text, the resource data can be stored as a hexadecimal string. Sometimes picture resource data is stored twice. It is stored as a display-ready image and as editable data. An example of this can be seen in RTF documents created with Microsoft Word for Windows.

Note that when resource data is stored as hexadecimal the size of it will double. Storing it twice will also double its size. When no editing needs to be done later, the editable version can be deleted. Embedded resources are best used when the resources are small and when the document is small. Fewer files are needed, and there are fewer chances of forgetting to copy something. If (temporary) files are being created for compilation, one should only use embedded resources:

- If the hypertext or hypermedia compiler does not accepts linked resources, or
- When all resources are used only once (this may be in either the same or in different projects).

This enables the editors to make changes only once for a resource that is used in several places. If the resource is embedded, each embedded instance of the resource needs to be changed.

10.2
Linked Resources

Linked resources are resources not included in the document itself. Only references, the names, and possibly the paths of the resources are in the document itself. The resources can be edited without having to change the document itself.

Linking the resources makes sense when the resources are large. It add less clutter to the textual part of the document. Also, resources stored in a native format tend to take up less space. Alternatively, resources could be converted to a supported format that takes up less space. Both Microsoft Windows and Macintosh System 7 platforms support the linking of resources. This is called Object Link Embedding or OLE for short on the Windows platform and Publish and Subscribe on the Macintosh platform. It depends on the applications used whether it is supported. Most applications that support the linking of resources by default still embed the resource. To link it a special menu option must be used: Edit–Paste Special on the Windows platform. On a Macintosh a resource must be published: Edit–Subscribe to... from the source application. Essentially this is the same as saving the resources with a special name and a special parameter. The resource can be subscribed after it is published. This is done with the menu item: Edit–Subscribe to... One should use the same name as when publishing it. This should be done from the application in which the document is loaded.

10.3
Hotspots Within Picture Resources

A hotspot is an area in a resource which can be activated by clicking or double clinking on it with the mouse. When a hotspot is activated the part of the document associated with the hotspot is shown. This association is called a hypertext link or simply a link. Note that this may be a different type of link then mentioned before. It may link to another file, but also to another part of the current file. Hotspots can also be stored in two ways, embedded within the textual part of the document or within the picture resources.

Embedding the links in the textual part has the advantage of being able to use the same resources in different instances with different links, from different parts of the resource. This feature is not supported by all hypertext systems. Storing the links with the resources has the advantage of being able to define the links without interfering with the textual part of the document. For Windows Help files, hotspots can be added to bitmaps that must be saved as Hyper Graphics (.SHG) files. This is done with the application SHED.EXE.

10.4
Conclusions

If temporary files are being created for compilation the choice of embedded or linked resources may depend on what the hypertext or hypermedia compiler accepts. Or a compiler must be found that accepts one's own input. Embedded resources are best used when the resources are small and when the document is small. Linking resources makes sense when the resources are large. It tends to take up less space.

11 Managing Hypermedia Documents

Managing hypermedia documents with the current generation of software tools is still a delicate and often tedious task. Production planning of new hypermedia titles can be very complex and must in any case be based upon earlier experiences. There is no single rule for how to do it.

As multimedia productions bring along different types of resources (audio, video, animation, and domain specific programs), each project should be divided into smaller parts, preferably each belonging to only one discipline. Only if the hypermedia production manager has knowledge in all of these fields (which is not probable) can he or she define the costs in terms of resources and time. For those fields in which the production manager has no knowledge (s)he should consult experts.

Because of their high development costs, hypermedia documents invite re-exploitation. In some cases documents must be re-edited before they can be reused for another versions. Re-editing brings along the need for an accurate bookkeeping of versions, royalties, etc. Other issues are the use of outlining tools, or equivalents for other non-textual resources, and the creation of author-editor plans.

11.1
The Management of the Production

While talking to different people about their approach to managing material and authoring, a number of different approaches became evident:

- Some publishers of paper-based material want to keep all typing, scanning, layout, and editing in-house. New material and remarks are provided to them on paper (or disk) and their typing and editorial staffs input and/or edit the material. Editing is done by annotating on the printed texts; the annotations are later edited into the texts by the typing staff. The use of paper is still very important.
- Other people who do the inputting, editing, and annotations use only computers. The use of paper is not important to them at all.

Given the differences between the paper- and computer-based approach, it is of prime importance to determine the various reasons for choosing one of them. There will be a description of the procedures followed for authoring and editing, so that what is needed for managing authoring and editing can be derived.

Depending on the type of material being used (paper or non-paper) some differences in approach may be determined.

11.2
Paper for Quick Annotations

Our experience to date has been that all or most of the information exchanged between authors on one side and the editors on the other is done using paper prints. Material from authors is received on paper or sometimes as unformatted texts on a computer diskette. This is then entered by the staff into their computer system. In later stages, the annotations are made by the authors on the paper prints and are then sent back to the publisher. The editors decide whether the annotations are used or not. If so, the changes are made to the entries. The current managerial procedure often is that each time a paper print is received or sent, this involves administration. Also each time a change has been made it involves administration.

11.3
Computer Assisted Document Management

Using computers for document management will not differ too much from using paper. The first text is uploaded to the system and then annotated or changed by editors and changed by the editors. The administration of annotations and changes should be automated. The automation gives management the capability to know the progress and status of the work at all times. Three types of document management are distinguished:

- *Creation* (Project). Creation of new documents or editing versions of old ones. Issues here are among others planning, managing, (co-)authoring, editing, versioning, copyrights, docinfo.
- *Librarian* (Archive). This would be what we call the pick-and-mix system. Issues here are among others retrieval, reuse, docinfo.
- *Production* (Delivery). The resulting documents are static, either on paper or binary documents, but access is provided after compiling and/or indexing the included texts. The media may be paper, floppy-based, CD(-I), etc. Issues here include delivery media, copyrights, royalties, accessibility, and pick-and-mixing.

For each of these types a list of applications can be made. Other important issues are annotating, revising, versioning, outlining (tools), planning, and managing, using author and editor plans.

11.3.1
Creation

Applications that can be used for creating documents include:

- Lotus Notes. Supports formatted text, and version 3.0 supports pictures. It can also be used as a vehicle for other documents as external formats may be attached to a text-formatted document.
- Microsoft Word for Windows. Supports formatted text, pictures, and OLE objects. It is possible to add summary information to a document, insert this in the document, and use this for finding the document after storage. Word also supports versioning. Using styles and templates will guarantee a uniform appearance for all documents within an application pilot.
- WordPerfect: Has approximately the same features as its main rival MS Word.
- Lotus AmiPro. Has approximately the same features as its main rivals Microsoft Word and WordPerfect.
- Others such as special SGML editors.

11.3.2
Librarian

Applications that can help in retrieving and reusing document information include:

- Lotus Notes. Supports formatted text, but does not directly support pictures. Pictures and other external formats may be attached to a formatted document.
- Microsoft Word for Windows. Although the feature seems to be rarely used, Word supports *Summary Information* for each document, using File-Find File, a search may be made for a document based on title, keywords, date, subject, author, or any text in the document. Also supports annotations for editors.
- Borland Paradox (for Windows). A database system that allows documents to be stored in BLOBs, for retrieval.
- MegaDoc (DEC, previously Philips). Paper-based material can be scanned and stored by the Office Standard Architecture (ODA). It is not a document management system by itself. It is a way data can be stored. Customizing needs to be done separately.
- Sybase (UNIX). A UNIX-based database application. Can be used for storing and retrieving documents.

11.3.3
Production

The delivery format for information to be displayed by a presentation application:

- Microsoft Windows Help files. Hypertext document database. If the documents to be publish are relatively small (a few megabytes or less) this might be a suitable format as it supports hypertext links and pictures. The documents need to be prepared (in an RTF syntax) before they can be compiled in one or more help files.
- IBM OS/2 Help files. Hypertext document database. As above.
- Microsoft Windows Multimedia Viewer files. This behaves much like the Windows Help system. It has some extensions to support hypermedia.
- DynaText. Imports SGML documents to create a hypertext document database. Supports larger documents. The documents need to be SGML tagged.
- OWL Guide. Hypertext document database. Also for larger document databases.
- BRS-search. Picking and mixing the selected documents might be possible.
- Folio Views. Used for instance for the Novell Help system.
- Topics.
- Adobe Acrobat.

11.3.4
Annotation

Annotation can only take place if it is supported by the system. If annotation is supported the editors must check the annotations and decide whether to use them. If the annotations are used the changes must be made in the text. If annotations are not supported the authors will have to change the text itself. These changes must be checked by the editors.

There can also be a situation where a main author is appointed. The main author could have the privilege of changing the texts of all co-authors who contribute to the main author's entry. In this case (s)he would have the same privilege, at least up to a certain time, as the editors.

The goal for some of the products goes beyond text or hypertext. The goal is multimedia. This does not change much in the managerial procedures. The actors are different: camera men and illustrators instead of authors, and producers instead of editors.

11.3.5
Versioning

After a text document (or any other type of material) is changed, the next decisions must be made:

- Must the old version be kept or deleted?
- If the old version is kept, must the new version have the same name?

Versioning is a problem. It is demonstrated by the fact that there are several computer applications on the market dedicated to solving this problem, but mainly for software projects. To keep this problem under control strict basic rules should be obeyed:

- Each user should have well-defined privileges to replace or add new versions in a certain domain, marked in terms of topic, author, time slot, or assigned classification by the main editor.
- One person, the main editor, should have privileges to delete or replace any version. The main editor must have the knowledge to make the decision if a version, or for that matter any document, is still relevant for the database.

There are several software products on the market for version and revision control for software projects. Most of these products are based on knowledge of the structure of software sources. This is especially true when the control software creates difference files. Both the authors and editors have to adhere to very strict rules using these products. Each time a file changes this has to be checked in with the versioning control software. Old or obsolete files need to be checked out with the control software. Creation of difference files by itself is a good idea. But it becomes very important to keep all of the files, for if one of the files is deleted, all older versions of that file may not longer be retrievable. In most cases the best solution may be to entrust the *main editor* of a document. He or she has the privilege of deciding which revisions and versions need to be archived and how. In this way only one person needs to do extra work to keep the project up to date.

Basically there are four ways of versioning or revising information (here actually old versions or revisions of a document):

- Only the previous version or revision is kept. This is at this time the only thing that can be done automatically by most word processors. Only in some cases might this not be enough.
- All the old versions are kept. This might not be practical because large storage capacity will be needed, especially if there are many versions and revisions. Also some tailoring to the word processor must be done. Otherwise each version or revision will have to be given a new filename manually.
- Files with the old versions are kept. From these all old versions can be recreated but with a smaller storage overhead. Again this will need some tailoring to the word processor; also a program must be available to create the difference files. We have not yet found a Windows application that can build difference files and rebuild the old files again. But there are several such applications for UNIX, most of which are for keeping track of versions and revisions.
- Only some revisions or versions are kept.

For the development of Macintosh software there is a tool available called Macintosh Programmers Workshell (MPW) Projector. It is actually a separate application which is called from within MPW. The users have to tell Projector what files are in a project. Every time the manager decides that a new version/ revision is ready (s)he can run it and numbered files are stored separately.

These files can be retrieved later on. Projector creates a directory tree to store a project.

New files have to be checked in and files that are no longer used must be checked out. This must be done by the developers. One of the weaknesses of Projector is that you may not move or rename any of the files or directories in the project. Doing this is dangerous for your project. Moving or renaming will destroy your project in most cases. The numbering scheme is simple: number-letter-number. The first number is a version, the letter is an indication of the state (alpha, beta, etc.), and the final number is a revision number. Each of the two numbers can be from 0 to 999999. As on UNIX systems, names on Macintoshes and Windows 95 systems can already be longer than in traditional MS-DOS systems, which makes things a lot easier.

As we do not like a system in which the authors and editors must do extra work, we developed a tool for Word for Windows. This small Word Basic macro for Word for Windows does what is described in Appendix B. Each time you want to save a revision, you run the macro and it will save the current document and a copy with almost the same name as the document in the same directory. Only the extension will be replaced by the revision number of the document. Each time the document is saved Word will add one to the revision number. So if the document was called TEST.DOC and has a revision number of 3, it will be saved as TEST.003. We hope to find a Windows applications that can compare different versions and make difference files out of them; adding a call to such an application would be easy, and remove some of the overhead. Different versions are not really supported, so you will have to rename the document to avoid problems with the numbering scheme. The listing of the macro:

```
REM Get current file name
OldName$ = FileName$()
REM Save it
FileSave
REM if next line is not done
REM Pos will err if there is a dot
in a directory name
LastDotAfter = Len(OldName$) - 4
Pos = InStr(LastDotAfter, FileName$(), ".")
REM get the Revision number and append it
to the filename
Dim dlg As DocumentStatistics
GetCurValues dlg
REM prefix zeros
Revision$ = Right$("00" + dlg.Revision, 3)
SaveName$ = Left$(FileName$(), Pos) + Revision$
REM Save as will also rename file
FileSaveAs .Name = SaveName$
```

```
REM close renamed file open file with
old filename
FileClose
FileOpen OldName$
```

To get this macro into Word for Windows, do the following:

1. Select the text of the macro and copy it to the clipboard and go to Word for Windows.
2. Choose Tools, Macro... (in Word for Windows).
3. Make sure that Global Macros is selected.
4. Type RevisionSave, or another name if it already exists, in the Macro name box and press Enter.
5. Paste the clipboard into the window which opened (this will be between Sub MAIN and End Sub).
6. Close the window, say yes to everything Word asks.
7. If you want you can add the macro to the file menu. To do this select Tools, Options..., Menus (this is one of the categories represented by an icon; at the left of the dialogue, you may have to scroll downwards), make sure Show Macros is selected and Context is Global. Select the Menu & File (this will be the default), select RevisionSave and choose Add. It will now appear in the File menu.
8. You can also add a shortcut key. To do this select Tools, Options..., Keyboard. Again make sure Show Macros is selected and Context is Global. Select the macro RevisionSave, check the Ctrl and Shift boxes, and type 'r' in the Key Box. Choose 'Add'.
9. Every time you want a new revision saved run the macro, either by selecting it in the Tools, Macro... dialogue and running it, or by selecting the menu item, or by selecting the shortcut key. You will only notice something if you list *all* files (*.*) in the directory the original file is in. The revision numbers in the extension will be the same as the one found in the File, Summary Info..., Statistics box (after saving) the document. This box also shows the total time spent on editing the document.

Note that the macro will not work for Mac Word versions older than Version 7. What is missing:

- Versioning is not really supported yet. This causes difficulties for MS-DOS and Windows 3.11 users, because names cannot be longer than eight characters with an extension of three characters. In UNIX you could do something such as:

THISISALONGFILENAME.VERSION.REVISION.STATUS

This was impossible under MS-DOS. If you really want to support version information in the filename (before the arrival of Windows 95) you will have to use either the first character of the extension or the last character(s) of the name itself. The question here is: Are 99 revisions enough? Because Word increments the revision number each time the document is saved, we are afraid it is not enough. After this the question becomes: Are seven or six characters enough for a document name or code? Happily, in Windows 95 file names can have as many as 256 characters.

For clarity:

- Revision. This is a revised document. Revised means that only small changes and corrections are made.
- Version. A new version of a document. This means that major changes have been made to the document, maybe because some kind of revolution has taken place or because this version is intended for a different target group.

11.4
Outlining Tools

An outlining tool supports the idea that before writing a document you should create a structure for it. You create the different headings and move them around until you have a structure which is appropriate for your purposes. If you wish to write a book about physics, an example of its outline could be:

- **Preface**
- **Table of contents**
- **Introduction**
- **First chapter: Ancient Greek physics**
  The lives of the ancient Greek physicists
  The theories
  Tests

- **Second chapter: Newtonian physics**
  The life of Newton
  Newton's first law
  Newton's second law
  Newton's third law
  Examples
  Tests

- **Third chapter: Einsteinian physics**
  Einstein's life
  Einstein's laws
  Examples
  Tests

- **Conclusions**
- **Solutions to the tests**
- **Index**

The above example is only a short sketch of a possible outline, which depending on the situation could be more compact or more detailed. Note that the outline in the example contains headings and titles for the text. Sometimes it may be different, and may also contain short descriptions of the content that are more than just a heading or title.

The process of writing a book may be initiated either by a publisher wanting a book to be written or because an author approaches a publisher. If an author approaches a publisher he or she may already have an outline (or indeed the whole book) ready.

When the decision has been made to write a book, the next step is to write an outline, if this has not already been done. The outline can also be used to plan the time needed to create the book (see *Author and Editor Plans*). Although outlines have been made on paper for a long time, many outlines are created today using computers with outlining tools. There are different types of outlining tools, most are integrated with a word processor (for instance Microsoft Word), and some are separate tools to be used beside a word processor or before a word processor is used.

Using tools such as Lotus Notes, the outlines created with any outlining tool can be exchanged among the authors and editors involved. If Lotus Notes is used this can be done by either importing the text into a note or attaching the created file to a note. We should state that this method was also used in creating this document. The work package leader attached an outline (in a spreadsheet format) to a note, and all authoring partners provided text appropriate for the given outline. Discussion of the outline is possible in this way, but we did not discuss it in this case.

11.4.1
Word Processor Outlining Tools

The outlining tool integrated with Microsoft Word, both for Windows and for Macintosh, uses styles. Nine default heading styles heading 1 through heading 9 are used for outlining the document. The heading styles are hierarchical, heading 1 being the top level and heading 9 the least important. The top level heading 1 can be used for parts of a book, heading 2 for chapters, heading 3 for paragraphs, etc. While creating structure for your document the headings can be moved around or changed from one level to another.

Because the outline tool is integrated with the word processor it can be used before, during, and after writing the document. To make it easier to use it during or after writing the document a special view of the document can be selected. In this view one can opt to show only the headings, a subset of the headings, and/or a selected set of paragraphs.

⇕ **First heading 1**
    ▫ Text of heading 1
      ⇕ **First heading 2**
        ▫ Text of heading 2
      ⇕ **Another heading 2**
        ▫ Text of another heading 2
⇕ **Second heading 1**
    ▫ Text of second heading 1

Figure 29a. Simple outline of a document

The screen dump above shows a simple outline of a document with everything displayed. Note that the All button is in the down position.

⇕ **First heading 1**
      ⇕ **First heading 2**
      ⇕ **Another heading 2**
⇕ **Second heading 1**

Figure 29b. Document outline with heading levels 1 and 2

The screen dump above only displays the headings 1 and 2. Note that instead of the All button, the 2 button has been pressed.

Using the left and right arrow buttons it possible to change heading levels. Using the up and down arrow buttons it is possible to move parts of the document. For instance, by putting the cursor on 'First heading 1' and pushing the down button, this heading and all normal text up to the next first-level heading will be moved after the text of 'First heading 2'. It is also possible to move a heading with all nested headings and text to another place by dragging that level to another place using the mouse.

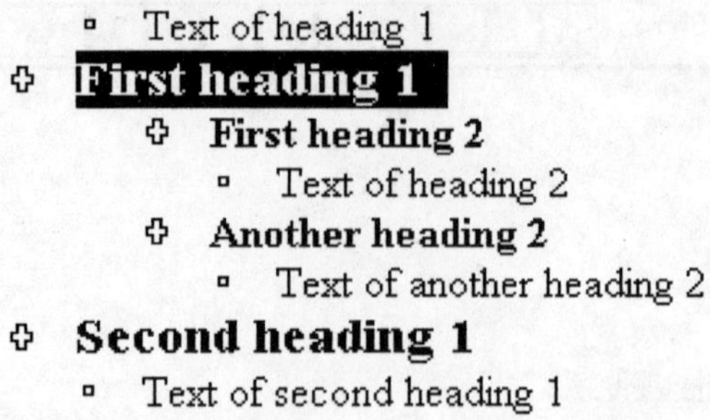

- ▫   Text of heading 1
- ✧   **First heading 1**
  - ✧   **First heading 2**
    - ▫   Text of heading 2
  - ✧   **Another heading 2**
    - ▫   Text of another heading 2
- ✧   **Second heading 1**
  - ▫   Text of second heading 1

Figure 29c. Dragging headings in the outline view

The heading styles can also be used to create a table of contents for the document. Note that because the outline tool is integrated into Word, it is possible to check and edit the outline in any stage of writing and editing the document, and if the outline is edited the document changes accordingly.

Word also supports the creation of the table of contents from the outline, which is a very handy option because in most cases the outline is the set of titles and headings which need to be in the table of contents anyway.

11.4.2
Groupware Outlining Tools

In its purest form a Groupware outlining tool is a tool which enables all authors, editors and managers involved to create and manipulate an outline together. All changes and additions will be visible immediately to all of the persons involved. This can be accomplished in (at least) two ways:

- One way is to use a normal outlining tool on one machine and to give all other persons involved the means to look at the screen of this host machine. This could be done by running an application such as Timbuktu on all the machines. One machine would have to run in host mode, and the other machines should run as clients. Editing should be enabled for all clients.
- Another way is to create an outline in one way or another and save this where other people can get to it, such as in a database on a Lotus Notes server.

Given the ways used to accomplish a Groupware outlining tool, it stands to reason that the way it works will be much the same as when using a normal outlining tool. In the first case, the difference will be that more than one person uses the same outline tool at the same time. In the second case the files will be loaded into the outlining tools, saved, and posted again on the Lotus Notes server.

11.4.3
Limitations of Outlining Tools

Although outlines help to create the frame of a document, they may have to change over time. Sometimes during the writing of a document it may become apparent that to make the document more readable some chapters will have to be moved. An outlining tool only helps to create the structure or framework. It does not create structure by itself. The creative work still has to be done by people. Groupware outlining tools may have additional limitations:

- If more than two people work simultaneously on a outline, it may become very difficult for all involved to follow what is happening. The problem would be much like a group of people all talking at the same time to all other people in the group.
- When Lotus Notes is being used for exchanging suggestions another problem may occur. Two people may have replicated the same version of an outline and have edited it off-line. When the edited versions are transferred back to the Lotus Notes server replication errors may occur. If each person made a copy of the outline, edited it, and published the edited copy on the Lotus Notes server, a whole bunch of outlines may appear overnight, giving the editor a real nightmare when confronted with the need to create a final or next version of the outline from all suggestions.

11.5
Author and Editor Plans

When planning the writing of a new document, the plans with the instructions for the authors and editors, about what to do and when to do it, are called author and editor plans (A/E plans.) The finished plan will be a kind of time-table.

The types of author and editor plans depend in many ways upon the way the organization involved functions. Most organizations hire external authors to write documents and use their own (internal) staff, sometimes helped by external experts, to edit the documents.

External authors and editors may be paid for their work in a number of ways:

- A fixed amount for each page, number of words
- A fixed amount for each document, independent on its size
- A fixed amount for each hour used writing the document and researching.

Internal authors and editors are (almost) always paid by the hour. When external authors and editors are paid for delivering a document of a fixed size, or are paid for the number of words written, it is not really important how much time an author or editor needs or uses to finish the document, as long as it is finished by a certain date. On the other hand, if authors and editors are paid by the hour, it is important how productive they are, because if they take longer to finish a document, the document will cost more.

The description about the document to be written may be different depending on the type of document or organization. If the document to be written is a text book about physics, a precise outline may be needed. An example of such an outline can be found in the part on outlining tools.

If it is an item in an encyclopedia about microscopes the description may be only:

- Write a description of a microscope in about a thousand words.

Sometimes an organization may have strict guidelines about how certain documents are written. An example of this would be a company that has guidelines about how a description of an object has to be written:

- First write down a general description of what it is, second describe what it is used for, third say who discovered it or invented it, and fourth list several special versions of these objects.

Given the guidelines above, a text for a microscope would be something like this:

A microscope is an object which enables you to see small things, invisible to the naked eye. It is used by doctors and researchers to look at bacteria and other small creatures. One of the first microscopes was built by the Dutchman Antony van Leeuwenhoek. There are two types of microscopes used today: optical microscopes can enlarge up to a thousand times and electron microscopes can enlarge millions of times.

From the above we can conclude that author and editor plans can have several forms:

- Unrestricted, write something about something.
- Strict in a time sense, an exact description when to have it finished.
- Strict in a quantitative sense, an exact description of how many pages need to be written or edited.
- Strict in a qualitative sense, an outline with all paragraph headers written.
- Strict in both a quantitative and a qualitative sense.

In many organizations computers are now used to create author and editor plans. The way these plans are created and stored depends on the organization, and the tools used. The plans may be created using different types of tools:

- Simple ASCII editors
- Word processors
- Spreadsheet applications
- Database applications
- Project management applications.

The first three types of tools will be used in more or less the same manner. The data will be typed in, or imported. Using any of the mentioned tools the creator will need to draw on his or her experience to create a timetable. Currently there are no expert systems available that can to suggest a timetable. However, expert systems for creating author and editor plans may be expected.

11.5.1
ASCII/Word Processor A/E Plans

ASCII and word processor author and editor plans are plans typed by the manager. These plans may have a simple tabular form, an outline form, or a combination of both. A combination of a tabular and outline author and editor plan is shown in Table 2. An example of a simple tabular author and editor plan is given in Table 2.

Table 2. Tabular and outline author and editor plan

Headings	Author ready	Editor ready	Part ready
Preface	January n. yr.	February n. yr.	February n. yr.
Table of contents		February n. yr.	February n. yr.
Introduction	January n. yr.	February n. yr.	February n. yr.
First chapter: Ancient Greek physics	September	October	November
Lives of ancient Greek physicists	September	October	November
The theories	September	October	November
Examples	December	January n. yr.	February n. yr.
Tests	December	January n. yr.	February n. yr.
Second chapter: Newtonian physics	October	November	February n. yr.
The life of Newton	October	November	December
Newton's first law	October	November	December
Newton's second law	October	November	December
Newton's third law	October	November	December
Examples	December	January n. yr.	February n. yr.
Tests	December	January n. yr.	February n. yr.
Third chapter: Einsteinian physics	November	December	January n. yr.
Einstein's life	November	December	January n. yr.
Einstein's laws	November	December	January n. yr.
Examples	November	December	January n. yr.
Tests	December	January n. yr.	February n. yr.
Conclusions	January n. yr.	February n. yr.	February n. yr.
Solutions to the tests	January n. yr.	February n. yr.	February n. yr.
Index	January n. yr.	February n. yr.	February n. yr.

By indenting the headings the outline can be preserved. In most author and editor plans more than just four columns are used. Possible columns are:

- Heading or title
- Planned author start
- Actual author start
- Planned author finish
- Actual author finish
- Planned editor start
- Actual author finish
- Planned editor finish
- Actual editor finish
- Planned author revision start
- Actual author revision start
- Planned author revision finish
- Actual author revision finish
- Planned proof-reading start
- Actual proof-reading start
- Planned proof-reading finish
- Actual proof-reading finish
- Actual status.

Which of these possibilities are used is totally dependent on the organization and the type of document being written.

11.5.2
Groupware A/E Plans

Groupware should be understood as software that supports editing of and interacting on information by a group of people. Thus groupware author and editor planning software would be software that supports editing of and interacting on author and editor plans by a group of people. There is no real dedicated groupware author and editor planning tool available. However, such a tool can be simulated in a few ways:

- Using an editor, word processor, spreadsheet, database application, or project management tool running on a computer that runs an application such as Timbuktu, a group of people can create and edit a plan together. Some care must be taken, because although the plan can be made together, only one person can effectively control the input at any one time. This is mainly due to the shortcoming of applications such as Timbuktu.
- Again using an editor, word processor, spreadsheet, database application, or project management tool, the manager can create a draft plan and save it as a topic in a Lotus Notes discussion forum. All authors and editors involved can respond to this plan and give suggestions as to how it could be changed.

Care should be taken, because off-line editing of the draft plan itself may cause replication errors.

The (Lotus Notes) Progress database made by us [University of Twente] in co-operation with Industriens Forlag Denmark on Lotus Notes is a prototype of a possible groupware tool using Lotus Notes. DTI, Denmark Technology Institute, made another database with the same function. All authors and editors using Lotus Notes in the COSYS project have access to these tools. The manager can make a new (draft) topic, put in the information (s)he has and get responses to this. When using Lotus Notes the responses could be in different forms. It could be a mail message, there could be an alternative plan or the original could be changed. The last form is dangerous and should be avoided, or replication errors may occur.

An advantage of using a groupware tool is that all the persons involved have access to the plans and can easily check what, if anything, is expected of them. If there are any delays or changes this can be put into the system.

11.5.3
Project Management Tools for A/E Plans

Project management tools and applications can be helpful when creating author and editor plans. Using project management tools only makes sense for complex plans, where many authors and editors are involved, or when authors and editors are already heavily involved in many other projects.

11.5.4
Limitations of A/E Plans

The currently available tools for creating author and editor plans do not have any intrinsic guidance by themselves. The creator of the plans must specify how long each step will take using his experience. In the future it may be possible to use expert systems that can suggest a timetable, but these facilities are not available yet. The progress database has limitations. All authors and editors need to make changes on-line, and versioning problems may occur. These problems may be avoided by saving every changed document under a different name. But then a manager needs to make all versions consistent again.

11.6
Why Still use Paper?

There are still a number of basic reasons for using paper:

- It is still easier to find errors on paper than it is on a computer screen.
- Often publishers do not trust anybody who is not an editor in their databases.
- The desired software tools are not available yet. Existing tools are very expensive and they do not have all the needed features, and/or are not user-friendly enough.

- Annotations by pencil on paper are easily made and checked.
- Paper-based text still gives a clearer (over)view while correcting or picking and mixing.

The first reason is a hardware problem that will not be solved for the next five years at least. It will remain routine to print texts and not only because we like to read while sitting in the train. The other reasons include some which may change over time given the right tools and privileges. The main problem will be giving authors the possibility to annotate while not changing any of the text they are annotating on, after which their changes may be made by the editors. The last reason can be overcome by building better editors which do provide the wanted features. The publishers give a list of what they would wish for in an SGML editor:

- Show fields instead of codes.
- SGML to typesetting conversions, independent of project and/or media.
- Flexible; possibility to split codes and fields.
- Find and select entries based on the appearances of any field in an entry or any appearance of a word or set of words within a field or set of fields.
- Update transactions in the hypermedia database should be interfaced with the publisher's administrative system.
- Multiple entries in a file. (There have been many problems with alphabetizing entries in the past because of language-dependent differences. A flexible way to sort the entries could also solve their problems.)
- Import of text files from WordPerfect, Microsoft Word, etc.
- Annotations should stay visible in the document's margin. This is a very important feature. It allows one to annotate a text without really touching the text but just (as on paper) having the annotations visible (beside the text) at all times.

As already mentioned, even if and when such an editor becomes available, the average publisher will still use paper in the majority of the preparation stages. Note that the multiple entries item is actually a database requirement and a result of how entries are stored at this time.

11.7
Conclusion

Updates or changes to documents should be communicated to the administrative system, and logged. If this is not done automatically it should be done by hand. It should be possible to derive the following information from the logging:

- When an item was created
- When an item was edited (parts deleted, inserted, or replaced)
- When an item was deleted
- If and when an item was annotated.

Thus if the update interface in the previous paragraph is provided some but not all of the administrative overhead can be reduced. This is a prerequisite for pro-viding good transparent management capabilities for (co-)authoring and editing.

11.8
Enriching Information: From Implicit to Explicit

Implicit information is information that can be derived from natural text. Humans are good at deriving implications from explanations, argumentation, and contexts. Humans are also good at benefiting from such typographical elements as styles, fonts, typefaces, and structure. Humans easily determine different parts of a text such as chapters, paragraphs, and titles. Humans also easily determine parts of sentences such as subjects, objects, names, numbers, etc. In order to allow computer systems to support the user, all relevant connotations of the text, sound, and pictures needs to be stated explicitly. For explicit information all important parts of the text and sentences must be tagged with labels that express the type and the function of the information. Figure 30 shows the different more or less implicit and explicit types of information added to a text.

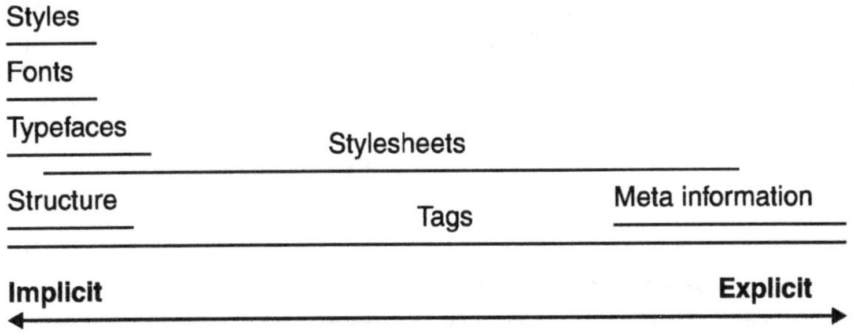

Figure 30. Implicit and explicit information

Structure, styles, fonts, and typefaces can all be used to add implicit information to a document. Style sheets and tags can be used to provide implicit or more explicit information. If the styles or tags are labeled as bold and italic, it will be implicit information, whereas labeled as *title* or *body* it will be explicit information. Meta-information, which is often added in the form of tags or totally separately, is always explicit.

Computers are quite oblivious to the semantic consequences implicit in the syntax of the texts. Everything has to made perfectly clear for them. If explicit information is not available it needs to be added. For hypertext and hypermedia systems explicit information is necessary to indicate which parts of the text are titles, keywords, and references. They are needed to make browsing by title, displaying the correct text with a title, searching for keywords, and jumping from references possible. If more needs to be supported, even more implicit information has to be added.

In certain cases it is possible to translate the text's typography, such as structure, styles, fonts, and typefaces, into explicit information. This is possible when there is a well-defined and strict relation between certain combinations of structure, styles, fonts, and typefaces and an explicit consequence.

An example of this is a document in which all paragraph headings are in large bold characters, normal text is plain and normal-sized, and references are bold. In this case conversion may be possible. It is possible when the document is indeed correct, which is often not the case. Thus checking the converted document is a must. Quite often lot of trouble can be avoided by checking and editing the original document before conversion.

Often the documents do not contain a computer-detectable structure or other implicit information that can be converted. This can be because the documents are raw ASCII documents or documents created by an OCR (Optical Character Recognition) application. The document can be enriched in several stages and using several tools.

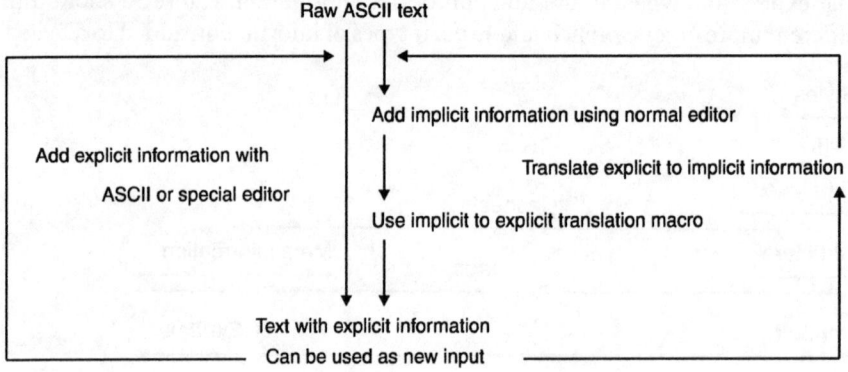

Figure 31. Adding explicit information

Explicit information can be added directly or indirectly. Often text editors or normal word processors are used. This is because there are relatively few editors capable of working with explicit information. Normal ASCII editors can be used if enough is known about the way the explicit information needs to be coded. In this way errors are easily made. Even very powerful word processors may be unable to work with real explicit information. Explicit information can be emulated using implicit information provided by using style sheets, styles, fonts, and typefaces. With translation macros implicit information can be translated to explicit information and vice versa. Each type of explicit informa-tion needs to be identified by a unique combination of implicit information. Errors can still be made, but their number can be reduced by adding validation parsers to the translation macros and adding special input macros for each type of explicit information. For some hypertext developments real explicit data is never used.

The explicit data is always emulated by using a list with unique combinations of implicit information.

In many projects combinations of tools (ASCII editors, word processors, and special editors) are used to enrich the documents. Often there are several enrichment stages using different tools for different stages or even different people. Before enriching a document the first question should be:

- What is desired and what is required?

This is closely followed by another question:

- What will it cost in terms of software tools and human effort?

Based on these two questions a decision has to be made. The quality of a final hypermedia system depends heavily on the proportion of explicitly encoded meta-information. However, richer data will cost more resources and time. Often a decision is made to minimally enrich the documents for the first title, and further enrich the documents for newer versions of the same title or other titles using the same material. Other issues pop up when documents are prepared:

- Consensus problems: Different experts will have different opinions on how the document should be enriched. This can be due to professional or personal preferences.
- Integrity and validation. The documents used for the hypermedia product should not conflict or contain errors.

What tools to use and how to enrich documents depends to a large extent on the target hypertext and hypermedia platforms to be used. Different platforms often need the input documents in different formats. The important aspect here is to create or enrich documents in such a way that they can either be used directly by the target platform or be easily converted to the format needed by the target platform. Conversion between SGML and RTF is possible, but as SGML can describe much more explicit information than RTF, explicit information can get lost when converting from SGML to RTF. Conversion from RTF to SGML can be simple if the same DTD or Document Template Definition can be used. The DTD is a part of an SGML document and can be compared with a word-processor style sheet. If the conversion has to work with any given DTD it gets problematic.

The problems with conversion between RTF and SGML, or with emulating explicit information with RTF, are almost the same for all types of formats that are functionally equivalent to RTF. The dangers of losing information are substantial.

Figure 32 gives an overview of the stages documents can go through. Figure 33 tries to give an overview of some prominent products and formats in hypermedia land. Relations between the formats, and the products, and the difficulty (as we perceive it) of moving from one format or platform to another are displayed.

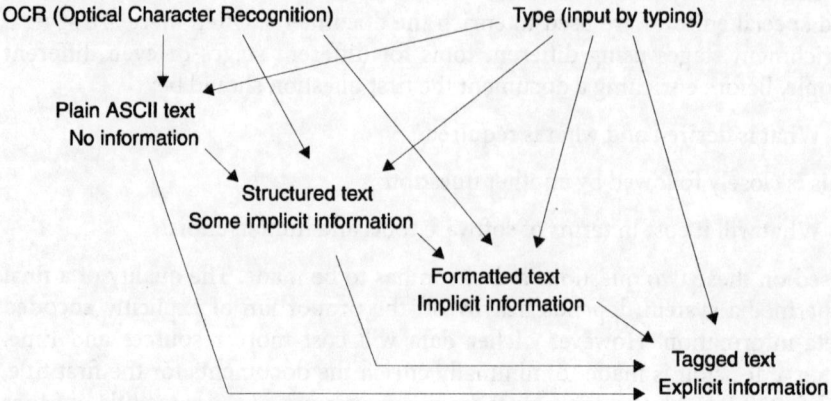

Figure 32. Stages in the document life cycle

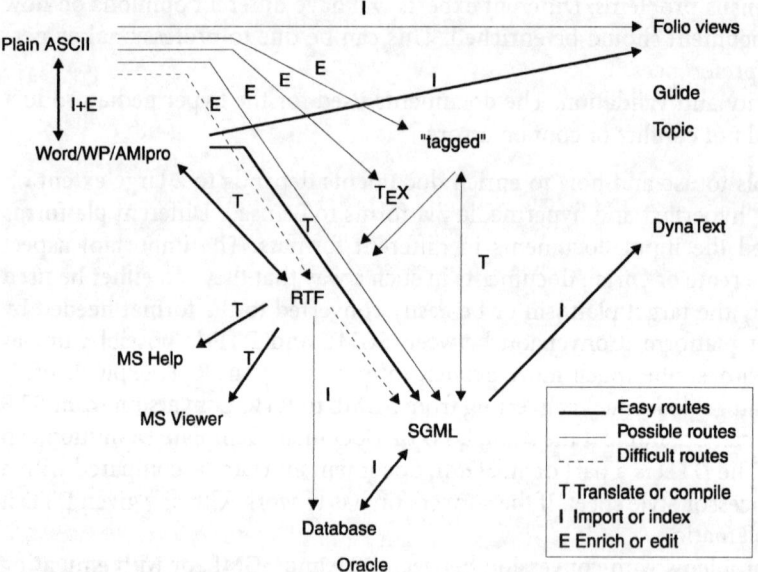

Figure 33. Products and formats

Notes on Figure 33:

- RTF is just one possible format. Some products may support other formats. In most cases a list must be supplied on how to interpret the styles, fonts, and typefaces. Thus implicit information can be translated into explicit information. Other possible formats are different word processor formats. Some products supply filters to enable them to read other formats.

- Although moving from plain ASCII to RTF is difficult there are a few products that are especially written to create RTF from ASCII without the use of a powerful RTF- supportive word processor.
- Even though importing SGML-tagged documents into a database is relatively easy, it is very probable that a special custom import filter needs to be written or modified to support the DTD used.
- Creating a DynaText book from SGML is fairly easy as long as one of the supported DDTs is used. If not, this may be a real problem.
- OWL Guide is one of the products where texts can be changed in the product using a clipboard. The first versions of Guide required the producer to type or copy in all texts in the right places. Hypertext capabilities were added in the production version of Guide. Needless to say, importing data in the Guide system requires a great deal of work and exporting the whole for use with other products was even impossible at the time when we did the evaluations.

11.9
DIS: Documentary Information Systems

A field where most of the problems mentioned in the previous section also apply is that of DIS. In fact DIS can be seen as a part of the hypermedia field. The difference between DIS and hypermedia is not so much how the information is accessed, but rather how much information is accessed and to what purpose. Most hypermedia applications are intended for leisure, learning, or reference. DIS is for companies that want to have all their documents accessible in an easy manner, not only their training and technical reference documents, but also sales documents, price lists, current orders, status of orders, etc. The following effects can be achieved for a company:

- Information can be kept more up to date.
- Information is more accessible.
- More documents can be reused.
- Documents can be (need to be) more standardized.
- Information can be accessed from different angles.
- Security and repair of the information is easier.

In order to put documents in a DIS the same things need to be done as when making documents ready for use with a hypertext system. Decisions need to be made about the required file formats to be used, for example, and the amount of explicit information that needs to be added.

12 Popular Multimedia Applications

12.1
Microsoft's Multimedia Viewer

Microsoft Help files enable not only help functions but also the creation of simple hypertext and hypermedia products. Having recognized this, Microsoft developed the next logical step, the Multimedia Viewer. The Multimedia Viewer has better support for audio and video and also supports a number of other features for generic hypermedia titles.

Microsoft Multimedia Viewer publishing tool kit can be installed on your hard disk from diskettes or CD-ROM and can require anywhere from about 6 MB up to about 30 MB. This depends on what needs to be accessible. There are programming examples, tutorials, support for different languages, etc. The CD-ROM is only needed for installation. Although Microsoft Word for Windows is not strictly required, it is required to get the full potential out of the Viewer development software.

The software includes a free runtime viewer that can be distributed with the titles produced. It also includes an installer which can be used to install titles. However, the installer still encounters problems on some machines. The first thing that strikes you when starting with the Authoring Guide is that the steps to be taken and the formats used are mostly the same as when developing a Windows Help file. But there are some differences.

Viewer for Windows supports most multimedia formats supported by the Media Control Interface (MCI), including the following formats:

- Wave form audio sounds
- MIDI music sequences
- CD audio (Red Book)
- Video (AVI) sequences created using Microsoft Video for Windows.

Playing video or audio sequences can be triggered by opening a topic or multimedia controllers embedded in topics (Figure 34).

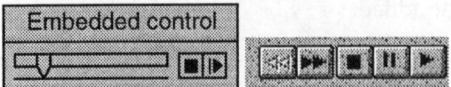

Figure 34. An embedded control and a custom control

It is possible to open a secondary window with your main window. The appearance of the Viewer windows can be changed, although some people find this hard to do.

As it was difficult to manage the files necessary for Windows Help file development, Microsoft has included a Project Editor application for easy access and editing of the project file. It can also start the appropriate applications to edit the files included in the project. Project files that are created with the Project Editor appear almost identical to the project files needed for the windows help compiler. The project files are in a simple text file format and the same sections can be found in both types of project files. While using a text editor it is possible to change the project's text file directly without touching the Project editor itself. This might be handy, for instance for tweaking during a presentation.

Editing topic files can be started by selecting the RTF tab to display the list of topic files, selecting the topic file to be edited and either double-clicking on it or choosing Edit File from the Edit menu. After this an application called the Topic Editor and Word for Windows are started.

The Topic Editor and Word for Windows can work together very well. When Word is started from the Project Editor, the Topic Editor is also started and becomes available to Word using a hot key. Using the Topic Editor viewer elements, such as "a hotspot here", "include a picture here", or "this is a keyword" can be inserted in the topic file loaded in Word. The viewer elements can also be edited in the Topic Editor. Viewer commands can also be added, deleted, or edited using Word, but you have to know the codes or styles. The codes and styles are essentially the same as those needed for creating the Windows Help files.

Some small macros are provide to use in Word. One of them is a macro to save the current file automatically as RTF. This macro can also be helpful if you are only creating RTF files for use with the Windows Help compiler. Other improvements over the help file compiler:

- Full text search. In this way occurrences of words can be found even if they are not in a key word or topic title.
- A flexible search dialogue, which can be replaced by your own if not appropriate.
- Search query operators that include Boolean, proximity, and range operators. The operators, by default AND, OR, NOT, NEAR, and THRU, can be redefined or aliases chosen from other languages or synonyms.
- Search fields to define categories of information within topics. These can be used in combination with topic groups to reduce the search scope and time. The search fields are also used with the search queries.
- Definition of parts of the topic texts as different data types. By default five data types are defined: text, numbers, dates, times, and epochs. This can be used in combination with search query operators to find for instance a list of all topics in which certain dates or ranges of dates are mentioned.

- Use of multiple simultaneous keyword lists. There is a limit to the number of keyword list. The exact number is not clear from the documentation, but is at least 62. The 62 possibilities mentioned are K0–K9, Ka–Kz and KA–KZ. K is regarded as the same as K0. The multiple keywords list can be used to define a number of categories for keywords. This can make searching faster and easier. It is not possible to use these different keyword lists combined. This can only be done by using search fields.
- Word stemming. If enabled while creating the title, searches can be done on the stem of words. An example would be metal, which is the stem of words such as metallic, metals and metallize. Searching for a word will return all occurrences of words with the same stem.
- Stop words can be defined. Stop words are words that when used for searches return unmanageable number of hits. Examples of these words are: as the, are, is, a, an, do.
- Ligature expansion. Ligature characters such as œ, æ, and ß can be used. These characters can also be expanded according to default or user-defined character-handling tables for sorting words containing ligature characters in the right order. The default translations for the ligature characters œ, æ, and ß are oe, ae, and ss.

12.1.1
Searching

As stated previously the Viewer supports multiple index lists and search categories or fields. For the user the main differences between the two are:

- An index list gives an alphabetical list of the whole index list to choose from. Only one item in the list can be chosen and no Boolean operators are possible. The index list dialogue presents a list of all indexed words with the number of topics in which the words appear.
- Free text search. Boolean operators can be used and the search is extremely fast even through megabytes of data.
- Searching using search fields or categories can be done by choosing "Search by category" in the search dialogue. Here Boolean operators can be used to combine search results of searches on different contents in different types of fields. It is important to note that wild cards can be used in the keyword boxes. As opposed to the index lists, you must have an idea of the words in the search field, because the words found in the different search lists cannot be shown. You cannot combine a search on category with a free text search, but it is possible to limit the search to one or more topic groups. This can be done for both search on category and free text search.

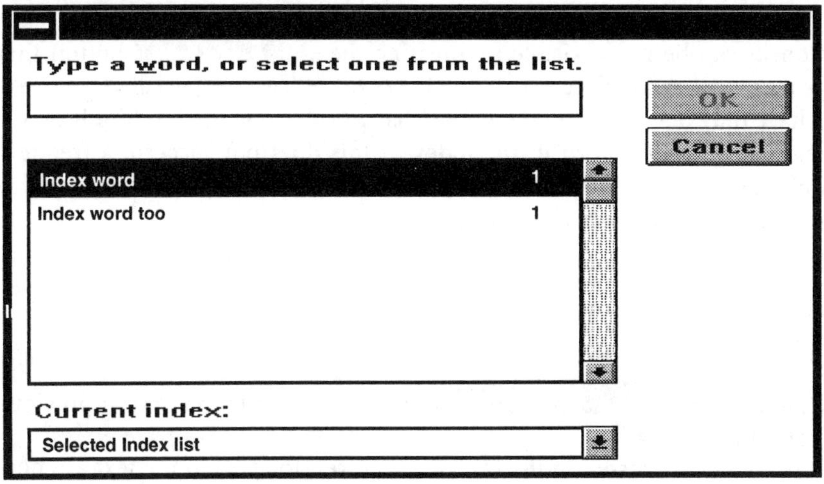

Figure 35. The index list dialogue

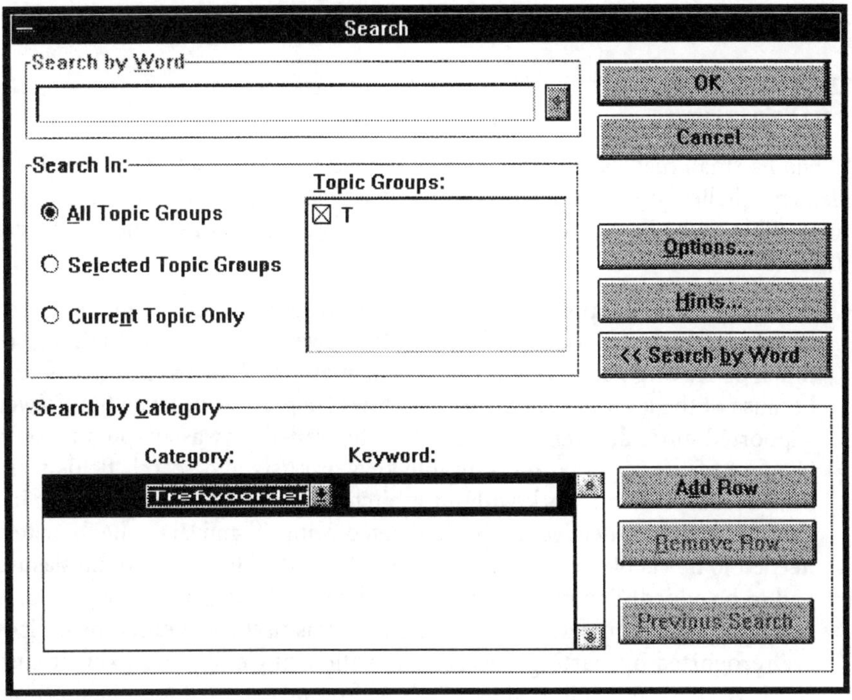

Figure 36. The full search dialogue

The search by category part can be removed by pressing the [<< Search by Word] button. It can be made visible by pressing the [Search by Category >>] button that appears on the same place. Using the index or indices is especially effective if you have only one word to search for. That word can be used to find it or another closely related word in the index. If this does not succeed, a free text search can be done. If you already know the category and (part of the) word to find, a search on category can be done.

12.1.2
Browsing

Browsing can be done by:

- Choosing the [<<] or [>>] buttons to go to the next or previous topic in a topic group.
- Clicking on a hotspot in the text or a picture. Hotspots in the text are normally highlighted by a green color.
- Using the history list to select a topic that was previously opened.
- Choosing the content to go back to the start of the title.

Browsing is in fact the same as in a Microsoft Windows Help file.

12.1.3
From Help to Viewer

We had a small medical encyclopedia converted to a Microsoft Windows Help file. The challenge was to adapt this medical encyclopedia so that it became compatible with the Microsoft Multimedia Viewer. This was done in several steps:

- First, a translator application was written to convert the original source material (which was coded with an SGML derivative), into RTF. In doing so, much of the original coding was lost, which at that time was not a problem because of the level of support by Windows Help. Now, because the Viewer supported more different types of data, the translator was adapted to keep in more of the information. Multiple keyword lists and search fields were introduced. It didn't work without a hitch. Search field codes, e.g., for including pictures, needed to be bracketed with /{ and /}as the brackets needed to be visible even after translation from RTF to word. So the slashes had to be added. The next problem was the way the different keyword lists had to be added. In each case a K footnote was used. The different indices are recognized by starting the footnote with a single digit number or case sensitive characters followed by a " : ". At first we assumed that the footnote name itself had to be K followed by that same digit or character. In the RTF file it should look like K{footnote K1:index one}. Note that keywords can be included in a more flexible manner in files used for the Viewer, as for the help compiler. In the former case there can only be one K footnote with all indices, which need to be in the header of the topic, and in the latter case there can be multiple K footnotes in different parts of each topic. Still, to keep it as compatible as possible the indices were kept together in the header, even though spreading them would have given the user the possibility to be taken to the correct paragraph of each topic where this index was first found.

- The second step was the conversion using the translator. This took about an hour after all problems were solved. The original files contained about 4000 topics, 2 000 000 characters. It takes so long because the original data contain references to topic titles which need to be converted to numbers for the Help and Viewer compilers to understand.
- In the third step a project file was created using the project editor. The project editor informed us when we tried to compile for the first time that it did not accept or understand Part III about Concept Mapping. This part is used by the Word help compiler to create a help file which can be used in combination with an application in such a way that the application can jump to a topic using a number instead of an index or topic title. These numbers are defined in the mapping part. So we deleted the mapping section. We also needed to add the names and corresponding numbers of the different indices and search fields.
- The fourth step is to run the help compiler. The compiler goes from 0 to 27% in a few seconds and then stays there for about half an hour. After that it goes with smaller and larger jumps to 100% and finishes about an hour later. The compiler works concurrently, so it is still possible to use your computer for other tasks. But it becomes very slow, and sometimes it will take a few minutes to react. The final file was about 10 MB, about three times the total size of the RTF files.
- Step five: Test the product.

To actually do this took a bit more than the total of two hours mentioned, mostly due to problems with understanding the RTF specs and finding out what the codes should look like in the RTF file. After that it worked quite fast. The total time investment in learning how to use the Viewer Toolkit and converting was about a week. It should be said that as yet no video or sounds are included, but bitmaps are, and including videos and sound is very straightforward. Com-paring the results with the Viewer compiler, however, it can be expected that it will take a bit more time than the previously mentioned hour when including sound and videos.

After converting the small medical encyclopedia, we did the same with a larger general encyclopedia with about 37 000 topics, a size of about 27 MB, and lots of references. The same steps were followed as with the medical encyclopedia. After adapting the translator, which took about one hour, the source files were converted to RTF. This took about a day, but the translator was not really optimized for speed. A Viewer project file was created and the RTF files were compiled. This also took about a day. It should be noted that compiling this general encyclopedia was impossible with the help compiler. The resulting RTF files are not totally compatible with the Help Compiler in the two cases mentioned above. The help compiler will probably have problems with the search fields and the added indices. But removing these will probably solve that problem. The help compiler has a mapping section, but it is not required. Topics in a help file can also be addressed using literal index words.

Maybe it would be nicer to use Viewer files instead of Help files, if only because of the built-in free text search. Two other important aspects are the extra index tables and search fields that can be used if the RTF files are adapted to include these. Using Viewer files instead of Help files is especially attractive in the case where the help files were previously used as a separate hypertext system anyway, that is, not directly connected to an application as a help file.

12.1.4
Conclusions

The Microsoft Multimedia Viewer publishing toolkit is quite a complete and robust product. Some types of multimedia titles could already be developed with the Microsoft Windows Help compiler, but as this took great pains previously, it can now be done more easily and with more features with the Viewer publishing toolkit.

The Viewer publishing toolkit can also be used for creating the old style Windows Help files. In this case only a subset of the Viewers features can be used, and before using the Windows Help compiler the .MVP extension of the project file has to be changed to a .HPJ extension. There are a few things that could have been better:

- The compiler is slow.
- Some words used to describe certain items, both in the documentation itself and in different Viewer dialogues are ambiguous or two words are used to describe the same thing. The best example of this are the words *field* and *category*. Different fields can be defined and used, but in the search dialogue the word *category* is used. You can search by category, not by fields.
- It appears impossible to combine a search on category with a free text search using the standard search dialogue. This might be possible by replacing the standard search dialogue by one of your own.
- The free text search is extremely fast. Searching on free text instead of text in categories is often faster. The drawback of this is that although more topics are found, fewer of the topics are those you really wanted. This because the categories can be used to make specific words more important in specific topics and situations.
- It is impossible to do a combined search on categories and certain index lists. This can be solved by putting the keywords in search fields too.

Microsoft Encarta is an example of what can be achieved with the Viewer. It is also an example of how much can be customized.

12.2
DynaText

EBT DynaText (we looked at version 2.0) is an electronic book index engine and browser. It is one of the hypertext development and delivery packages. The index engine expects SGML (minimally) formatted documents using one of the supported DDTs. Before indexing, a file needs to be made to inform the index engine how to interpret the different SGML codes. This makes the system flexible. Different types of hypertext can be developed using the same SGML documents, where for example different tags can be used to indicate keywords or references.

The index engine builds a full text index and derives the hypertext links to tables, figures, and footnotes. The index engine supports ISO, AAP, and ArborText SGML DDTs. It also supports SGML equations and even non-SGML T_EX equations. It appears that indexing the document does change the SGML documents, as the resulting textual documents used by the browser/viewer do not contain any normal SGML < > delimited tags.

The viewer supports text, hypertext links, and pictures. Hotspots or links from within a picture are not supported. Tables and pictures can be made visible either in the same or separate windows. Using separate windows makes it possible to view these whilst continuing to scroll through the text. The structure of the title can be made visible in a table of contents. Its appearance is akin to that of an outliner. End users can make annotations to the document and even add hypertext links using the browser.

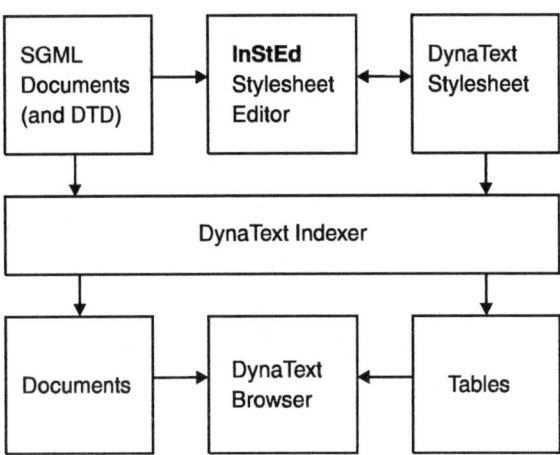

Figure 37. DynaText scheme

12.2.1
InStEd

The interactive style sheet editor InStEd is an add-on for DynaText. It is a power-ful tool to add styles to tag names. It provides an intuitive graphical user inter-face for viewing and editing DynaText style sheets.

Each SGML tag can get a style attached to it. A style can consist of typographical information (called style property settings), a short description, and one of four logical categories. The style property settings can be inherited by high-level elements. While using the style sheet editor, one can use the DynaText browser to instantaneously view the effects of changes made with InStEd. InStEd outputs commented style sheets in valid SGML format. This makes it easier to convert documents used as input for the DynaText index engine for use with other publishing system formats.

DynaText and InStEd are developed by Electronic Book Technologies (EBT).

13 Recipes

13.1
Introduction

Creating a hypermedia or hypertext system needs strong discipline and a good awareness of available document tools, especially when the information is not yet stored in a computer, and when the information is plain. To give an idea of how to start, a few recipes are given for paper, plain text, and for MS Windows Help.

13.2
Paper Recipes

Converting paper material to a hypertext system is one of the most costly and time-consuming way to create a hypertext system. It is still the case that often the material for a hypertext system is only available on paper. There are a number of possible reasons for this:

- The original material was typed with regular typewriters.
- Typesetting tapes, computer punched tapes or cards, or magnetic tapes or disks have been destroyed or lost.
- Typesetting tapes, computer punched tapes or cards, or magnetic tapes or disks have become unreadable. This may be because of degradation of the media, because the machines that can read the media have been destroyed, sold, or scrapped, or made unavailable, or because the needed computer programs have become unavailable.

Given the high costs of conversion, the last two points prompt us to conclude that it might make some sense to think twice before destroying or scrapping all the material associated with a medium, or all machines or computer applications able to read certain media, before it is clear whether the material can still be used with new machines or before it is converted to the new media or new computer applications. The most difficult steps of converting from paper to a hypertext system are still the entry of the available texts, figures, and pictures on paper into a computer system.

13.2.1
Figures and Pictures

Figures and pictures can also be entered by hand, using scanners, or with a combination of both. Most OCR applications will not store pictures found with the texts on paper. Thus entering the figures and pictures will have to be done separately. Files of a scanned figure or picture will often be quite large. This has its consequences for both the space needed for storage and the retrieval speed. To reduce the space needed for storage and to enhance to storage speed some actions may be taken:

- The figures and pictures can be loaded into special computer applications and everything not part of the intended figure or picture can be removed from it.
- Special computer applications may be used to trace schemes and drawings and make vector oriented drawings which will take up less space.
- An artist may take the appropriate scanned figures and pictures and use a computer application to trace these by hand (or more to the point, by mouse) to make vector oriented drawings. This will often take less time and produce more accurate results then doing it all by hand.
- Using special computer applications figures and pictures can be converted to ones with fewer colors, with or without using dithering, and can also be converted to smaller ones or ones with lower resolution.
- The figures or pictures can be compressed to a format known by the application.

Which actions will be taken depend mostly on what is expected of the end product. In practice it is almost impossible to have no hand work.

13.2.2
Computer Applications

To give some idea of which applications can be used, we give a list, which is not intended to be complete:

Function	Platforms	
OCR	Omnipage	Macintosh, Windows 95
editing photos	PhotoShop	Macintosh, Windows 95
editing pictures	Pixelpaint	Macintosh
tracing figures	COREL Trace	Macintosh, Windows 95
editing figures	COREL Draw	Macintosh, Windows 95
editing figures	MacDraw	Macintosh

13.3
Plain Text Recipes

Often texts that have to be used in hypertext systems are plain, sometimes because the OCR application could not read or save it as anything but plain text, or just because the original texts was created using a editing application only supporting plain text.

There are two approaches to upgrading the plain text for use with a hypertext system.

- Import the plain text into the hypertext system and upgrade it within the hypertext system.
- Upgrade the plain text, by tagging and/or formatting it, and than importing it into the hypertext system.

Combinations of the two methods may also be possible. Figure 38 illustrates the two paths.

Some hypertext systems still do not support importing of tagged or formatted text. In these cases it does not make sense to follow path A.

Upgrading plain text to tagged and/or formatted text is very sensible. Most hypertext systems do not support exporting of tagged text. Having the formatted and tagged text handy can have the advantage that it can also be used for other purposes besides hypertext systems. An example of this is the extraction of all parts of the texts that have to do with one or more subjects. In this way a derivative work can be made from a larger work. At least one publisher uses this system to derive special subject encyclopedias from a main encyclopedia.

Before starting to upgrade the material the following questions have to be answered:

- How much time, money, and effort are you willing to invest in upgrading the texts? This also has to do with the intended result. Tagging and/or formatting all of the information in the texts and parts thereof will obviously always cost more than only tagging headings and a few generic references. Note that more tagging and formatting may enable the hypertext system more search and navigation options, if the hypertext system used supports it.

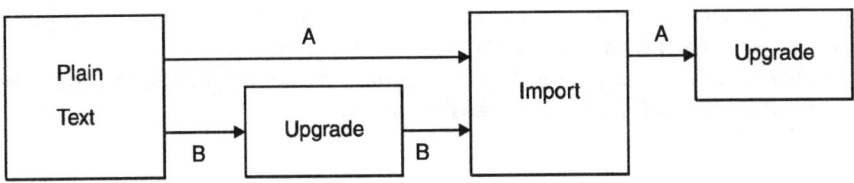

Figure 38. Upgrading paths for plain text

- If little time, money, and effort will be invested, is this a one-time operation, or is the result intended to be upgraded further at a later stage?
- Can any tagging or needed formatting be derived from the structure of texts using special applications? This is often not the case. Also, when it is possible it is often very difficult to create the special applications.
- How much of the tagging or formatting needs to be done by hand? Our experience is that almost all of it needs to be done by hand.
- Can a tagging mechanism be used to provide formatting or typesetting information latter on? Given the right tools the answer to this is yes.
- If tagging is not used, can the texts be formatted to derive tagged texts from them later? As long as the different types of information are formatted uniquely the answer is yes. But this is very difficult to achieve in most cases. Especially if the result needs to be upgraded at a later stage, formatting alone of text is not recommended.
- What is the format needed for importation into or use with the target hyper-text system(s)? For a Windows Help system RTF files formatted in a distinct manner are needed. For some systems SGML files are needed. In both cases you can either directly format or tag the files in the necessary format, or in another format. In the latter case, you will need one or more conversion utilities. It is recommended to create the necessary files immediately if possible and if the target format supports all the necessary tagging and for-matting. This will almost always be the case with SGML or an extension, but it may be different for RTF documents.
- What parts of the texts need to be formatted or tagged in what way? Parts that can be considered are: headings of different levels, body text, questions, answers, footnotes, endnotes, keywords, different types of references, synonyms, homonyms, different types of names, different types of dates, different types of numbers, quotations, captions, headers, footers, and tables of contents, to name but a few. Which of these are to be used depends on the desired result.

In a low-budget, minimal-upgrade situation, normal plain text editing applications that support the use of macros will be what is needed. Only the parts with information of the types selected in the texts need to be tagged. An example would be adding tags to headings and references. In a situation where more needs to be done there are two possibilities:

- It is possible to use either a WYSIWYG word processor with macro support and optionally with style sheets (MS Word, WordPerfect, AmiPro),
- Or one can use a specific tagging editor. One for tagging SGML could be used. This is still the more expensive option.

13.3.1
Conclusion

What to use and what to tag depends strongly on the desired result.

13.4
Microsoft Windows Help Recipes

The Microsoft Windows Help system is one of the most widely used hypertext systems. It supports references, pop texts, keywords, different font styles and sizes, pictures, and hotspots in pictures. Windows help files are normally created to provide help with a specific application, but they can also be used to store any other kind of information that can be retrieved in a similar manner, for example, small encyclopedias, dictionaries, and other reference works.

Obviously Windows help files have limits, the most important being that there is no authoring system. But once the material is stable and available in the formats accepted by the help compiler, it can be compiled once, reproduced, and distributed. The latest help compiler accepts more formats and can create larger help files then the earlier version. It also support OLE, which makes it possible to include even the most alien formats in the help file.

13.4.1
Creating Windows Help Files from Existing Material

In many cases the texts and other material for encyclopedias, dictionaries, and other reference works are already available (although publishers are not very eager to part with them). In many cases this material is already in machine readable form and tagged or formatted, and making a help file from the material should be quite easy. To create a help file the help compiler must be used. This help compiler accepts input in the form of Rich Text Formatted (RTF) texts, Windows bitmaps (BMP) files, HyperGraphics (SHG) files, and Windows Meta-Files (WMF). This implies that all other types of file that your existing material will probably be using must be converted to the ones mentioned.

13.4.1.1
Using Untagged Material

If the existing material has some formatting from which tagging can be derived it may make sense to write or use an application (or macro in a word processor) to convert the formatting information to tagging information. When no convertible formatting is available, you can just load your material into a word processor and start adding tags, or simply adding the necessary formatting or RTF codes.

This can be made easier by using tools such as RoboHelp, DocToHelp, or HelpWizard.

13.4.1.2
Using Tagged Material

If the existing material is already tagged, for instance SGML-formatted material, a translating application can be written to translate the SGML tags to RTF codes. How the resulting RTF file should be composed will be addressed later.

13.4.2
Rich Text Format

RTF is a Microsoft standard for formatting text. It supports paragraph styles, colors, typographical formatting, headers, footers, and embedded or linked pictures, drawings, tables, and formulas. An RTF file only contains ASCII characters so it can be read as text, and does not have to be handled as a binary file.

13.4.3
RTF and the Help Compiler

The Help compiler does not use all the features supported by RTF; styles are among the features it does not support. The following is a description of the basic structure of a minimal RTF file as needed by the help compiler. Knowing the structure and formatting of the necessary files is especially important when not using RTF-capable word processors, or when translating another format to RTF for compiling into a help file. If an RTF-capable word processor such as Word is used most of the codes given need not be known. However, it is necessary to know what typographical information is needed to code the different parts of the text.

The fixed codes are in `Courier` roman and the variable texts are in *Courier italic*.

An RTF file should start with:

```
{\rtf1\ansi {\fonttbl{\f0\froman
Times New Roman;}
{\f1\froman Symbol;}}
```

Each topic in the file may start with a title, in this case in bold (by the \b code):

```
{\b Title}
```

A unique key or code should be declared. The key can be any unique combination of alpha-numerical characters and some special characters such as the underscore and minus.

```
#{\footnote # UniqueKey1}
```

For referencing the title should be declared:

```
${\footnote $ Title}
```

The browsing order can be declared, and you can use one or more subject names followed by a colon and a number. To avoid problems always pad leading zeros before the number to give numbers the same length. If this is not done Subject:9 will appear after subject:10 because of the way sorting is done.

```
+{\footnote + Subject:00001}
```

Keywords can be declared to a maximum of 1023 characters (including the separators). The ; is used as a separator.

```
K{\footnote K keyword1;keyword2;another
keyword; this is a sentence, it can also be
used as keyword; spaces, and all punctuation
except the separator may be used; keyword 6}
```

All footnotes should be in one sequence without other text between them.

Carriage returns and linefeeds (CR/LF) are ignored by the help compiler, so paragraphs must be separated by:

```
\par
```

A reference may be included thus:

```
This is a text with a {\uldb reference text}
{\v UniqueKeyOfTopicReferredTo}
```

The text between {\uldb and } is the text which will appear green within the hotspot. The text between {\v and } contains the key and is invisible. No characters of any kind are allowed between the } at the end of the reference text and { at the start of the key. A pop text may be included in much the same way as a reference:

```
{\ul press mouse to popup}
{\v This text will appear in a popup box}
```

Each topic must end with:

```
\page
```

The file must end with: }

Note that each { must be paired with a }.

All characters with a value of above 127 (0x7F) should be replaced by a string starting with \' and directly followed by the hexadecimal value of the characters. A few examples:

```
\'80 \'FF \'A0
```

13.4.4
Pictures

It is also possible to include bitmaps. This may be done by one of the following:

```
\{BMC FILENAME.EXT\}
\{BML FILENAME.EXT\}
\{BMR FILENAME.EXT\}
```

The first includes a bitmap as a character (BitMap Character}, the second left aligned (BitMap Left), and the third right aligned (BitMap Right). The help compiler supports Windows bitmaps (.BMP), device-independent bitmaps (.DIB), Windows metabolize (.WMF), and also the HyperGraphics format (.SHG).

13.4.4.1
HyperGraphics

The HyperGraphics format is a special format that may contain hotspot information, co-ordinates of the hotspot, and a reference to a unique key, the same as defined in the RTF file. A .SHG file can be created by using the hotspot editor application that is included with the help file compiler package. The hotspot editor accepts all formats mentioned above and is able to save the result as a HyperGraphics file. Because the data is always stored in a compressed format in an HyperGraphics this is another advantage over normal Windows bitmap files.

13.4.5
Typefaces and Fonts

It is possible to create an RTF file with different typefaces (i.e., Times, Courier, Helvetica, etc.), font sizes, and appearances (different colors, bold and italic). Because underlined and double underlined text is already used for activating hotspots (pop texts and links), these cannot be used merely to adorn the text.

13.4.6
Extending Help

Help can be extended and customized using the available macros. It is also possible to start applications, jump to other help files, add or remove buttons from the button bar, etc.

It is possible to create multiple help systems that refer to each other. This makes it possible to overcome some of the limitations of the help compiler. If a help system becomes too big to be compiled by the compiler it can be divided into chunks that can be compiled separately and that refer to each other. Referring to other help files can be done by using the JumpContext or JumpId macros. First, using the double-underline formatting, type the text or insert the graphic you want to appear as the hotspot. Second, immediately following the text or graphic, use hidden text formatting to type the following items (do not separate any of these items by spaces):

- An exclamation mark (!)
- Either JumpContext (or JC) or JumpID (or JI) with the appropriate parameters.

In RTF it has to appear thus:

```
{\du This is the hotspot}
{h !JumpContext(THEFILE.HLP, MYHELPTOPIC)}
```

It is possible to add buttons or other information to the help system. This can be done by inserting a button that activates an external DLL when pressed or by auto-executing a function in an external DLL when a topic is made visible. To use an external function it must be registered first. Once the function is registered, it can be used in the same way as standard Win Help macros.

```
RegisterRoutine("DLL-name",
"function-name","format-spec")
```

Any of the following tasks could be done by using functions, if contained, in a DLL:

- Adding a full-text search engine
- Displaying animated graphics
- Sound effects.

If you want to use a DLL function throughout a Help file, you should register it in the [CONFIG] section of the Help project file. The documentation mentioned the possibility of creating multiple keyword lists. But we could not get this to work, probably due to some misunderstanding on our part.

13.4.7
Weaknesses

One of the weaknesses of coding the RTF files is the fact that much information needs to be coded twice. Examples of this:

- Titles must be declared in a footnote for referencing, even though a title may already be coded.
- Keywords must be declared separately in a footnote text. The keywords cannot be marked within the normal text.
- Keys need to be declared for each topic, even when the title is unique.
- References always need have a key added even if they are an exact duplicate of the title of a topic.

These weaknesses make it harder and more time-consuming to create a help system.

13.4.8
Examples

Over the past years we have had good connections with one of Netherlands' leading encyclopedia and dictionary publishers. They have provided us with some of their material to use for testing in different environments and for testing our own applications.

The publisher's material is tagged in an SGML-like manner, which they call GML. There are no document type definitions or DDTs. In fact to make SGML, they would only need to add a DTD and replace their special character descriptions by the standard SGML character descriptions.

An application (GML_to_RTF) was written to translate all their files to RTF files. The translation was done in several stages.

- First a list of all files was compiled for use with the help compiler project file.
- Then a list of all titles of all topics in the material was composed. The list was saved on disk with the names of the files where the topics could be found and a unique context string or key for each title.
- The list of titles was alphabetically sorted, and saved again. The sorting was only done on the first character, for small sets of titles in memory and for large sets on disk. This was because of the 64-kilobyte memory limit of one memory segment in MS-DOS. A list of pointers to the file with the list of topics was made. Each of the pointers pointed to the next first character in the file. So there was a pointer to the listing of the topics started with the characters A and a, one for B and b, etc. This was done to reduce the amount of searching in the list. This simple method reduces searching time by over 95%. Although it is possible to reduce the search even further and not much has been done to optimize either this or the process as a whole. It was not optimized mostly because it did not make sense to make a system that was much faster than the help compiler itself, as it would only be used a few times and would have taken more time to implement.
- The translation of tags to RTF tags was done on a file by file basis. If a title was found, it was first written to the output file (with some formatting) and then the unique context string was retrieved from the list and also written to the output file as the appropriate footer, where the title was written again but now as footer. All words marked as keywords in the topic were put into the keyword footer and the text itself was written to the output file. If a reference to another topic was found, the context string of that topic was retrieved and added. If commands to insert pictures were found, these commands were translated, with the filenames to the appropriate RTF codes and file types. The picture files were not translated, it was assumed they could be better handled by specialized batch translation applications. For reference a list of all expected picture files was generated.

After these steps some problems might still exist:

- Some titles may not have been unique, so two topics may have got the same context string. The help compiler will generate warnings when this occurs, but will continue.
- The picture files had to be translated. In this case the pictures were already in BMP format so not much needed to be done.

- Some references were not found, either because the articles referred to did not exist or because the title was slightly different from the referencing text. The differences were mostly plurals referring to singulars and vice versa.
- Sometimes small errors in the original material were not detected by the GML2RTF translator and the translator in turn produced errors. When detecting nested references, which should not exist, at times a } too many was produced.

The translation of the four megabytes of text, almost 4000 topics, from the original format to RTF took about 30 minutes. Optimizing the translation application may provide up to a ten-fold speed increase. But the help compiler took about 45 minutes to compile the help file. The resulting help file is about four megabytes, half of which is used for pictures. It is very well compressed, and using ARJ or PKZIP only produced a 3% space saving. The performance of this help file is quite good.

Part III
Navigational Support

Authors, editors, and secondary authors use documents in quite an intense way. If we think about document management and navigational support it is obvious that these roles need it quite urgently. A typical task for editors is reusing existing texts for new text books. This "pick-and-mix" job can be tedious if there is no descriptive information about the available documents. Indications about the concepts in these documents and their relations have proved to be helpful in ongoing projects. On top of these concept networks, graph computations can be performed to get a grip on their complexity.

14 Graph Computation in Structuring Hypermedia

Authoring hypermedia is a multi-actor process as it needs several types of expertise and may even need many different actors in the same phase of preparation (see Part II). Here graph theory is introduced as a formalism to represent and evaluate complex patterns of relations between information elements (items) in hypermedia. Hypermedia are essentially based on the interrelations between information elements. Static presentation frames like texts and pictures, but also dynamic frames such as fragments of video and sound, can be called from the current state in the presentation sequence. The call typically manifests itself as the user wanting to see or hear more about a certain aspect of the current information. To anticipate this hunger for related information the authoring phases of hypermedia should pay special attention to the structure in the inter-relations between information elements (items). As we saw in Chapter 2, authors and editors of hypermedia face the task of verifying and consolidating the dif-ferent levels of item descriptions and the links between them. This task is not only a practical problem in the sense that browsers should meet sufficient hot-spots to digress. The main criterion for assigning relations is that they must be valid and important enough for meaningful reading. The DELTA research project, in which we were involved, examined a number of alternatives to reduce the mental load of editors in the phases of interrelating hypermedia documents.

Based on previous experiments with editing (Frisse 1988a and Castelli, Colazzo, and Mic 1990) we know that contextual awareness is a decisive factor in the cognitive load on hypermedia authors. Contextual awareness is the ability to validate assigned relations on the basis of the structural position of an item in the total network of items and relations between them. For instance, hypermedia items on predators may evoke relations to food like meat, plants, etc. The editor will be helped, however, if he/she is prompted that specific birds of prey suffer from pollution like DDT more than animals who eat fruit, etc. In other words, the context of specific instances of a concept can be prompted to the author so that new links (e.g., from birds of prey to environmental health) may be installed. This increases the density of the hypermedia network and supplies more mean-ingful associations to the final reader or learner. Contextual awareness may also prevent the editor from assigning new relations. For instance, in the case of the detected relation between prey animals and environmental health, it would not be effective to elaborate on specific examples of the decline in specific species of animals if the generic principles of food rationing and the food cycle are not explained anywhere in the hyperbase.

The function of contextual orientation has been analyzed and explored in the DELTA HYPERATE project. The network of interrelations between the items is considered as an unlabelled directed graph, whose function is to prompt the hypermedia user as to where to find conglomerates of references. The hypermedia database (Kibby, Tanner & Hardman, 1991) can store the results of the graph analysis of the graph structure in the properties. An extra field could be installed to store the structural centrality of the item in the total hyperbase. The reason for storing the outcomes of graph analyses in the boundaries of the permanent item information, rather than recomputing them when they are needed, is that it save time. Recomputing a network of 4000 concepts (which is a typical size of a concept domain in a reference manual) will cost some hours. The main reason for choosing graph theory among other formalisms is twofold:

- Existing information resources as deliverable by traditional publishing companies can easily be transformed into directed (unlabeled) graphs via SGML interpretation.
- The graph representation is close to the conceptual map needed by hypermedia authors and end users for efficient navigation (see, e.g., Travers 1989).

Two levels of graph representation can be distinguished:

- The complete (global) configuration of assigned relations between the hypermedia items. In a realistic system we may expect several thousand nodes and more than ten thousand links. They can never be shown simultaneously. We need dedicated rules and even heuristics to decide which part of the network should be displayed to provide users with sufficient information about where they are now and where they can go in n steps.
- The local state of the user as a function of previous browsing sequence and the first order browsing step as an exclusive alternative of all possible continuations (see Waterworth et al. 1989). Designers of hypermedia face the problem that adequate anticipation of all particular states of all particular users would entail speculations about the cognitive states in users as they emerge from their prior knowledge and the confrontation with the information in the last visited items. This complexity for the hypermedia author becomes manifest as he/she faces the task of assigning hotspots in the items. Hypermedia for learning should not only support the local interest of the user but should trigger cognitive effects which are useful in the current phase of learning and development.

The representation of hypermedia relations (level 1) is different from the concrete level of hotspots (level 2) which links together the pieces of information (items) in a hyperbase. The first one is virtual and can only be detected after browsing through all possible transitions of the hypermedia network or by providing special network visualizations on the screen. The second one is obviously present as the user (or author) moves along from one item to another. In one way or another we may presume that the first level of representation is necessary to support contextual awareness for hypermedia users: Just seeing the hotspots prompting where to go next restricts the user to a local view and prevents him/her from making a global plan for the browsing session. Graph theory can assist in reducing the complexity at level 1. To provide prescriptions to the user at specific moments in the browsing tour, we need the decisions of directing producers who arrange a well-defined goal to be met by the user, for instance, the teacher or the curriculum designer who tunes the hypermedia system for specific learning goals. This chapter describes several types of graph representations and their subsequent evaluation procedures to assist the author of hypermedia systems.

14.1
Formalisms for the Representation of Relational Patterns

The creation of relations between hypermedia items is a necessary step before browsing by the user is enabled. The complexity of the patterns in the hypermedia relations is often underestimated and becomes a problem in the phase of maintenance and sometimes even already during the authoring process itself. Elm & Woods (1985) described the orientation problem as follows:

> The user not having a clear conception of the relationships within the system, or knowing his present location in the system relative to the display structure, and finding it difficult to decide where to look next within the system.

In case the hypermedia relations do not contain cycles, it is easy to determine the 'top node' in the taxonomy of the network by taking the node(s) having only outgoing relations. However, if nodes are located at one or more cyclic tours, we need a more indirect criterion to evaluate the level of entailment.

14.1.1
Unlabeled Directed Graphs for Representing Hypermedia Relations

Graph computation is a well-described formalism to typify several structural characteristics of the hypermedia elements in a complex network of relations. A directed graph can be defined as a pair $D(P,A)$ where P is a non-empty finite set of elements, called nodes; and a non-empty family A of ordered pairs, called arcs of elements of P. Arcs go from origin to destination nodes. Symmetric relations can be made by defining two relations in opposite directions.

Two approaches can be made:

1. The hypermedia relations as declarative references, reflecting the dependency in the descriptions within the item. In the network below, the description of visualization of item 4 entails the items 1 and 5. In other words, the author of the hypermedia graph considers it useful to refer to two adjacent descriptions in the exposition of item 4.

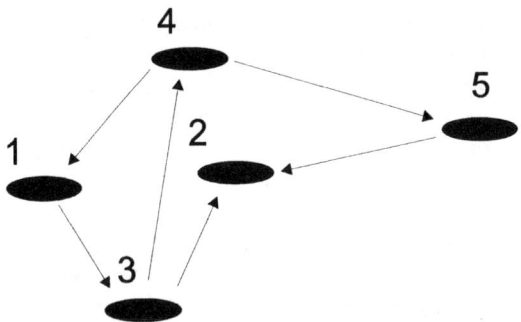

Figure 39. Level of hypermedia relations

2. The hypermedia relations as potential browsing transitions. In this case a hypermedia link is a procedural assignment: if you arrive at item 3 you may browse to items 2 or 4.

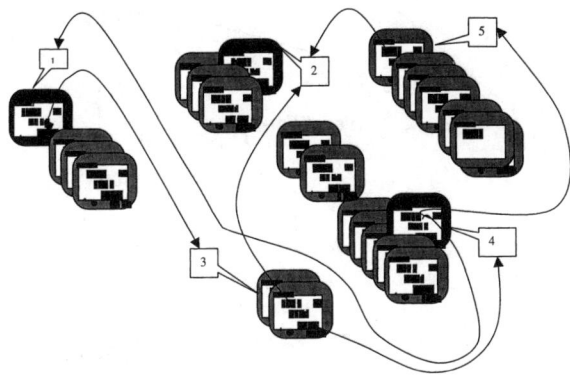

Figure 40. Browsing

This dichotomy between the declarative and the procedural approach to hypermedia relations needs further analysis, as it may confuse the discussions about the epistemological status of hypermedia networks on the one hand, and the consequences for browsing and navigation on the other.

14.1.2
Hypergraphs

A hypergraph can be defined as a pair $H(P, HL)$. P is a non-empty, finite set of elements, called nodes, and HL is a non-empty, finite set of non-empty subsets of P. HL is the set of hypergraphs. The use of hypergraphs in the context of hypermedia systems is in the phase of Editing as subsets of the overall network prove to be more interrelated than the rest of the network. Sub-graphs in the case study with the Medical Encyclopedia were called rubrics or sections. Examples of sections in the medical domain are diseases, parts of the body, diagnoses, symptoms, medical interventions, etc. The detection of sections was based on the SGML encoding in the text resource. Graph analysis of the directed graph as it emerges from the hypermedia relations can be used to detect subgraphs. Let us study the next concept map, in order to demonstrate the use of sub-graph detection.

The coherence within and between detected sub-graphs in a hypergraph can be expressed in terms of 'weak' and 'strong' components: 'Strongly connected' means that there is a path between all pairs of points of the sub-graph.

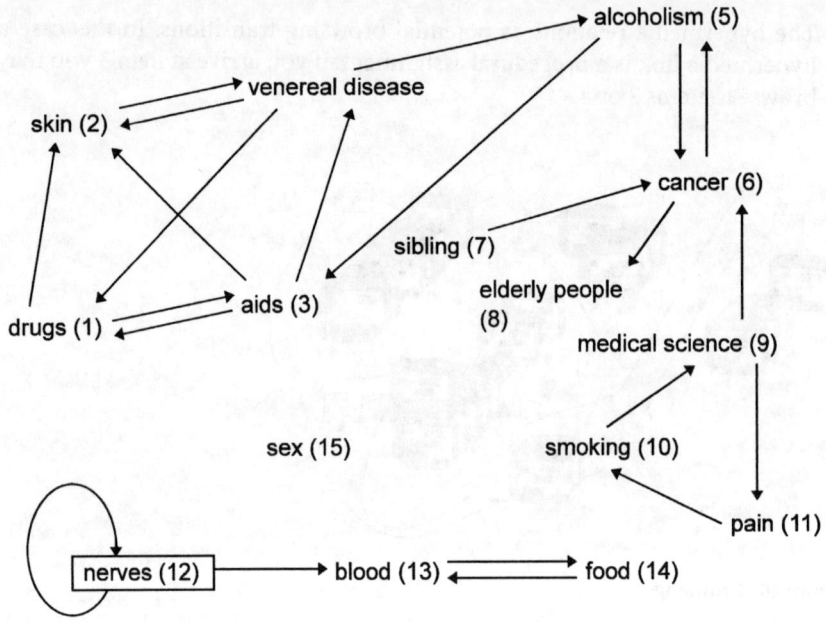

Figure 41. A sample concept map

According to Harary, Norman & Cartwright (1965), there is a path between all pairs of points of the sub graph. The essential difference between weak and strong components is found in the degree to which components are connected: semi-paths versus paths. In terms of hypermedia, items which embody points on a semi-path can only be reached or only be left exclusively. So strong components of a hypermedia network are those sub-graphs which are located on continuous chains of browsing routes. They can not only be reached but also give immediate access to at least one other node.

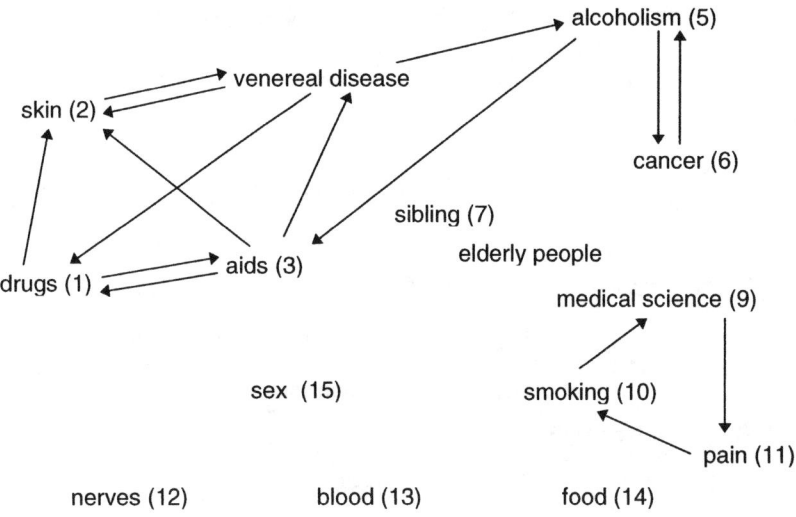

Figure 42. Strongly connected (directed) sub-graphs

A *block* in a directed graph is a maximally connected sub-graph having no point p such that B–p is disconnected. A *cutpoint* of a graph is a point which removal increases the number of (weak) components. A *bridge* of a graph is a line whose removal increases the number of (weak) components. Hypermedia authors should be aware of the items and links which are essential for browsing tours.

A clique is a maximal complete sub-graph of a graph G. Complete means that lines exist between each pair of points of the clique or that the distance between each pair of points is equal to one. An N-clique C of a graph G is a maximal sub-graph of G such that for all pairs u,p of C the distance in G is smaller than or equal to N, that is, $d\{ G(u,p) \} \leq N$. In terms of hypermedia networks we can say that cliques are those groups of items which may cause short cyclic tours by the user.

14.1.3
The Bipartite, Directed (Conditional) Graph or Petri-Net Graph

A Petri-net graph can be defined as a quadruple: $C=(P,T,I,O)$ where

P is a finite set of elements called places, T is a finite set elements called transitions, and P and T are disjunct.

- *I   is the input function and is defined as: I: $T \Rightarrow P$*
- *O   is the output function and is defined as: O: $T \Rightarrow P$*

(see Peterson 1981).

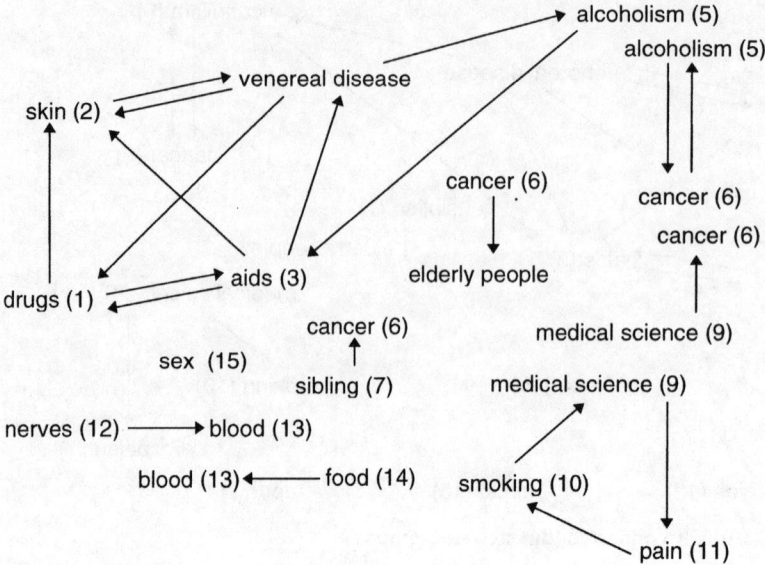

Figure 43. Blocks in the graph

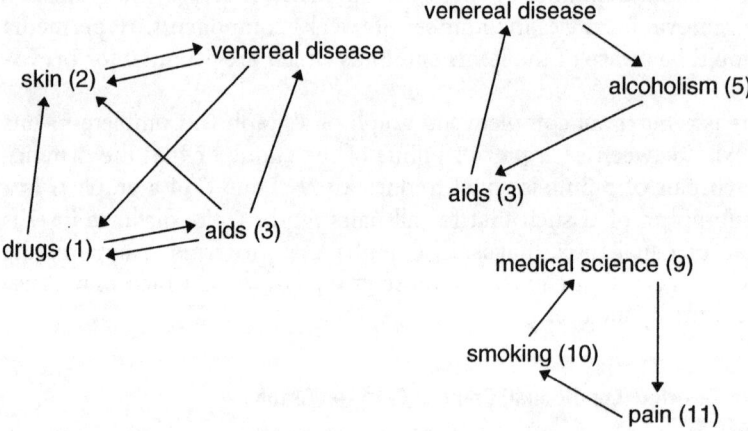

Figure 44. Three cliques in a graph

Furuta & Stotts (1989) have reflected on the potential of Petri-net mechanisms for the synchronization of hypermedia actions. The Trellis system they designed and implemented is based on a notational and analytical framework uni-fying two critical aspects of hypermedia:

- The logically linked information
- The experience the reader has when browsing the structure.

The declarative part of conditional transitions enriches the concise unlabeled graph underlying traditional hypermedia. The basic problem, however, is how hypermedia authors can assign dependency relations to concepts and their semantic context. The same problem arose when cognitive psychologists tried to establish sequencing principles for teaching concepts. The only argument for doing this would be the availability of a clear task analysis.

The user interface management system could be synchronized by Petri-net representations. In our opinion, however, hypermedia authors should be freed from these problems. You could compare it with double-declutching in old cars.

14.2
Unlabeled Directed Graph Reflecting Conceptual Entailments

Characteristic for the pattern of hypermedia relations is its implicitness: Authors only become aware of the topological consequences of the assigned relations as the system mirrors one or more of the graph-analytic results. Castelli, Colazzo & Mic (1990) mention four basic structures concerning the topology of hypermedia items which constrain the browsing behavior of the user:

1.	Sequence:	Offering the reader a linear transit from item to item similar to text and pictures in a book or video program.
2.	Branch:	The user is offered several alternatives to continue.
3.	Convergence:	Several browsing paths come together in one node.
4.	Loop:	Longer or shorter cycles in the hypermedia relations occur and finally bring the reader back to the item of departure.

The four basic structures can be combined into complex entailment patterns which can hardly be represented and imagined without powerful analytic tools. Especially the evaluation of cycles in hypermedia networks needs special care to avoid confusion during the stage of authoring.

14.2.1
The Problem Space of the Hypermedia User and the Need for Graph Computation

The elementary reference structure in hypermedia can be considered as a directed graph. Each arc represents the incident of a main concept pointing to a help concept in its description field. As authors of a hypermedia database can define concept relations by direct or indirect recursion (referring backwards to an earlier mentioned concept), it is obvious that a hypermedia network can contain cycles. None of the research attempts made so far addresses the specific complications of cyclic hypermedia relations. Cycles complicates hypermedia relations in the sense that they can no longer be described as a taxonomy or (more generally) a tree in which the upper nodes are hierarchically higher than their 'descendants'. This complicates notions like 'level of detail', 'pruning a network' (e.g., for displaying where you are), or 'defining the centrality of a node'.

This is the reason that hypermedia tools need a more complex type of graph evaluation. Graph analysis in the field of social networks has been equipped to deal with cycles and the algorithms to deal with NP-completeness (Hoede 1978, Bakker 1987).

This study into the connectivity of hypermedia graphs restricts itself to un-labeled relations. The type of the relation between main and help concept will not be specified, and the strength of the relation will not be taken into account. Characteristic for the use of hypermedia is the ease of operation, while the cogni-tive costs to orient in the network of relations are high.

During hypermedia authoring, you can simply digress on one of the terms in a current description. The same is true for the learner who wants to see more about a certain aspect of the current item.

Local assignments can be helped by an adequate 'direct manipulation' user interface, while the consequences on a global scale can still be obscure for the user. In fact the comfort of assigning hypermedia relations hides an enormous anticipation complexity for the author (see also Neuwirth & Kaufer 1989). On the level of manipulation it is quite simple to digress on a certain concept, by in-stalling new sub-concepts and relating new concepts to existing concepts. At the level of semantics however, the problem remains, and will soon exceed human imagination as the size of the network increases. The problem for the author is how to keep the network of relations centered around the key issue to be covered in the information rather than how to digress along the many aspects of the topic under concern.

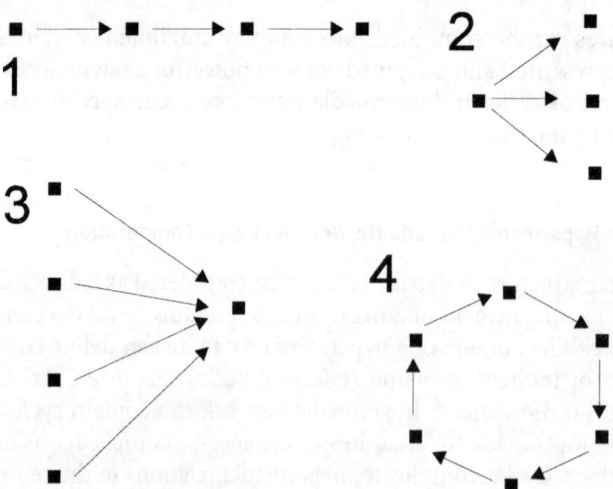

Figure 45. Basic structures

Practical questions the author should answer while creating or extending a hypermedia base:

- How crucial is this concept within the overall subject area? Is it essential enough to act as a root for further digression? The root is not necessarily important to understand the current item, but it should provide sufficient access to other important items.
- Am I forgetting to relate words in this item to already existing concepts, so that they stay unreachable?
- Did I use a synonym for that concept before?
- Did I use this word for another concept before?

One way to diminish this complexity and uncertainty for the author is to supply configuration information, prompting him/her how long the chains of entailments after a concept already are, and how influential it is to connect two previous unconnected concepts. If they are parts of two totally separate sub-graphs, this addition will be of importance, especially if they already had a central position in the two separate graphs before. As far as the reader of hyper-media adds new information, the same problem arises. As the reader restrains from authoring, the graph representation is of importance for navigation and anticipation of the new information. The quality of hypermedia facilities is heavily dependent on the correctness with which local help concepts anticipate the information that can be expected along their entailments, not only because it is demotivating for the user if he/she misses the expected information, but also because the way the user arrives at certain information influences the final effect in knowledge acquisition. In our experiments users were aware of this and reported some of their permanent questions during browsing in Explain:

Does the current item give the answer to the question or interest that arose in the former item?

or

Does it give a more precise indication where I can find the actual information I am looking for?

If the answer to the first question is yes, then there are two main possibilities. The first is that the user may want to go backwards to the item where the question originated, and may continue the original line of interest. The second possibility is that the user may want to elaborate on a point of interest that came into being in the current or in one of the intermediate items. If the answer to the first question is no, again there are three possibilities:

1. The user returns to the former item and tries to find the fact of interest via another branch.
2. The user backtracks even further than the former item, in order to find a more promising direction to pursue his/her points of interest.

3. The user is caught by one of the elements in the intermediate items, and shifts his/her attention to another point of interest.

14.2.2
Problem at the Level of a Complete Hypermedia Network

The problem of assigning local hypermedia relations stresses the need for textual coherence and the need for sufficient and valid connections to other items. Much of the effort of authoring hypermedia items focuses on decontextualization, so that they can be read independently, apart from a fixed position in a presentation sequence. The author's care to keep the complete network representative for the information to be transferred is even more delicate, though it has only seldom been mentioned in literature so far. One of the reasons is obvious from Nelson's permanent plea for democracy in hypermedia additions and the elimination of supervisors to maintain integrity and correctness of the information.

The real problem in hypermedia design is not so much the user interface at the level of manipulations as the transparency needed for creating a valid and logical structure of references:

... creating sound data models that can be maintained.
... hypermedia relations soon turn into a morass of meaningless,
    obscure connections and references.

(citations from Fiderio, 1988)

The second problem Fiderio mentions is that some hypermedia systems give you control when, in fact, you may need guidance. The reader may get lost following obscure links before getting a firm grip on the basics of the subject he/she is trying to research. The third issue she mentions refers to the level of local hyper-media relations: the problem of segmentation into items. She claims that not all literature is suited for hypermedia structures. Breaking the theme into decon-textualized parts of information can be done prematurely so that the logic of the subject may be obscured. It may be clear that Fiderio's first two signaled prob-lems cannot be solved by graph considerations solely. But they can contribute to the solution of her first two problems as they are the only way to unravel highly interconnected networks.

Local and global assignments of hypermedia relations are delicately interwoven as we have to design a hypermedia user interface. This should both elicit the author to be aware of the consistency and integrity of the individual items and at the same time, should prompt the author to be aware of the total configuration of links, as it develops, implicitly expressing the ideas to be grasped by the consumer.

14.2.3
Computational Approaches of the Hypermedia Entailment Complexity

Representation of hypermedia relations aims to delegate the management of complexity to a computer medium. A fundamental trade-off between expressiveness on one hand and the tractability on the other hand has been proposed by Levesque & Brachman (1985). They present the dilemma by saying that it can be more difficult to reason correctly with one representational language than with another, and moreover that this difficulty increases dramatically as the expressive power of the language increases. In other words, defining more types of relations (as already announced for hypermedia) makes it more difficult to have the language evaluated by a computer system. The examples they give concern first-order predicate logic (F.O.L.), database query languages, semantic networks, and frame representations. In their conclusions, Levesque & Brachman assert that different representation formalisms take different positions on the trade-off dimensions expressiveness and tractability.

> The tractability concern we have here is much deeper and involves whether or not it makes sense to even think of the language as computationally based.
> Even when these languages can be viewed as special cases of F.O.L.; What really counts is that these special cases be interesting from the point of view of what they can represent, and from the point of view of the reasoning strategies they permit.
>
> (citations from Levesque & Brachman, 1985)

Smith (1982) restricted the representation paradigm to those expressions that support at minimum a sufficient level of detail to be causally responsible for the behavior of the system.

> Any mechanically embodied intelligent process will be comprised of structural ingredients that (a) we as external observers naturally take to represent a propositional account of the knowledge that the overall process exhibits, and (b) independent of such external semantic attribution, play a formal but causal and essential role in engendering the behavior that manifests that knowledge.
>
> (citation from Smith, 1982)

As we accept Smith's knowledge representation hypothesis it is clear that only a few of the current hypermedia system can be considered as knowledge representation devices. The user-controlled main event loop, as it allows freedom to browse, does for instance, not satisfy this criterion, as the (human) user is the main actor in selecting the next item. However, any kind of navigation automatism will be based on a representation of the links between the nodes. We will summarize three distinct ways of formalizing hypermedia relations so that a computer can help us in reducing complexity:

1. Hintzman's resonance theory,
2. Frisse's implementation of a hypermedia query processor,
3. Structural centrality based on recursive graph computation.

14.2.3.1
Hyperspace Search Based on Hintzman's Resonance Theory

Kibby & Mayes (1988) envisage the need to find appropriate methods for the automatic computation of relatedness between nodes in hypermedia, of conceptual connectivity or semantic proximity. The technique they explore incorporates Hintzman's simulation model of human memory. Hintzman's MINERVA system is based upon the idea that all activated memory traces respond in parallel during retrieval. Kibby and Mayes try to transplant this idea so that finally a hypermedia system could bring the user automatically to the most appropriate node after he/she had activated one or more nodes of interest. The general idea is that extended hypermedia networks can hardly be encoded with relations between every pair of nodes. Hintzman represents an experience or an event as a list of features, each having a three-state value:

    0 = not present
 − 1 = present in a negative form
 + 1 = present in a positive form

An experience leaves behind a list or vector (i), for instance:

$\mathbf{v}(i)$ = $(1\ 0 - 1 \ldots - 1\ 1\ 0\ 0\ 1)$.

Each new retrieval event ('probe') results in a similarity index which reactivates all existing experience traces in memory. The echo $\mathbf{e}$ is computed by summing all reactivated traces.

$\mathbf{e} = \sum \mathbf{w}(\,i\,).\mathbf{v}(\,i\,)$

Each retrieval is evaluated on its similarity to the probe, and is expressed in a weight function $\mathbf{w}(i)$. The echo after a sending a probe in the concept space can be computed by summing all weighted traces, and comprises intensity (the number of traces matching the probe) and content (the pattern of properties that is returned after the matching of the probe against all individual traces).

Kibby and Mayes have experimented with various measures of relatedness, mainly evaluating two-state properties of vectors x and y because of efficiency. They propose the Hamming distance and the Tanimoto similarity measure as alternatives to Hintzman's model for associative memory retrieval. All three are based on rapid bitwise match evaluation.
Hamming distance:

D = bit count ((not x and y) or (x and not y))

Tanimoto similarity:

S = members(intersection of x and y)/members(union of x and y)

If the hypermedia base consists of a very large quantity of nodes, and only little information about the interlinking relations is available, then maybe these measures can solve the problem of combinatorial explosion during search. But if the hypermedia base has more consistency and the number of nodes is less, then it is doubtful whether these so-called bit-mapped classifier approaches will fit. The balance between Levesque and Brachman's expressiveness versus tractability in this case tilts strongly to the right.

14.2.3.2
Frisse's Implementation of a Hypermedia Query Processor

One of the most prominent computational approaches to hypermedia query processing has been proposed by Frisse (1988a, 1988b). His concern is about the situation when graphical browsers and precise title and heading searches return too many documents to the user. Examining them would cost too much time and would lead to distraction.

Especially when the subject domain is less structured and the semantics of the links is not clear, the traditional hypermedia query is not useful. Frisse mentions four criteria to be met, for increasing the probability of selecting useful starting points for browsing:

- The utility of a card,
- The intrinsic card weight,
- The extrinsic card weight,
- The relative weight position of the card among other candidates.

The utility of an item is approximated by computing the numeric weight of two components: The intrinsic component, computed from the number and identity (names) of the query terms contained within the item, and the extrinsic component to be computed, from the weight of immediate descendant items.

The intrinsic component is proportional to the number of times each query term occurs in the item and should be inversely proportional to the number of items containing each query term. (The more cards that contain the query term, the less typical are the coincidences.)

The extrinsic component should be inversely proportional to the number of immediately descendant items. An item with many immediate descendants should have a lower weight than an item with fewer descendants, provided that in both cases the descendants contain the same number of query terms.

Frisse claims that hypermedia systems should respond to text string queries by providing the user with one or more optimal starting points. After this initial query, graphical browsing should start with items with the higher weights down to those items with lower weights. The second candidate is the item with the next highest weight that is not a descendant of any item with higher weights. If the next item is an immediate ancestor of any previously identified starting item, the ancestor item should assume the descendant's role as a starting point item.

Intrinsic weight is defined in the algorithm below, assigning term weights to cards both as a function of the term frequency in the entire database, and as a function of the number of items containing the term (derived from Salton's algorithm, Salton & McHill, 1983):

$$\text{WEIGHT}(i,j) = k \times \text{FREQ}(i,j) \times \{\log(n) - \log(\text{ITEM.FREQ}(j))+1\},$$

where *weight(i,j)* is the weight component of item *i* due to concept *j*; *k* is a constant; *freq(i,j)* is the number of occurrences of concept *j* in item *i*; *n* is the number of items in the hypermedia base; and *item.freq(j)* is the number of items containing concept *j*.

As a second determinant for an item's utility, Frisse mixes the intrinsic weight component with the relationship of the item with its context (directly related items). The *extrinsic weight* describes the component of a card's total weight contributed by the propagation from neighboring cards. In other words: an item's extrinsic-weight component depends on the weights of its immediate descendant items:

$$\text{TOTALWEIGHT}(i) = \Sigma_j\text{WEIGHT}(i,j) + (\Sigma_d\text{WEIGHT}(d)/y)$$

where *y* is the number of immediate descendants of item *i*, *j* is a search term in *i*, and *d* is an immediate descendant of item *i*. Frisse proposes to start the propagation function recursively upwards from the leaf items up to the root.

Frisse (1988b) gives an example of how the computed item weights can be displayed in list boxes and graphical maps for browsing. The extrinsic weight component can only be computed for non-cyclic graphs. Frisse proposes to prune down cycles in what he calls aberrant cases. The experiences in our current study show that cycles in concept references show up quite often. Especially if the hypermedia base has been created bottom-up (declaring concepts while composing the text in the items) a lot of confusion would be introduced if the system forced the author to avoid reference cycles.

The importance of Frisse's notion of intrinsic and extrinsic weight still has to be proved in terms of retrieval effectiveness, but its main approach has already been acknowledged in another field: citation indexing (Garfield 1980,1983). The background notion of Frisse's work (based on Salton's algorithm) and Garfield's idea of expressing the relevance of a document in terms of its number of descendants (citators) are quite similar in the sense that they both are aware that the context decides the status of a document.

Garfield's work was rewarded when he proved that the relevance researchers assign to a publication correlates positively with the number of citations to it. Garfield's citation index does not include a weight factor for the status of the person citing. It would be useful to explore the surplus of power for the relevance prediction if we correct Garfield's outcomes for the status of a citator. The trade-off between content versus context is quite related to the notion of intrinsic versus extrinsic weight as introduced by Frisse. Neither Frisse or Garfield solve the problem of cycles, which is too essential for hypermedia structures to be disregarded.

14.2.4
Structural Centrality Based on Direct and Indirect Influence

In order to get an idea where to find the structurally important areas in a hypermedia graph, we can make use of a rich tradition in applied graph analysis. The basic notions about structural centrality have been presented by Hoivik & Gleditsch (1970) and Freeman (1979), and concern point centrality and graph centrality. In relation to the analysis of graphs in hypermedia systems we will restrict our attention to graph algorithms concerning point centrality as this enables us to identify central and peripheral areas in a hypermedia graph.

Freeman (1979) distinguished between adjacency, betweenness, and distance for undirected graphs. Freeman's three parameters in fact allow us to assign centrality properties to concepts in a hypermedia graph, except that hypermedia need a directed graph representation. Let's first see Freeman's connotation of the three of them:

1. **Adjacency** defines centrality of a node as the number of relations with other nodes. Freeman's application of this measure was to define the position of a person within a communication network: Persons with many direct (undirected) relations with other members of the group were highly enabled to exchange ideas. In the case of hypermedia, nodes with many in- and outgoing relations have a good opportunity to be visited by the reader, and also supply many relations good for (long) further digressions. The transfer of this notion to hypermedia differentiates between the in- and outgoing relations of a certain item. Outgoing: An item embedding many help concepts enables the user to browse away according to his/her point of interest. Ingoing: An item embodying the explanation of a concept which has been mentioned in many other explanations has a high probability to be visited by the user.

2. **Betweenness** defines the number of times the node will be visited on the way between two other nodes. One could say: Which nodes have an important gate-function? In terms of hypermedia: Which nodes are extremely important for connecting sub-graphs in the network of relations? If a node connects two previous unconnected sub-graphs, it is important to know how big these sub-graphs are, and if the connection has been made with central nodes in the sub-graphs.

3. **Distance** reflects the sum of the distances to every other node. Some hypermedia systems provide a directory item, listing all the names of the nodes in the text base. Differentiating between in- and outgoing relations again comes down to Departure versus Reachability.

Freeman's classification of the three aspects of structural centrality does not cover analyses of influence, which says that the position of a node cannot be characterized exhaustively by taking into account the first order relations. In terms of hypermedia, the position of an item can only be qualified if we regard all the possible routes that finally lead to this particular item. Also the indirect and redundant ways should be taken into account.

The work of French (1956), Hoede (1978), Hubbell (1965), Katz (1953), and Taylor (1969) went into this problem of so-called *n-sequency*. This means that in computing the centrality of a point, it is not assumed to be sufficient to state how many relations are going to or coming from a specific node, but an attenuation factor should be included to reflect the importance of the adjacent node.

14.2.5
Adjacency Matrix Representing Hypermedia Relations

A crucial representation in regard to graph computation is the adjacency matrix: A square matrix with one row and one column for each node, in which the entry is $p(i,j)=1$ if the hypermedia item i contains a help concept j, while $p(i,j) = 0$ if the main concept of item j has not been assigned as a help concept in item i. In the first case we say: item i is *adjacent to* item j, while in the second case we say item j is *not adjacent from* item i.

The adjacency matrix of a concept i lists the nodes that can be reached in one step. The adjacency matrix provides a quick analysis of potential browsing sequences as it is easy to jump to one of the adjacent nodes of concept i, and again its second-order descendants show up. The adjacency matrix enables analyses in two directions. Following the hypermedia links brings us to the final descendants of a node i, while starting from the column, it traces us back to the predecessors of concept i. Adjacency matrices enable quick visual inspection if the hypermedia graph is small. This shows which of the items are isolated, and whether or not relations are symmetric (direct recursion). The hypermedia graphs we meet in real situations are too large for visual inspection, and we need to rely on coefficients of graph and point centrality.

14.2.6
Small Scale Example

The hypermedia network analyses throughout the experiments have been performed by means of the GRADAP (GRAph Definition and Analysis Package) software on the CYBER mainframe of Groningen University, and the GRADAP PC-version later on.

Before deciding which of the many procedures would be most adapted to screen concept networks as they arise in hypermedia, some small scale networks have been calculated for the different aspects of point centrality. One of them serves as a demonstrator for the reader to get a basic feeling for the influence of recursion networks.

The example has been taken as a subset from top-level concepts in the network on Medical Science, as derived from a currently available Medical Encyclopedia. Only the direct relations between the top-level nodes have been drawn, but this does not mean that browsing in the complete network can only be done along these lines.

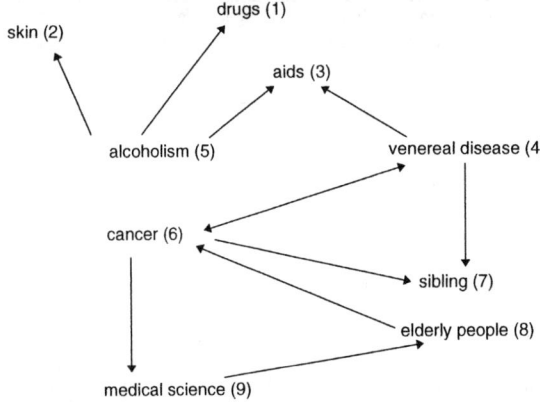

Figure 46. Example of recursions

The computation is for point centrality based on n-sequences. Centrality computation starts from the adjacency matrix. The rows and columns of the matrix represent the points of the graph, indexed with the numbers 1, 2, ... , n). The cell $a(i,j)$ denotes whether there exists a directed line from point i to point j in the graph, where index i is for the rows and j for the column position. The convention will be followed of choosing a 0 for the absence of a link and a 1 for the presence of a line from i to j.

The matrix above enables a first quick search for the most central and the most attainable items (based on first-order relations). In this case the concepts labeling items 4, 5, and 6 are central in the sense that they all point to three other concepts. The n-sequency computations will differentiate in the weight of contribution of the links. Concepts 3, 6, and 7 belong to the most attainable nodes, based on first order relations again.

To	Law	Gazette	States General	Queen's Speech	Royal Decree	Budget Debate	Budget	Right of Budget	House of Commons	Total OUT degree
From										
Law	0	0	0	0	0	0	0	0	0	0
Gazette	0	0	0	0	0	0	0	0	0	0
States General	0	0	0	0	0	0	0	0	0	0
Queen's Speech	0	0	1	0	0	1	1	0	0	3
Royal Decree	1	1	1	0	0	0	0	0	0	3
Budget Debate	0	0	0	1	0	0	1	0	1	3
Budget	0	0	0	0	0	0	0	0	0	0
Right of Budget	0	0	0	0	0	1	0	0	0	1
House of Commons	0	0	0	0	0	0	0	1	0	1
Total IN degree	1	1	2	1	0	2	2	1	1	11

14.2.7
Hoede's Status Index

Freeman's (1979) concept of structural centrality is based on the three classes: adjacency, betweenness, and distance. However, it does not comprise the analysis of influence structures.

Among graph theorists who included 'influence' as a fourth type of point centrality, Hoede (1978) introduces 'Status Index' as the sum of direct and indirect influences via all possible sequences in a relational network. Hoede's Status Index is quite similar to Katz' Index, except that Hoede replaces the uniform attenuation factor by weights $w(i,j)$ that satisfy $0 \leq w(i,j) \leq 1$.

Hoede (1978) adopted the idea of Katz (1953) to compute the relational status of elements in a network as the sum of all direct and indirect influences via all possible sequences. Influence or status is seen as a process to which not only direct connections or shortest distances between points are contributing, but also indirect and redundant connections. Though the intuitive notions of influence and status in the graph theory on 'centrality' computation have mainly been applied in sociometry, they are in fact context-free.

$$s(i) = \sum_{j=1}^{n}[w(i,j)] + \sum_{j=1}^{n}[w^2(i,j)] + \sum_{j=1}^{n}[w^3(i,j)] + \dots$$

An element $w(i,j)$ represents all sequences of length k from point i to point j, weighted by a factor that is the product of the weights attached to the lines in the sequence. Katz' (1953) attenuation factor b is replaced by W_{ij} that satisfies $0 \le W_{ij} \le 1$. (Hoede, 1978, p. 4).

$$s(i) = d(i) + \sum_{j=1}^{n} w(i,j) \times s(k)$$

The transformation sequence is mentioned in the GRADAP user manual (Sprenger & Stokman 1989, pp. 346–348) (see also Appendix A). Hoede's Status Index is closely related to those of Katz (1953) Taylor (1969) and Hubbell (1965). They are all based on adjacency and n-sequency. The status index as defined above can be transformed into:

$$s = ((I\text{-}W)^{-1}) \times d$$

in which I is the identity matrix, W is the matrix of weights, and d the degree (in- or out degree depending on the reference or the hierarchy criterion).

The final computation of Hoede's status index has been performed for the entailment structure of 4255 concepts in the explored domain of medical concepts by means of the GRADAP package. In order to demonstrate the computation of centrality indices (both out- and indegree) we will restrict ourselves to a subset of the top-level medical network as displayed in Figure 46.

14.2.8
Centrality Computation by Hoede's Status Index

The main concepts can be coded by integers, and are tabled with the status indices after Hoede's centrality computation was performed.

Table 3. Hoede's status to in- and outdegree

Index	Concept label	Status to:	
		Indegree	Outdegree
1:	Drugs	0.3	0.0
2:	Skin	0.3	0.0
3:	Aids	0.6	0.0
4:	Venereal disease	0.6	2.0
5:	Alcoholism	0.0	1.3
6:	Cancer	1.3	3.0
7:	Sibling	1.0	0.0
8:	Elderly people	0.8	1.5
9:	Medical science	0.6	1.3

In order to compute Hoede's status index, the graph as displayed in the scheme above has to be transformed in the adjacency matrix. Value 0 is chosen for the absence of a relation, and value 1 for its presence. As the hypermedia entailment graph is directed, the adjacency matrix will not be symmetric.

14.2.9
Alternative Graph Computations for Structural Centrality

There are alternative graph algorithms for the computation of structural centrality. Hubbell's status score has an offset of +1 on its minimum value, compared with those of Katz. In the overall pattern they both go in parallel.

Hoede's status score is more sensitive to the more indirect influence, caused
by the difference in weight w(i,j), while they are uniform in Katz' definition of
status. The high Hoede status score to indegree of *cancer* even causes a
swapped rank position between *cancer* and *sibling*. Again this can be attributed
to the sensitivity for cyclicity of Hoede's status score as shown by the cycle:

cancer $\Rightarrow$ medical science $\Rightarrow$ elderly people $\Rightarrow$ cancer.

14.2.10
Rush: A Measure to Unify Centrality Based on In- and Outdegree

The concept of rush has been formalized by Anthonisse (1971) to quantify the
proportion of flow that passes a point. The metaphor explored in rush is a
communication network in which the flow of information can be distorted or
withheld by persons at strategically located points, who can partially control
channels of information between other points in the network. In terms of hypermedia structures, one can say that rush measures the impact of certain concept nodes on the permeability for browsing. Some nodes in the network are
essential to browse as they connect two or more sub-graphs, while others will
only isolate themselves if they lose a link. As we can see in the next table showing
the relationship between the rush and the Centrality values in the demonstrator
network, both attainability and centrality (based on outdegree) play an important role. In other words, the rush measure can be imagined as a compounded
entity. Its first element is the chance to arrive at a certain node, and the second is
the chance to depart from it towards a node with high centrality again. The consequence of being a node with a high throughput is that it is highly sensitive to
any change in in- and outgoing relations. Any change in those points will severely influence the total connectivity in the graph. Connectivity or permeability
is the average ease to travel from one node to another in a graph. If the connectivity of the hypergraph is low, the reader needs long chains to browse from one
item to another, or may even not be able to reach certain nodes. In computing
the flow between two nodes, the shortest paths only are taken into account.

$$r_i = 1/C \sum_{j,k} e_{j,k}(i) / e_{j,k}$$

where

C is the total number of units flow that are sent

$e_{j,k}(i)$ is the number of shortest paths from the sender j to reachable point k upon which i is located,

e_{jk} is the total number of shortest paths from j to k.

(Anthonisse, 1971)

The *RUSH of a line* is defined as the proportion of flow that a *line* transmits. A first intuitive concept of rush was formulated by Bavelas (1948) to signal that a strategically located point in a communication network can easily distort or withhold information, especially if the point is a member of short lines between central points the network. In terms of hypermedia one could interpret the *RUSH of an item* as a predictor for the frequency of visitation as users are browsing. At the same time, those items with a high RUSH value are essential for the overall connective pattern. If those items (or the links to and from them) are removed, large areas of the hyperbase will become isolated.

Table 4 shows the shift in centrality outcomes due to second and higher-order influences. Cancer derives much of its status from the relation to venereal disease and also from the recursion to itself via elderly people and medical science.

Another strong n-sequence effect from Hoede's status index can be seen in the comparison of Aids with elderly people. While Aids has 2 incoming relations, and elderly people has only 1, we see that the second one scores higher on Hoede's status index for indegree, due to the impact of the weight factor via budget debate.

In general it can be concluded that Hoede's status index is highly sensitive to recursiveness that emerges in cyclic structures, and which is indicative for descriptions and conversations.

Table 4. Structural measures for concept nodes in a graph

		A	B	C	D	E
1	Drugs	0	0.000	1	0.250	0.0000
2	Skin	0	0.000	1	0.250	0.0000
3	Aids	0	0.000	2	0.643	0.0000
4	Venereal disease	3	1.965	1	0.573	0.1304
5	Alcoholism	3	1.333	0	0.000	0.0000
6	Cancer	3	2.955	2	1.292	0.3913
7	Sibling	0	0.000	2	0.993	0.0000
8	Elderly people	1	1.515	1	0.797	0.1739
9	Medical science	1	1.258	1	0.594	0.0870

A:	First order (out) degree
B:	Hoede Status based on outdegree
C:	First order (in) degree
D:	Hoede status based on indegree
E:	Rush

The need to embed cyclicity in conceptual representations has been stressed by Pask (1975, p. 177):

> There is no serious dispute over the existence of self-referential entities; with rare exceptions all of the entities in a conversation are self referential.

To perform adequate and efficient analyses of medium and large-size networks (containing cycles), several computational approaches have been tried out, and have been compared to their adequacy for hypermedia.

We finally chose the status index of Hoede as a reference for browsing behavior in our experimental hypermedia prototypes. The reason for choosing Hoede's status index (to outdegree) is twofold:

- The notion of hierarchy is well known to those who are familiar with tree diagrams and the distinction between general (top nodes) and specific (bottom nodes). In the context of learning and study skills, the idea of hierarchical organization is common nowadays.
- Hoede's status index gives an articulated impression of the higher-order influences of remote concepts and the function of recursive influence in a cyclic network.

Both graph centrality and RUSH are based on the assumption that every branching element has the same probability of occurrence. To make it clear by an analogy: Traffic behavior in the one-way streets of a big city can partly be predicted by studying the connective patterns. Squares where many one-way roads are coming in, and less one-way roads are going out, will be crowded. The few roads that are going out will be quite busy. The reverse is true for squares with many outgoing roads and only few ingoing ones.

The pure graph representation as used to describe centrality in hypermedia structures abstracts from the fact that human users choose their routes on the basis of local interest, or because they expect to find information somewhere further on in a specific direction.

This means that for the more inert users of hypermedia, the graph representation will be a better predictor for browsing routes, than for the more involved users who are obsessed by the content elements of the text base. For those users even the conceptual reference paths pre-defined by the hypermedia author are too narrow. They will create bypasses by directly referring to unpredictable concepts, and will even extend the subject area by adding new concepts and new texts.

Though hypermedia linkages (and their graph equivalent) may be useful to examine the potential of highways in browsing behavior, we should be aware that it is only a dim determinant for the psychological space of the user. If the user of hypermedia gets absorbed by the content of the text base, the characteristics of the route become subservient to the adventure of being caught by the meaning of the information itself.

14.3
Graph Structures as Concise Conceptual Representations

In case of conceptual relations as in hypermedia, graph theory offers computational algorithms to process cyclicity in an efficient way. This is the major advantage of the graph formalization beyond dynamic indexing, path algebra, and Petri networks so far. Traditional graph analyses have been performed for directed and undirected graphs. The most elementary representation of the relations in a hypermedia structure is a directed graph. The nodes in the graph represent the items, and the arcs represent the references from one concept to another. Graph computations, as we know them from sociometric research, use unlabeled and unconditional graphs.

The computational possibilities with graphs enable hypermedia systems to recompute the consequences for structural changes during network editing. In order to tackle the problem of recursion in cyclic structures, we need the most advanced algorithms from graph theory and matrix algebra. As most of the problems in graph computation are NP complete, it is good to be aware that current computer power is only capable of processing small networks within acceptable limits of time. Concept networks derived from full-size encyclopedias contain about 20 000 to 50 000 nodes should be parsed into sub-graphs first (see Kommers 1989a and 1989b).

A problem not addressed here is that when links are added or removed after the graph computation has been done, the concept networks should in fact be recomputed for each change. It is not clear whether partial recomputations, or approximations can also give satisfactory results in a short time (seconds). The key concept to be explored is centrality. Tree structures as they can occur in hypermedia structures are the most elegant situation for the definition of centrality. The centrality derived from computations using graph theory can be used for structuring the hyperbase in such a way that the attention of the user is called to the items computed to be most important. This enables us to perform a strict top-down or bottom-up strategy, without intensive computations. If the tree is unbalanced then the extrinsic-weight computation of Frisse can give a better estimation of centrality: The nodes with a larger domain of sub-references can be raised in status. This leads to the facility that on the same level of distance from the root concept there is a differentiation in status, due to the number of subordinate concepts.

If we disregard the actual content of the concepts, graph computation can offer some indication of their role in the configuration of relations. In case of hypermedia relations we should be aware of how the graph representation reduces the actual information.

1. The order of creation has been omitted. If we were to take into account that some of the concepts were created initially and some of them as an appendix, then it would be easier to generalize the conclusions.

2. The different types of relations in hypermedia links are omitted. Traditional graphs are restricted to one type of relation. The recent work of Bakker and Hoede (Bakker, 1987) go into the potential of 'knowledge graphs', expressing the types of relations, in order to extract formalized knowledge from scientific documents.
3. The strength of the relations between concepts in hypermedia is disregarded. In many cases there is a good reason to ask from the author how strictly or how strongly the relation holds. If the domain of knowledge has been formalized before, it is reasonable to constrain the relation by adding a rule or precondition that has to be satisfied before the relation obtains.

The question whether computer power should be used to act on a lean, austere representation or a more expressive one, brings us to the trade-off problem between tractability and expressiveness. Levesque & Brachman (1985) argue that this dimension is fundamental for the choice of symbolic structures and for the selection of appropriate processing algorithms. Hypermedia as we have defined it for human access to large text domains can be seen as one of the many steps on the long way to meaning representation and the processing of knowledge by computers.

15 Graphical Display of Concept Maps

15.1
Displaying Two-Dimensional Concept Maps

Displaying two-dimensional concept maps is problematic. In most cases standard solutions may be less then satisfactory. Standard solution are:

- On a line (Figure 47),
- In a circle (Figure 48),
- Evenly distributed (Figure 49).

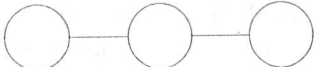

Figure 47. On a line

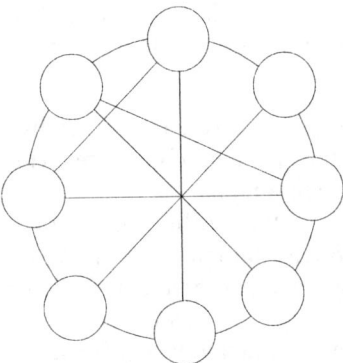

Figure 48. In a circle

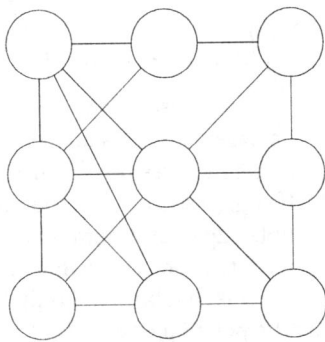

Figure 49. Evenly distributed

With larger concept maps the problems are:

- The number of crossings of relations with other relations. In graph theory relations are called edges. The words link or arc may also be used in this context. They are displayed as an arc or straight line from one concept to another concept.

- The intersections of relations with concepts they are not related to. In graph theory concepts are called vertices. The word node may also be use in this context. They are displayed as a circle.

The resulting graphs are not neat or easily interpretable. There is quite a lot of literature on research done on the display of graphs (see Appendix A). From the literature at least eight criteria for drawing a satisfactory graph can be derived:

- A drawing should be as symmetrical as possible.
- Paths should be as straight as possible.
- Concepts on a straight line should be distributed equidistantly.
- The number of line crossings should be minimized.
- If possible the graph should be split up into separate hierarchical graphs that may be drawn separately.
- A hierarchical parent should be centered above its siblings.
- Hierarchical siblings of the same parent should be placed equidistant from each other.
- Users should be able to tinker with the drawing.

Satisfying all of the above criteria in the same graph may be impossible. Thus the target would be to satisfy as many of the criteria as possible for any one graph.

P. Leenes (1990), a member of our project team, implemented a combination of algorithms to optimize a graph's topology. A graph is considered complex if it has many cycles, and large when it has more than twenty vertices and more then forty connections. This is not a real obstacle given the context, the display of concept maps, in which the algorithm is used. It is based on hierarchical method of Sugiyama et al. (1981) and adaptations based on Rowe et al. (1979), and has three phases (see Figures 50–55):

1. A level is assigned to each concept. Each concept will have a lower level than its parents. Cycles are removed by reversing the direction of the edges. This is stored to restore the direction before drawing the graph.
2. If edges are long, i.e., they skip one or more levels, they are broken into multiple edges, and dummy concepts are inserted. The dummy concepts are inserted in such a way that each edge will only go from one level to the next. Its effect is that lines will only change direction when crossing a level.
3. The position of the concepts is sorted so that a *minimum number of crossings* is reached. This is done by swapping positions on each level to reduce the number of crossings between this and the next level. The process starts at the first level and is repeated for each next level. This process is done several times, reversed on the even times, to get an optimal result.
4. The concepts are moved to get *straighter lines*. Positions are also moved to get *concepts centered above their siblings*.

Figures 50–55 give a simple example of how the algorithm works. Table 5 shows the relations used in the example.

Six levels are necessary. Directions are not important for the algorithm itself, so they are not drawn.

Table 5. Graph Connections

From	To
1	2
1	6
2	3
2	5
3	6
4	1
4	5
4	7
5	3
5	8
6	5
6	9
7	6
7	8
9	8

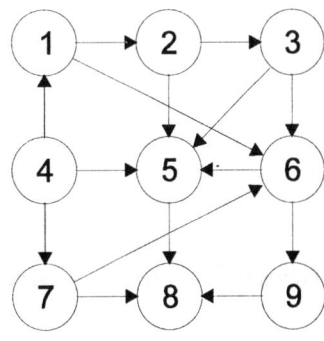

Figure 50. The standard graph

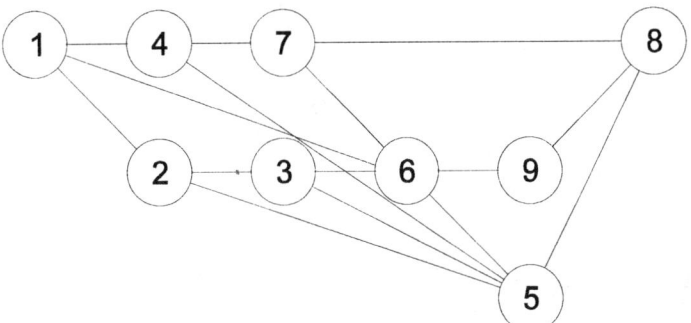

Figure 51. First part of the first phase: Assignment of levels

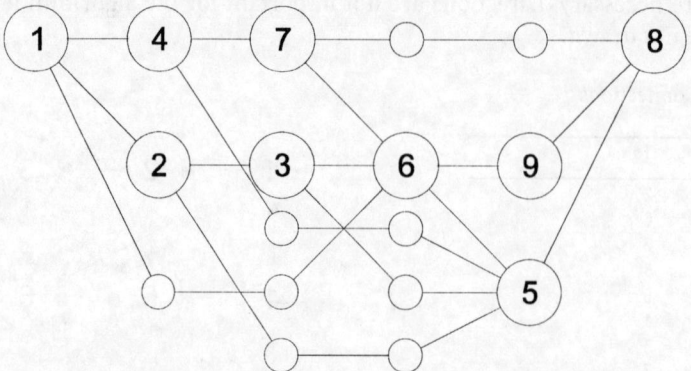

Figure 52. Second part of first phase: Addition of dummy nodes

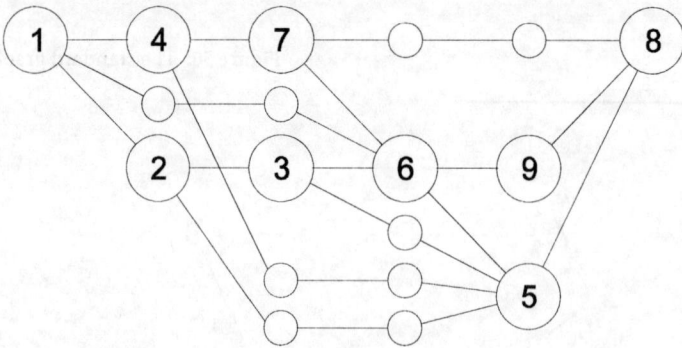

Figure 53. Second phase: minimizing the number of crossings

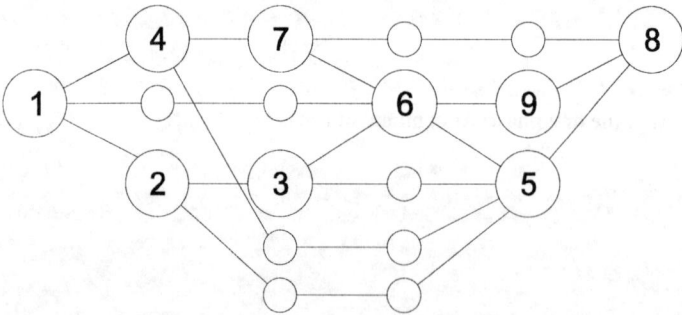

Figure 54. Third phase: Parents (where possible) centered above siblings and straightened lines

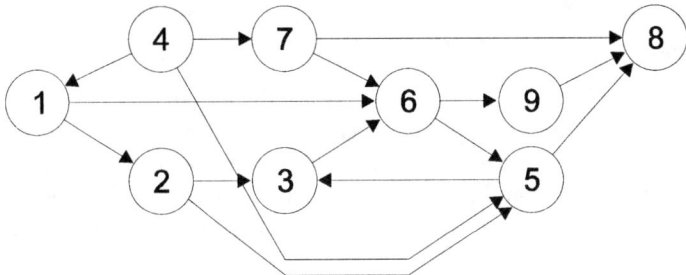

Figure 55. The final graph. The dummy nodes get a radius of one and the direction arrows are drawn in again.

Note that the algorithm does not detect the fact that swapping the levels of 4 and 1 will make it possible to remove the two crossings left. Note also that the algorithm tries to fulfill the criteria mentioned above either implicitly or explicitly. The time needed to calculate a graph with this algorithm is linear with the product of number of concepts and number of relations. The reduction of crossings depends on the graph, but the data suggests that it will be 50–80%.

The algorithm was used in the hypertext programs developed by us (Depart-ment of Educational Technology, University of Twente). A large list of literature is provided for further reading about this and other algorithms to display graphs (Appendix A).

15.2
Displaying Three-Dimensional Concept Maps

15.2.1
Illusions of Depth

Displaying a three-dimensional concept map posed an interesting problem, how to display the concepts and relations in such a manner that an illusion of depth is created. The following paragraphs contain a list of the possibilities considered.

15.2.2
Vagueness

Objects in the distance always seem to be a bit vague, less colorful, and a bit hazy. This effect might be used to create or strengthen an illusion of depth. Only a small amount of programming code is necessary to implement this feature. Given the small amount of code it can be assumed it will not slow the drawing of the picture too much. The drawback of this measure is that the computer should support either shades of gray or colors to make it possible.

15.2.3
Radius of the Concepts

In the original version of TextVision the concepts are displayed as circles, so it stands to reason to display the concepts as spheres. An illusion of depth can be created by giving a concept it a larger radius when it is to the front of the picture and a smaller radius when it is at the back (see Figure 56). The tiled floor helps to suggest a depth in the concept space. Each sphere throws his shade on the floor.

Using the radius for this presents a problem. The original TextVision version used the radius of a circle to represent the centrality, which will not be possible if this method is adopted. The solution to this problem would be to color code the centrality. Gaudy red-colored concepts have the highest centrality, green concepts a median centrality, and blue concepts the lowest centrality. Color nuances between red, green, and blue can be used to represent centralities in between the highest, median and lowest values. If color cannot be displayed, shades of gray could be used, or different types of dithering patterns.

15.2.4
Shading Spheres

To enhance the illusion of depth the spheres could be shaded. The spheres could be illuminated by a light and be shaded on the unlighted side. This method was considered too time-consuming to implement, and ultimately it would have been too slow drawing the spheres themselves.

15.2.5
Shadows

Another way to enhance the illusion is to illuminate the spheres from above and display shadows on a grid beneath the space the spheres are located. The disadvantage of this is that this method will only work well if the grid is visible. A large screen for displaying large numbers of spheres is recommended. To speed up the drawing the shadows of the spheres are not drawn as ovals, but as circles.

There is one bonus in using the shadows. Moving a sphere up, down, left, or right can be easily achieved by dragging the sphere with the mouse. Moving a sphere backward or forward can be done by dragging its shadow to the back or to the front.

15.2.6
Text Size

Each sphere will have a label with its title. The size of the text of each label may be varied. A smaller label can be shown at the back and a larger one at the front.

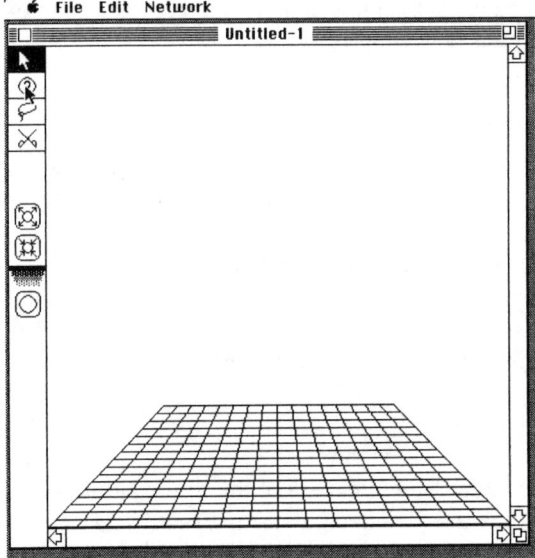

Figure 56a. The 3D concept space

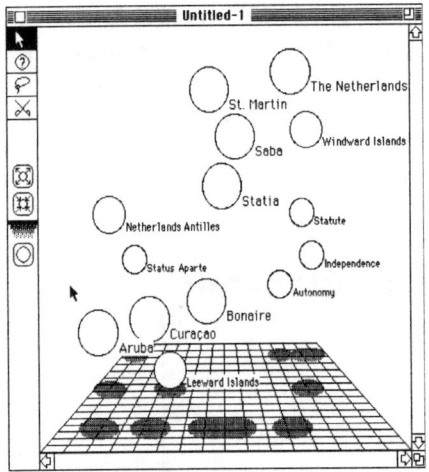

Figure 56b. A sample 3D network display

15.2.7
Inner Sphere

Another method suggested was to divide each sphere in an inner sphere with a ring around it. The ring would be gray or black. The circle would be colored where possible, to code the centrality as mentioned before. The total radius would provide for a depth effect, while the radius of the inner sphere would provide an indication of the centrality, a larger radius indicating a larger centrality.

15.2.8
Algorithms for Showing 3D Concept Maps

The algorithms for showing three dimensional concept maps in TextVision-3D are very simple. Everything is assumed to be drawn within a cube of a fixed size. This cube has a vanishing point that is placed at the center of the cube. The bottom of the cube is drawn as a grid as shown in Figure 57.

Spheres at the front of the cube are full sized. When a sphere is moved to the back it will become smaller. A choice has been made to have the spheres become linearly smaller until they are only half-sized at the back of the cube.

$$R = R_{max}(1 - \frac{Z}{2Z_{max}})$$

The same is done for the connections. The thickness of the connections is calculated for both ends. To enhance the 3D effect, a starting point and ending point of the connection on the two spheres is calculated. This is done because connections only starting at the edge or the center of a sphere corrupt the 3D effect. Only shadows of spheres are drawn. Because calculating and drawing the correct ovals would cost time, the shadows are drawn as circles. Rotation of the spheres is done around the center of the cube. If the co-ordinates of a sphere would place it outside the cube the sphere is moved inside again. Simple sine and cosine functions are used to calculate the new co-ordinates. To reduce the number of sine and cosine calculations, all those needed are done once and stored in a matrix. The values in the matrix are used to calculate the new co-ordinates.

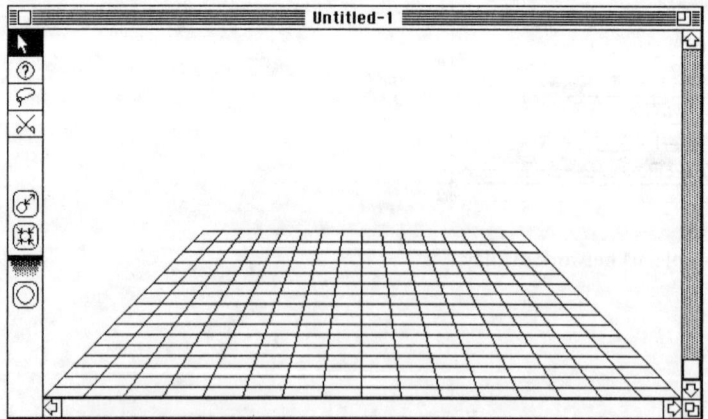

Figure 57. Grid

15.2.9
Conclusions

Some of the possibilities will only work when the monitor and computer support the use of colors. However, these are those which give the best results. Each method has one disadvantage: It will cost time to calculate and draw the result. Thus the time the computer takes to draw a new picture will be slower for each method used. A compromise had to be made between speed and the effect of the illusion. The following choices were made:

- The centrality was color coded.
- Shadows were drawn on a grid.
- The radius and the size of the title of each sphere were resized according to its position.

16 Rule-Based Navigation in Hypermedia Systems

Due to the enormous amount of information available to the user of a hypermedia system, the user is likely to get lost. To avoid this, steps must be taken to guide the user during his or her session. Although several navigation methods are possible there are two main groups of navigation methods:

- The method of valuing certain nodes to the user as he or she makes moves. This method is called coaching.
- The method of preparing a path at the start of a session.

16.1
Coaching Methods

The first method should use as much information as possible to guide the user. There are several sources of information that can be used.

Node information

- Centrality: This is the outcome of a complex recursive calculation of indegrees and outdegrees of a certain node, as defined by Hoede (1978).
- Rubrics or categories and other meta-information: This should be provided by the author of the hyperbase.
- Added semantic and meta-information: This could be all sorts of extra information like bookmarks, etc.

History information

- Visited nodes, differences in centralities and rubrics.

User information

- The user's goal.
- Previous sessions.

The second method asks the user to define his or her actions thus that as much information as possible will be provided.

16.2
Navigation Tools

The task of choosing the right tools for hypermedia navigation is quite consequential and delicate. It helps if the hypermedia designer is explicit about the type of search support that is essential for the target users. The task confronts the system designer with possible mismatches between the required database oper-ations and the precise meta-information needed for them. From the technical side one could opt for hard-coded rules programmed in the same computer language as the hypermedia system itself. This will have the advantage of speed and all elements of the program will fit together perfectly. But then no flexibility whatsoever is provided. Any change of insight concerning navigation will lead to rewriting and recompilation of at least parts of the program.

To avoid such a situation one could consider the use of an external rule database which would be readable by the navigator. This would improve the flexibility of the navigator but it would also decrease the possibilities of using the ready-made database routines.

A third way of navigating is to combine the original programming language with an Artificial Intelligence language like PROLOG. By using an interpreter version of this language instead of a compiler, it is possible to alter the programming code without having to recompile it. An extra advantage of using PROLOG is that calls to the database-engine are possible. The main problem with using PROLOG is speed, or rather its lack of speed.

16.3
Navigation Rules

Many navigational rules can be thought of, each with its own functions and requirements. A short list will be provided:

Avoid the unwanted retrieval of pages you've already visited

Methods:

- Prompting/warning the user when he/she tries to do so.
- Making it impossible. A possible way of doing so is to instruct the navigator to mask any used pages.
- Providing a list of all visited pages, for example by using footprints.

Usefulness:

- Recommended in almost all the literature, potentially with the possibility of jumping to these pages (almost a contradiction).

Additional requirements:

- Keeping a history of the user's moves.

> *Conditional relations: A link between two nodes will only be visible when the user satisfies one or more conditions.*

Methods:

- One condition could be the visiting of other (major) nodes in the network. Another condition could be the kind of user, for example in a learning environment where a teacher has more privileges than a student.

Usefulness:

- Very useful when many different kinds of users are to be served, or in case the navigation rules should be adapted to the developing skills of the users.

Additional requirements:

- Hierarchical structure required, which has to be encoded in the SGML text by the primary author, or put there by the secondary author.

> *Allow the user to visit only nodes with a certain minimum centrality during the first part of his/her session.*

Methods:

- Prompt the user when he/she tries to go outside the current class.
- During the first part of his session, the user is only allowed to visit the main nodes of any class.

Usefulness:

- Disadvantage: The user can't go straight to his/her goal, but has to go through some major points.
- Advantage: The possibility of getting lost becomes less.

Additional requirements:

- Hierarchical structure required, which has been encoded in the SGML text by the primary author, or has to be put there by the secondary author.
- New index files for accessing only major points.
- Keep track of some kind of time, or number of nodes visited.

> *Bookmarks.*

Methods:

- Give the user an opportunity to mark an important node.

Usefulness:

- Recommended in almost all the literature because this gives the user the unconditional power to pinpoint a certain node.

Additional requirements:

- Keep a list of bookmarks.

   Backtrack possibility.

Usefulness:

- Compared with the opposite, this avoids the unwanted retrieval of already visited node.

Additional requirements:

- Keeping a history of the user's moves.

   Landmarks in combination with Furnas' fisheye view.

Methods:

- This gives the possibility of showing a large part of the network. The center of the network will be very detailed but as one goes further to the edge of the screen, one may see just some major points (compare this to a photograph made with a fisheye lens).

Usefulness:

- This gives the user a broad overview of the network, but at the cost of the number of nodes of the local structure that can be displayed.

Additional requirements:

- Select landmarks.
- Develop a fisheye function. Furnas' function requires a weight on links, which in this case may be the same as centrality.

   Present also the preceding and following word of the keyword. (Lesk 1989)

Usefulness:

- Worth taking into consideration. Not useful in an encyclopedia, because keywords won't have preceding or following words.

Additional requirements:

- Index files for every keyword, to ease the access to the preceding and following words. These files can become very large.

   Give additional (category) information to the user when he/she has to choose from different keywords.

Usefulness:

- It eases the user's choice of the correct keyword.

Additional requirements:

- Category information for every keyword.

  Try to keep track of the user's moves through the hyperbase.

Methods:

- One should look at:
  - Locality: How large is the area in which the user has been?
  - Path followed: Has the user often made mistakes?

  These points can be evaluated with the help of the theory of Canter (1985).

Usefulness:

- It is always important to inform the user, so he/she can learn from his/her previous sessions.

Additional requirements:

- Keeping track of the user's moves through the hyperbase.

  Preparing a path for the user which he/she has to follow.

Methods:

- The user can also be allowed to leave this path for a moment, after which he/she should return to the place where he/she left the path.

Usefulness:

- Especially for students this strategy can be very useful. For an examination the teacher can prescribe a path which is to be followed by the student. If the student does not know an answer, he/she can search through the hyperbase to find a solution. Another possibility is skipping a difficult question to answer it later on.

Additional requirements:

- Path facility.

16.4
Implementation of Coaching Methods

A few of these strategies are implemented in an existing hypertext system which is connected to several encyclopedias.

In this system hard-coded strategies as well as PROLOG rules are combined in one 'navigation engine'. All strategies can be made active at the same time to study the effect of these rules as they co-operate. To explain the working of this system we will look at the simplified structure of this hypertext system shown in Figure 58. Whenever the user instructs the hypermedia system to show a topic (1), every possible link within this text (2,3) is checked by the navigation system (4). If the navigator is hard-coded it will check with the Database Management System (DBMS) if necessary (5a); otherwise, if the navigation rule is PROLOG-based, then it will instruct the PROLOG engine to get the matching PROLOG clause from the PROLOG program (5b) and execute it. It is also possible to include a statement in this PROLOG program to access the DBMS (6). In the existing implementation several strategies can be selected (Figures 59 and 61). The first four are hard-coded in the program itself; the following four are programmed in PROLOG and can therefore be modified by the user if he/she wants to. The latter can be achieved by clicking the PROLOG 'Edit' button. Pressing ReRead causes the program to carry out a Reconsult to check for possible syntax errors. Figures 60 and 62 display two screen dumps of a session at which two articles about breathing are opened. In no navigation rules whatsoever are active, so all hyperlinks are displayed. (To make this clear in print, instead of using colors as the original program does, we chose to use bold, underlined, and italic type to display the various types of links.)

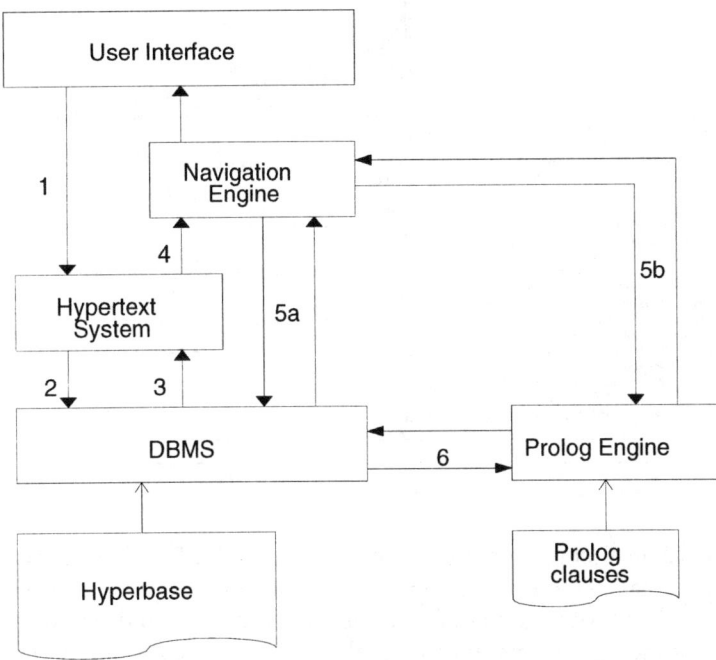

Figure 58. The simplified structure of hypertext system used

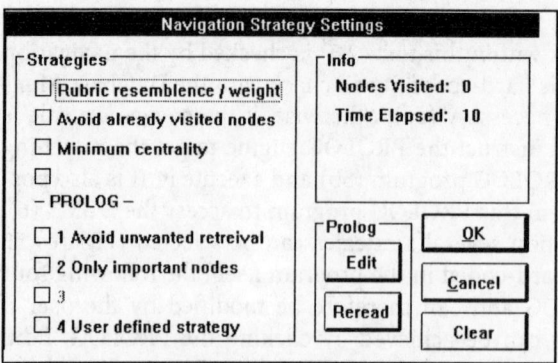

Figure 59. Nothing selected in the navigation strategy dialogue

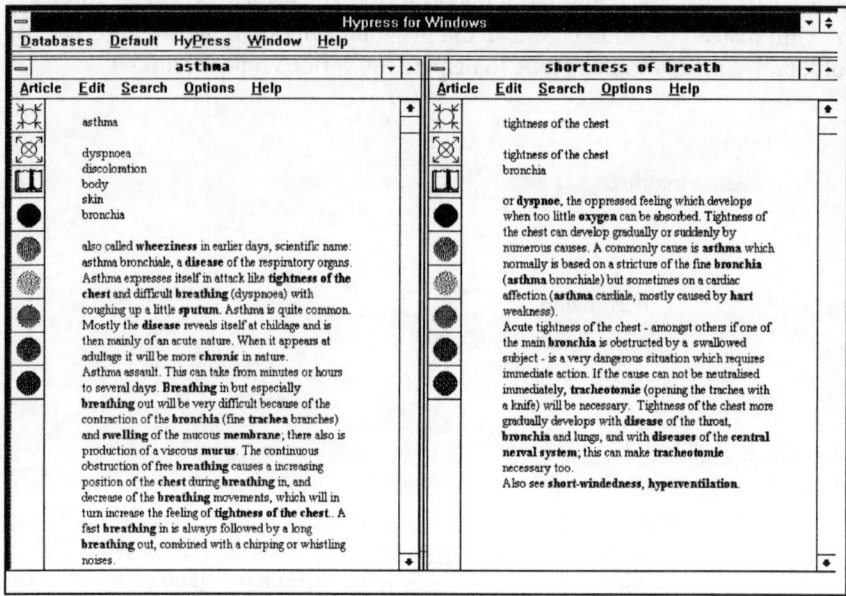

Figure 60. Outcome of Figure 59

In Figure 62 the first strategy rule has been made active. This rule checks out to what degree the outgoing link is a member of the same rubrics at the original article. Summarized with the centrality of this link it gives an indication of the importance of the link. Importance normally varies form dark blue to bright red, indicated in this print by a graduation from italics (= minimal importance) to bold and underlined (= maximum importance). The current implementation of navigation could be extended by adding a weight to the different strategies. For example, one could choose to give an absolute importance to not displaying already visited nodes, whereby other nodes should be displayed according to centrality.

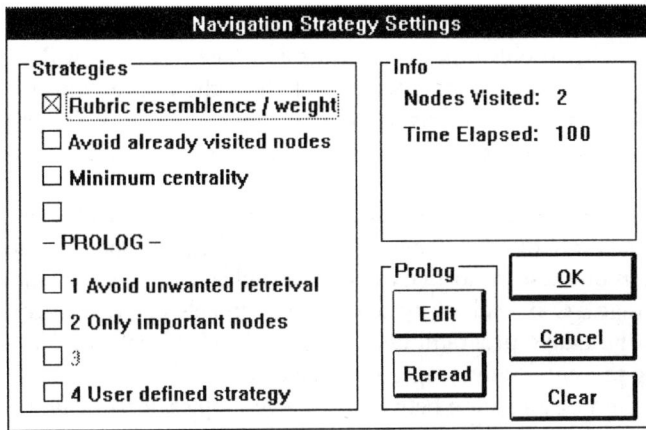

Figure 61. First strategy selected in navigation strategy settings dialogue

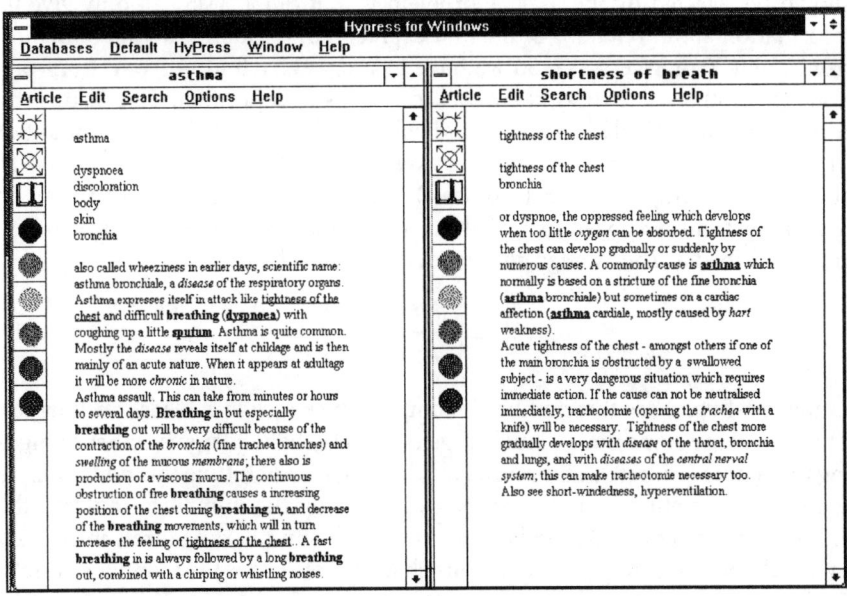

Figure 62. Outcome of Figure 61

16.5
Preparing a Path

If the user has a good idea of what he/she is going to do, it may be advantageous if he/she can define his/her problem prior to the session. The computer will ask the user for certain information, whereupon it will show the user a choice of nodes he/she is likely to visit. In our current program we chose to ask the user for two entries, at which the program calculates the most important neighboring nodes.

As stated earlier we like to use PROLOG for these kinds of purposes because of its flexibility. But a severe disadvantage of PROLOG, namely its speed, turns out to be a problem in this case. A normal calculation will cost up to one or two minutes on an average PC nowadays; which is unacceptable for a real-time browser. Coding in the native programming language (= C++) will solve this problem but will also present disadvantages as stated before.

Next, we explain finding a relation between two given topics. First of all, the exact problem is to be defined. This is finding all possible paths between two given nodes with a maximum of 2^{n+1} nodes on this path, including the two nodes themselves, where n is the number of search levels. This number of search levels should be selected by the user. A problem is that our DBMS can only give us information about relations of the first degree, that is, point X an outgoing link from point Y or vice versa. So we have to recursively find our way from one node to another. The most likely way to do this is depth-first. This also is the reason why this calculation is slow and will quickly be limited by the amount of memory that can be used. While recursively walking through the tree we have to check all outgoing references (= outrefs), through the number of outrefs can be quite large. This is applied to a test-hyperbase which was a medium-sized medical encyclopedia. The average number of outrefs is calculated by:

$$W = \left(\frac{\# outrefs}{\# nodes} \right)$$

In the test-hyperbase this number is about 7. The effective value is much larger. This is because some nodes with a large outref also have a large number of ingoing references (=inrefs). This results in a high chance of hitting this node. Where the normal weight of a node can be expressed by the number of outrefs, the effective weight of a node can be expressed by the number of outrefs multiplied by the chance of hitting this node. This chance is of course the number of inrefs. So the average effective weight of a node is expressed by:

$$W_{weighted} = \frac{\sum_{i=1}^{n} \left(inrefs_i \times outrefs_i \right)}{refs}$$

Calculated in the test-database this comes to 18, which is an increase by a factor 2.6. This number can be decreased by using an intelligent way of walking the tree, which stops the recursion whenever an already visited node is encountered (Kwak, 1996). To visualize the distribution of nodes of the test hyperbase by their inref/outref product, a graph was made (Figure 63).

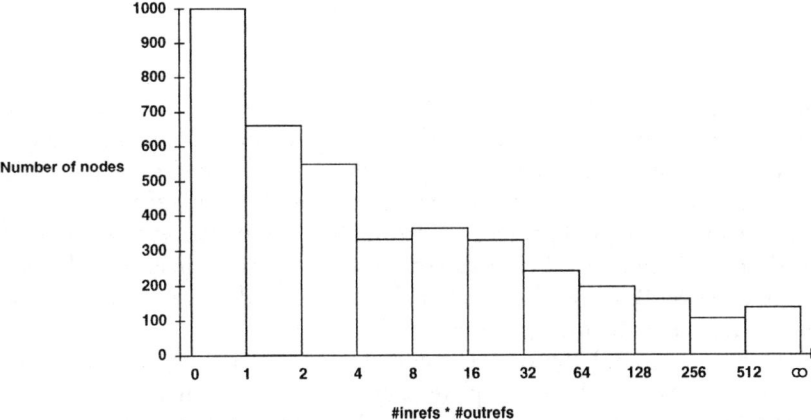

Figure 63. Distribution of number of nodes with certain weights

17 Calculating a Path

In the following example (Figure 64) the two given nodes are 1 and 2, and the maximum search level is 3. To find a relation between these the points, we will try to find all points 1′ and points 2′ so that there is a relation between point 1 and 1′, and a relation between point 2 and 2′ of a level one less than indicated. Then again, in order to find points 1′ and 2′ in this example, we will have to find nodes 1″ and 2″ because the DBMS can only give us information about relations of the first degree. When we have found all nodes 1′ and 2′, we intersect these two sets to find all nodes that give us a path from 1 to 2.

Now we have found the middle nodes for our relation, which does not mean that we have found the complete relation. First of all, there is no way of remembering the relation between the middle nodes and the start nodes because of the huge number of nodes we encountered during our calculation. So we have to recal-culate the relation between the middle node(s) and the start node in the same way as before, but with the number of level decreased by one.

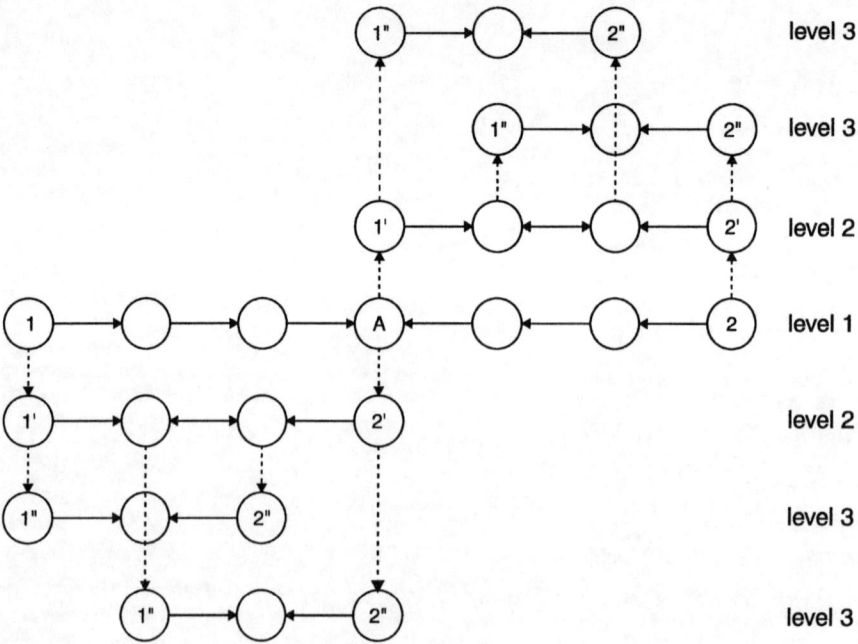

Figure 64. Finding a relation between nodes 1 and 2

Having found all nodes which form all possible paths between the two starting nodes, we will have to recheck the (first-order) relations between all these nodes. For it is possible that we missed a direct relation between two nodes because they previously were members of two different paths. The resulting PROLOG program finally became quite complex. It is shown at the end of this chapter.

In the following figures we will show the outcome of three different queries, which are the relations between coughing and sneezing. Note that the maximum depth is limited to two instead of three. This is a because of the memory and performance problems as stated before.

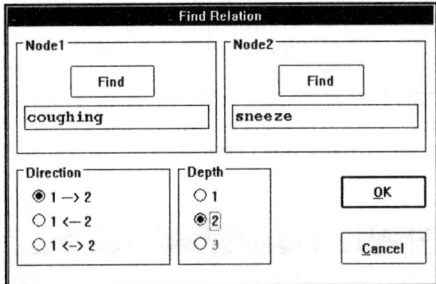

Figure 65. 'Find Relation' dialogue with instruction to find the relation between coughing and sneeze, one way only and with a maximal depth of two

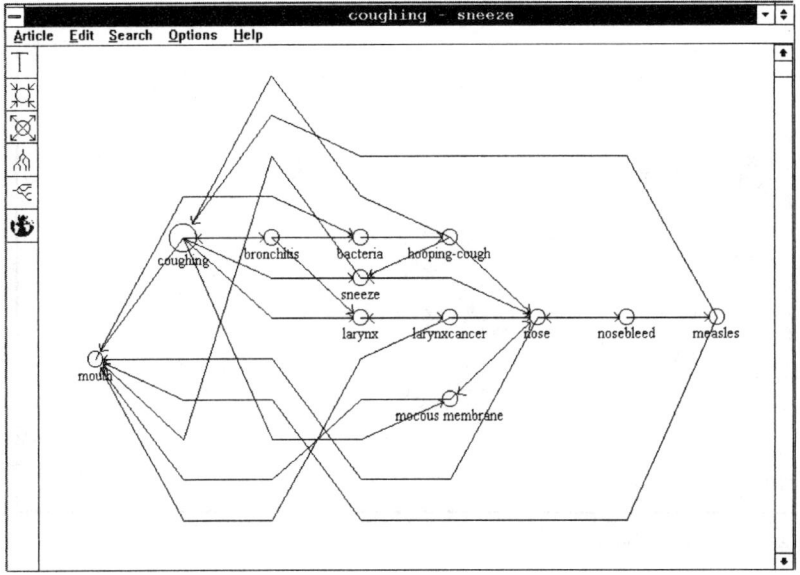

Figure 66. Outcome of Figure 65

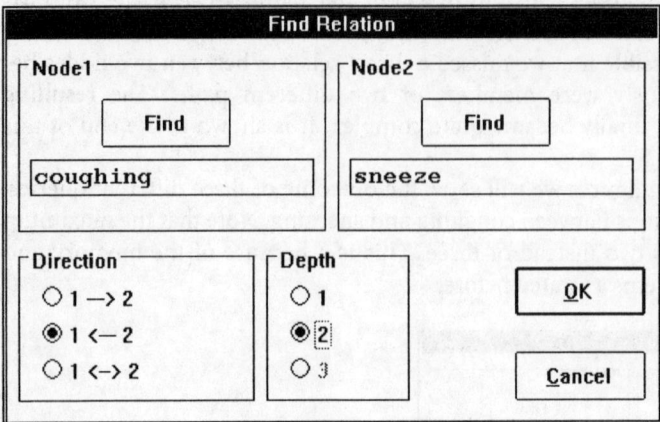

Figure 67. 'Find Relation' dialogue with instruction to find the backwards relation between coughing and sneeze, one way only and with a maximal depth of 2

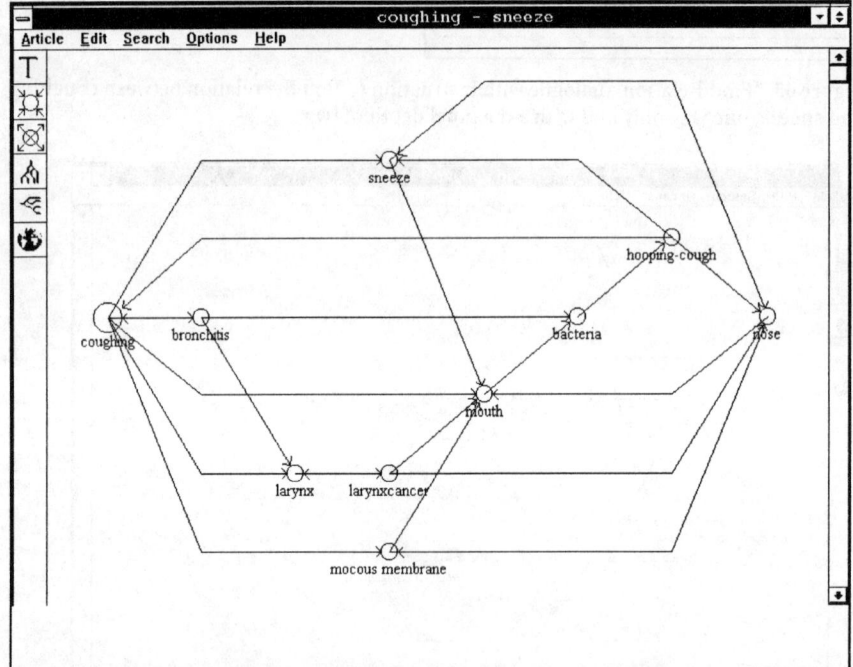

Figure 68. Outcome of Figure 67

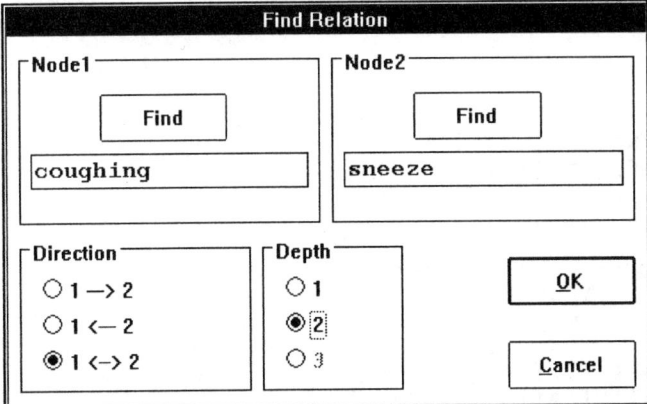

Figure 69. 'Find Relation' dialogue with instruction to find the relation between coughing and sneeze, both ways and with a maximal depth of two

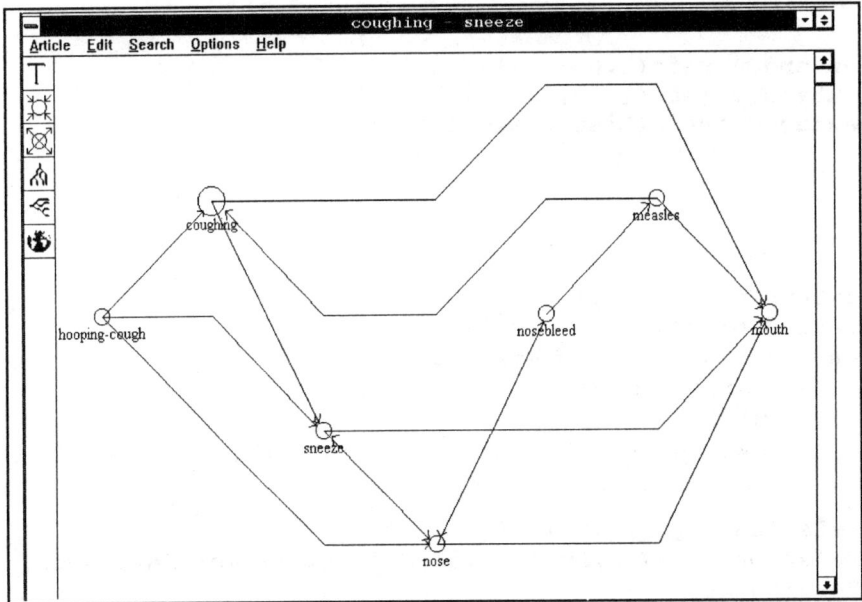

Figure 70. Outcome of Figure 69

17.1
Prolog Clauses

RELATION FUNCTIONS

```
outrefs2outrefs([  ],[  ]).
outrefs2outrefs([F|[A|[  ]]],L) :-
     outrefs(F,A,L).
outrefs2outrefs([F|[A|L1]],L2) :-
     outrefs2outrefs(L1,L3),
     outrefs(F,A,Lfa),
     unionpair(Lfa,L3,L2).

inrefs2inrefs([  ],[  ]).
inrefs2inrefs([F|[A|[  ]]],L) :-
     inrefs(F,A,L).
inrefs2inrefs([F|[A|L1]],L2) :-
     inrefs2inrefs(L1,L3),
     inrefs(F,A,Lfa),
     unionpair(Lfa,L3,L2).

extendOutrefs(_,0,[  ]).
extendOutrefs([  ],_,[  ]).
extendOutrefs(List,N,NewList) :-
     outrefs2outrefs(List,OutList),
     N1 is N - 1, !,
     extendOutrefs(OutList,N1,ExtOutList),
     unionpair(ExtOutList,OutList,NewList).

extendInrefs(_,0,[  ]).
extendInrefs([  ],_,[  ]).
extendInrefs(List,N,NewList) :-
     inrefs2inrefs(List,InList),
     N1 is N - 1, !,
     extendInrefs(InList,N1,ExtInList),
     unionpair(ExtInList,InList,NewList).

relation(_,_,_,_,0,[  ]).
relation(FileId1,ArticleId1,FileId2,ArticleId2,Depth,
ResultList) :-
     extendOutrefs([FileId1,ArticleId1],Depth,
     NewOutList),
     extendInrefs([FileId2,ArticleId2],Depth,
     NewInList),
     intersectpair(NewOutList,NewInList,ResultList).
```

```
getrelation(_,_,_,_,0,[ ]).
getrelation(FileId1,ArticleId1,FileId2,ArticleId2,
Depth,ResultList) :-
     relation(FileId1,ArticleId1,FileId2,ArticleId2,
     Depth,ResultList1),
     Depth1 is Depth - 1,
     getlistrelation(ResultList1,FileId2,ArticleId2,
     Depth1,ResultList2),
     getlistrelation(FileId1,ArticleId1,ResultList1,
     Depth1,ResultList3),
     unionpair(ResultList2,ResultList3,ResultList4),
     unionpair(ResultList1,ResultList4,ResultList).
getrelation(_,_,_,_,_,[ ]).
getlistrelation([ ],_,_,_,[ ]).
getlistrelation(_,_,[ ],_,[ ]).
getlistrelation(_,_,_,0,[ ]).

getlistrelation([FileId1|[ArticleId1|L]],FileId2,
ArticleId2,Depth,ResultList) :-
     getlistrelation(L,FileId2,ArticleId2,Depth,
     ResultList1),
     getrelation(FileId1,ArticleId1,FileId2,
     ArticleId2,Depth,ResultList2),
     unionpair(ResultList1,ResultList2,ResultList).

getlistrelation(FileId1,ArticleId1,[FileId2|
[ArticleId2|L]],Depth,ResultList) :-
     getlistrelation(FileId1,ArticleId1,L,Depth,
     ResultList1),
     getrelation(FileId1,ArticleId1,FileId2,
     ArticleId2,Depth,ResultList2),
     unionpair(ResultList1,ResultList2,ResultList).
     getlistrelation(_,_,_,_,[ ]).

findrelation(1,FileId1,ArticleId1,FileId2,ArticleId2,
Depth,ResultString) :-
     open_lib,
     getrelation(FileId1,ArticleId1,FileId2,
     ArticleId2,Depth,ResultList),
     list(ResultList,ResultString),
     close_lib.

findrelation(2,FileId1,ArticleId1,FileId2,ArticleId2,
Depth,ResultString) :-
     open_lib,
     getrelation(FileId2,ArticleId2,FileId1,
     ArticleId1,Depth,ResultList),
```

```
        list(ResultList,ResultString),
        close_lib.
```

**findrelation(3,FileId1,ArticleId1,FileId2,ArticleId2,
Depth,ResultString) :-**
```
        open_lib,
        getrelation(FileId1,ArticleId1,FileId2,
        ArticleId2,Depth,ResultList1),
        getrelation(FileId2,ArticleId2,FileId1,
        ArticleId1,Depth,ResultList2),
        unionpair(ResultList1,ResultList2,ResultList),
        list(ResultList,ResultString),
        close_lib.
```

findrelation(_,_,_,_,_,_,[ ]).

Part IV
Seven Hypermedia Project Cases

This part presents descriptions of several cases. The cases are based on prototypes and studies done for a number of institutes and businesses. Two types of
cases can be distinguished here:

- Incremental growth. Each day or week new data is added that must be accessible immediately.
- Delivery plan for a hypermedia title. The data is used to create a new title.
  The data for the title is selected and then compiled or indexed for the final
  data.

The first three cases are incremental growth. New material has to be added, preferably without having to re-index or recompile all data.

The last cases are more concerned with delivering new titles. The data may be
recompiled or re-indexed for each new title. In all of the last cases it can be handy
to have an incremental growth system, within the company publishing the titles,
to view new data and select data for new titles.

Case I
Publishers' Documentation Support System

A documentation department in the publishing area of weekly journals was planning to store as much of their material as possible on computer media. The documentation department stored all articles of a selected set of newspapers and magazines in different folders. In most cases articles were copied and distributed among several folders. This was because they already had large sets of rubrics. An example would be that if a leading politician somehow attracted publicity, the documentation director would normally decide to store this news both in the personal file of the person and also in the folders of political parties, discussion reports of the House of Commons, etc. Some articles could wind up in as many as six or seven folders – reason enough to change from the traditional copy tradition to a multi-dimensional database with hypermedia facilities. You too many see reasons in your situation to migrate from linear (chronological) storage to this new method.

When information is needed by a person, he or she can send a request to the documentation department for relevant articles about a person, institute, etc. The documentation department will then get the appropriate folders, select the appropriate documents, copy them, and deliver them to the requesting person.

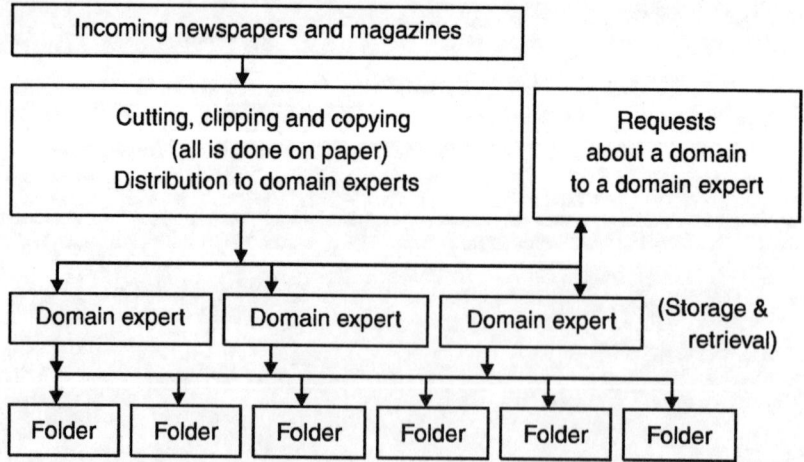

Figure 71. Paper document flow

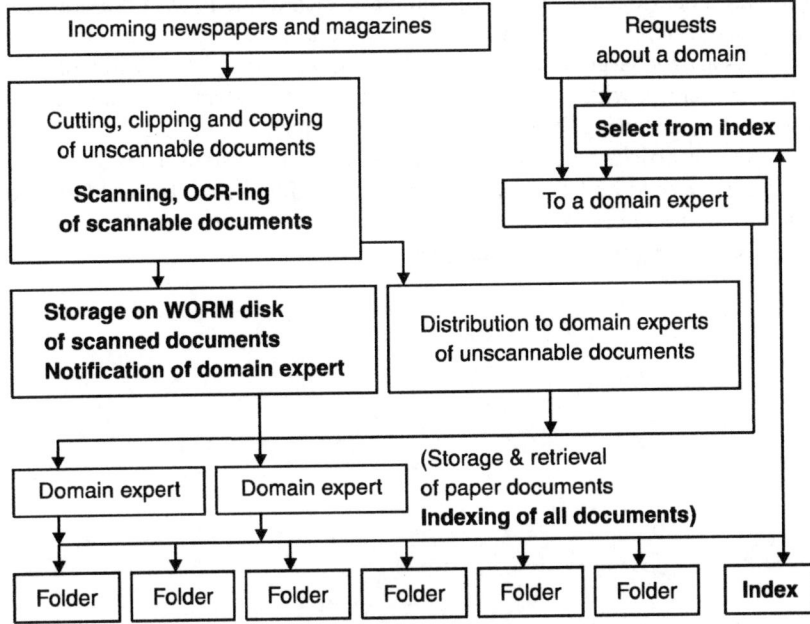

Figure 72. New document flow, added steps in bold

Storing all document on paper makes large storage rooms necessary. This is made worse by the need for multiple copies of each article. Searching and retrieval is also a lot of work. Using computer media for storage provides a number of benefits:

- Less space needed for storage. Articles can be stored once with references from each appropriate (logical) folder.
- Faster and easier retrieval of data. A decision was made to use some kind of WORM disk technology.
- The possibility to do searches on the data in ways that were previously impossible, such as searching on free text, on articles stored in or referred to by a specific set of folders.

There were some staggering problems:

- Scanning the articles into the computer would be a very large job.
- Some articles may be impossible to scan because of size, colors used, etc.
- Some articles may cost so much computer space if stored as bit images that it would not be affordable to store them that way.

To cope with these problems the following three solutions were suggested:

- All articles will be stored only once. And references from the relevant (logical) folders will be stored in an index. After this the index will contain a list of domains, a list (logical) folders contained in each domain, with the domain, and a list of references to the articles contained in each (logical) folder.

- If articles are too large or too costly to store as a bit image, they will either be stored as before, with references in the computer system, or scanned and converted to text using OCR, and only stored as text, not as a bitmaps.
- Only the new articles would be put into the computer system. The old articles and folders would be left in paper form for the time being. It would cost to much time and effort to put those in the computer system also. Possibly references to the right folders would be added.

Case II
Genealogical Research Support

Doing genealogical research is similar to seeking the proverbial needle in the haystack. It requires browsing and searching through large amounts of paper looking for the occurrence of names of people and dates to find possible parents, grandparents, nephews, etc. A hindrance can be the fact that some of the papers are in a terrible state or have to be handled with great care to keep them in a fair state. If all the texts and other information could be put into a computer system it would be much easier to search for the right documents and names and dates in them. It might even be possible to ask the computer if two persons were or are related. The related material was delivered as flat ASCII texts in several files. Each of the files contained several parts:

- Table of contents
- Inventory (numbered)
- Footnotes
- Index (one or more)
- Introduction
- Addenda (numbered)
- Literature listing.

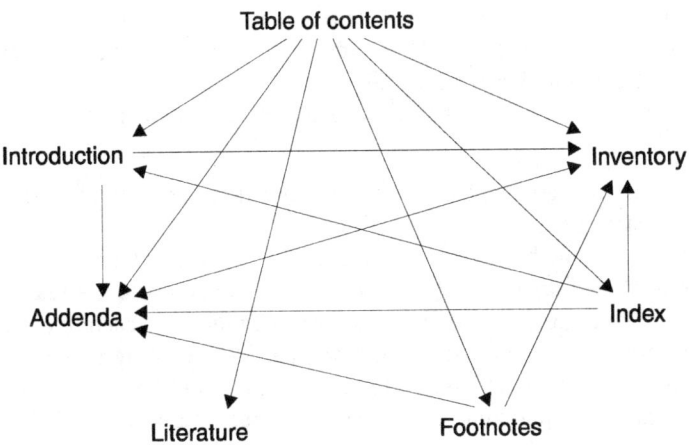

Figure 73. Structure of references

The table of contents refers to all headings and subheadings within each file. The parts containing inventory, footnotes, index, introduction and addenda had references to inventory numbers and addendum numbers. The required search methods:

- Systematic search on part, hierarchy, addenda and inventory,
- Free text search,
- Combination of the above.

To make this possible, all the texts were loaded into WordPerfect for DOS 5.1 for mark up. The texts were marked up in two ways, automatically using a few macros and manually. Codes were added to get unique titles and search keys. Words like 'a' and 'the' were removed from headings to facilitate searching on headings. Keywords, topic texts, and references were marked by using styles. Paragraphs were marked by placing an end of paragraph code before all hard carriage returns. Because items in both the addendum and inventory list were numbered, codes were inserted before the numbers to make a distinction between the two types of numbers. Codes were also inserted before all numbered references to match the right type. This was done using a macro or search and replace functions where possible. Where it was not possible to use a macro, changes where made manually. After this, the text styles were used to finish the mark-up of the files. A macro was used to add the correct mark-up codes before and after where the styles were used.

Because the old structure of the files was kept intact the old search methods using the table of contents and indices can still be used.

The added functionality:

- Searching for a heading starting with a specific word was made possible. Matching headings can be easily found, and the topics of those headings viewed.
- Using a special tool, all words or parts of sentences matching a heading were marked as an automatic reference. These added references, invisible before using the tool, gave a new view over the files.
- Using the concept map views, relations between families can be made visible to some degree.

The prototype version worked very well but at that time did not support free text search or Boolean search criteria.

The conversion was done by someone who had just joined our team. He did all of it in six weeks. One of the things that went wrong was that he did not realize that it made sense to split the different files into seven smaller ones, each of these smaller files containing one of the parts of the original file. By doing this some operations that were previously difficult to do automatically could be done more easily. This was because the parts themselves were all structured rather well, but the compound file was more difficult to dissect. Writing macros to use on each part was easier than writing one big macro to do it all.

A step that was not taken, but which would have made the system even more usable, would have been to mark up words of the texts that would have provided interesting keywords, such as other family names, cities, or items.

Case IV
Document Maintenance via CD-I[3]

This is already done quite often. For instance the aircraft manufacturer Boeing and the car manufacturer Renault, to name just two large corporations, store some or all of their technical documentation in hypertext systems. They store mostly maintenance information.

One of reasons to do so is that previously they needed stacks of books meters high whereas now they can fit their technical documentation on one or a few CD-ROM disks. These are easier to distribute and much cheaper to reproduce. Because of the low reproduction costs it is easier to send new disks with updates incorporated. In the past only additions and corrections (on paper) were sent. These had to be inserted into the original documentation in the right places. This takes some effort and time and is prone to errors, something which airplane and car manufacturers can ill afford.

Searching and browsing the documentation can also be made simpler on a hypermedia system. Searching for keywords, category, model, or part, requesting more information on a part in an illustration, or seeing a blow-up of a part of an illustration can all be supported. Especially hotspots in illustrations for infor-mation and blowups are considered important extras. The data on the CD-ROMs needs to be structured so that printouts of texts and diagrams, if necessary, can be easily made. Technical hypermedia documentation is created in several stages. In most cases there is already technical documentation available on paper and/or in computer-readable format.

The paper material must be converted into computer readable format. The texts can be converted using scanners and OCR applications or by using typists. More often than not the graphics, drawings, schemes, etc., need to be redrawn by artists. Scanning the graphics, drawings, and schemes first for tracing can speed up this process. If the computer readable format does not contain any coding, this has to be added. Before adding the code some thought has to be given to what to code. Headings and keywords are a minimum. Depending on the hyper-media package used, hotspots, if supported, must be added to the graphics, drawings, and schemes before or after importing or indexing it for final use.

The final title can then be mastered and reproduced on a CD-ROM or a WWW server.

---

[3] CD-I is Philips technology to implement hyper- and multimedia titles for both the industrial and the consumer market on a read-only compact disc.

Case III
Newspaper Archiving and Delivery on CD-ROM

This case is similar to that of the documentation department. Newspaper articles must be stored for later retrieval in order to create new articles. The main difference here is that the articles are already in computer readable format. The following mark-ups were already available:

- Date in YYMMDD format.
- Section and page it was placed on. This made some type distinction possible. Possible sections are among others main news, national news, sports, culture, economy, and foreign news.
- Theme, a code to indicate what the news is about.
- Field containing the name of the person the article is about.
- Field containing the subject the article is about.
- A numerically coded category.
- A nation field with a code, containing a code for the nation followed by a category code.
- Author(s).
- Heading.
- The bold or larger first part of the article.
- The main body of the article.

Not all fields were used at all times. Further, the use of the fields was not yet really consistent. But it provided very nice material for a prototype which functioned very well. After indexing articles, it could be searched on date, heading, subject, country codes, persons, etc. Even Boolean functions could be used, such as give all articles from date one to date two, written by author one or two. Examples of possible searches:

- All articles between January 1st, 1991 and April 1st, 1991 about person Mr. Person.
- All articles between the January 1st, 1992 and April 1st, 1992 about person Mr. Person in which the words war or peace were used.
- All articles between the January 1st, 1993 and January 1st, 1994 about sports in the country Luxembourg.

The resulting articles were listed alphabetically by heading in a list box from which one or more of the articles could be selected and opened. To scan or not to scan illustrations and photographs for display was the only choice left to make.

Case V
Preparing Encyclopedias for CD-ROM

Searching and browsing in paper-based reference works and encyclopedias is especially difficult when you need to browse through multiple volumes. Creating a hypertext system with a complete set of reference works or a complete encyclopedia on it can make it a lot easier for someone to find the information he or she is searching for. To make it easier and better for the user, such a hypertext system should contain the following search mechanisms:

- Search on (partial) keywords. Sometimes it may make sense to distinguish different types of keywords: generic, names, dates, etc.
- Search on (partial) topic titles. The system should be able to produce an alphabetical list of topic titles to browse through and select from.
- Search of topic titles within subject fields. The system should be able to produce an alphabetical list of all topic titles of a selected set of subject fields. Subject fields could be as wide as physics or as specialized as chaos theory, which may be a subset of the first.
- Browse subject fields. A hierarchical list of the available subject fields.
- Hypertext links from references to the related parts of the reference work or encyclopedia.
- Free text search. Because this can be very slow, due to the possibly large volume of text in which to search, it might be a good idea to have the user select a subject field first.
- History list. To give the user an overview of all topic already seen, and to retrace his steps.

To enable all of the search actions above, the material going into the hypertext system needs to be tagged appropriately, so that the compiler or indexing program can distinguish the different topics, subject fields, references, different types of keywords, etc. In this case the publisher preferred an indexing program over a compiler because in that way modifications could also be used for new paper versions of the material. The original material of a small encyclopedia provide by the publisher was based on typesetting tapes and contained mostly typographical codes.

The original material was improved in a number of steps:

- Some of the typographical codes were converted to meta-codes. Topic headings, references, explanations, and paragraph ends were marked. This provided a base to continue from.
- All dates and numbers were marked.
- Names were marked, by forename and family name.
- All text parts that matched with headings were marked as a special kind of reference. The method used was quick and dirty. The matching procedure was case-insensitive and did not check for synonyms, plurals, or singulars of headings. In retrospect, it would have been fairly easy to include case-sensitivity. All headings started with an uppercase character, but otherwise, except for the first word in a sentence, a word only started with an uppercase character if it was a name or an abbreviation that always did so. The matching would have been foolproof for every word but the first word of a sentence.
- Classification codes were added to each topic.
- A number of pictures were scanned to be used with the texts.

All of the above were modifications to the original files. These files could be used both for normal printing purposes and multimedia purposes. One of the spin-offs of this test was a tool to check if references matched with headings. Using this tool inconsistencies were removed from the original material. The inconsistencies had appeared because headings had been changed or removed or because the author or editor adding the references had made a mistake. The removal of the inconsistencies provided the publisher with more consistent files which could also be used for their paper version of the encyclopedia. The same procedures were also used for the publisher's other reference works.

Case VI
Managing Instructional Material

The step from reference works to instructional material is a big one. It does not have to be so, but when a hypertext system is developed for instructional use there is always the wish to include the following:

- *Tests*. In many cases it is expected of an instructional system that it is able to test the users on their knowledge of the subject matter. The problem with this is that in many cases simple multiple choice questions, which can be easily handled by a computer, are not enough. Another possibility is to use blanks exercises: The student has to fill in the correct word(s) on open places in the text. Questions that require an open answer are still too difficult for com-puters to comprehend. In this cases the teacher or instructor will have to evaluate the answers.

- *Coaching or navigating*. The user has to be coached to navigate through the material along one of the paths selected by the instructional designers. De-pending on a set of criteria, such as results of tests, the user either has to redo one or more of the previous items, or can continue with a new item which covers something extra, or may skip a number of items. The use of Petri nets is one of the possibilities to overcome the typical problems that arise while authoring 'programmed instruction'. 'Skill learning' based upon evidence of having taken the prerequisite steps (detected in a task analysis) makes it quite possible to sequence a learning dialogue. However, planning 'knowledge acquisition' creates a notorious problem for the instructional designer, as it is the person's prior knowledge that defines which concepts are adequate to start with. Giving the student the navigation job still leaves the need to orient him/her in the conceptual dependencies as experts see them. These expert assertions might be definable in so-called Petri net-works. They will prompt the student which way to go, but always give the student the authority to overrule this advice.

These points make it difficult to develop an instructional hypertext system. If tests, coaching, and navigating were not issues it would be the same as deve-loping normal instructional material. However, then tests and coaching would have to be done by the teacher or instructor.

Case VII
Product Catalogues for Delivery on Demand

Travel organizations are already producing hypermedia applications in which the customer can select a destination and have a preview of sights and scenes of that destination. Details about travel costs, arrangements, and accommodations can also be provided.

Because of the fast-changing details in those offers that start less than a month before the actual travel date, changes must be easy to make.

A product catalogue should offer several search methods:

- By product type, in the case of travel organizations by the different countries and price classes.
- Simple browsing through all different items, much like the way browsing is done in a normal catalogue.

Mail-order firms are also a good example of the 'delivery on demand' concept. The input data vary from fixed-format descriptions, like the technical specifications we expect with electronic equipment, to a complete lack of data for, clothes, sweets, or toys. However, we may expect that product documentation in general will gradually appear in all stages of business transactions. As we pointed out already in Chapter 5, the start of CALS, Computer-aided Acquisition and Logistics Support, as initiated by the American Department of Defense, will likely become a default criterion for any product description. CALS will make it more convenient for EDI (Electronic Data Interchange) services to anticipate descrip-tion formats so that they become a standard component in pre- and after-sales, training, maintenance, and experts' assessments for insurance, etc.

We have seen the last four years that high quality hypermedia products have begun to be used in the sector of POI (Points of Information) and POS. (Point of Sales). Especially POS applications belonged to the pioneers, as they had a relatively quick return on investment. After several products the hypermedia development costs came down steeply. We even see nowadays that many companies start the CD-ROM hypermedia programming and resource preparation in house. This book is meant for the first generation of in-house pioneers, as they might meet many problems in the field of document management.

Part V
Appendices

A. References

SGML

Bryan, Martin (1988) SGML, An Author's Guide to the Standard Generalized Markup Language, Addison-Wesley, Wokingham, UK

Herwijnen, Eric van (1990) *Practical SGML*, Kluwer Academic Publishers, Dordrecht, The Netherlands

T$_E$X

Knuth, Donald E. (1984) *The T$_E$Xbook*, Addison-Wesley, Reading, MA

Graphical Display of Two-Dimensional Concept Maps

Bos, W. (1988), *How to draw a graph*, Ph.D. dissertation, Dept. of Computer Science, Univ. of Twente, Enschede, The Netherlands

Eades, P., Hickey M. and Read R. C. (1984), Some Hamilton paths and a minimal change algorithm. *JACM* 31(1), 19–29

Gansner, E.R., North, S.C. and Vo, K.P. (1988) DAG – a program that draws directed graphs, *Software-practice and experience*, 18(2), 1047–1062

Leenes, P. (1990). M, *TEGA (Teken Een Graaf Algoritme)*, Dept. of Educational Technology, Univ. of Twente, Enschede, The Netherlands

Nelson, T.H. (1967) *Getting it out of our system, information retrieval: a critical review*, Thompson Books, Washington D.C.

Newell, A., Simon, H. A. (1972) *Human Problem Solving*. Prentice Hall, Englewood Cliffs, NJ

Ozawa, T., and Takahashi, H. (1980) A graph-planarization algorithm and its application to random graphs. In: Saito, N. and Nishizeki, T. (eds.) *Graph Theory and Algorithms*. Sendai, Japan, October 1980, Proceedings. Lecture Notes in Computer Science 108, Springer-Verlag, Berlin, pp. 95–107

Reiner, D., and Brown, G. (1985) *Heuristic layout for DDEW ER+ diagrams*, Manuscript, Computer Corporation of America, USA

Rowe, L.A., Davis, M., Messinger, E., Meyer, C., Spiriakis, C., and Tuan, A. (1979) Tidy drawings of trees, *IEEE Trans. on Software Engineering*, 5 (5), 514–520

Sedgewink, R. (1988) *Algorithms*, 2nd edition, Addison-Wesley, Reading, MA

Sugiyama, K., Tagawa, S., and Toda, M. (Feb. 1981) Methods for visual understanding of hierarchical system structures, *IEEE Trans. on Systems, Man, and Cybernetics*, 11 (2), 109–125

Tamassia, R., Battista, Di G., and Batini, C. (Jan./Feb. 1988) Automatic graph drawing and readability of diagrams, *IEEE Trans. on Systems, Man, and Cybernetics*, 18 (1), 61–79

Tutte, W.T. (1960) Convex representations of graphs, Proceedings. *London Math. Soc.*, Vol. 10, pp. 304–320, London.

Vaucher, J.G. (1980) Pretty-printing of trees, *Software Practice and Experience*, 10, 553–561

Woods, D. (1982) *Drawing planar graphs*, Ph.D. dissertation, Computer Science Dept., Stanford Univ., Stanford, CA, Tech. Rep. STAN-CS-82-943

General

Anthonisse, J.M. (1971) *The rush in a directed graph*. Mathematical Center, Amsterdam

Bakker, R.R. (1987), *Knowledge graphs: Representation and structuring of scientific knowledge*. Dissertation University of Twente, The Netherlands

Bavelas, A. (1948) A mathematical model for group structures. *Applied Anthropology*, 7, 16–30

Canter, D., Rivers, R., and Storrs, G. (1985) Characterizing user navigation through complex data structures. *Behavior and Information Technology* 4, 93–102

Castelli, C, Colazzo, L., and Mic, L. (1990) Lost in hyperspace: Hypermedia structures and subjective variables. Paper proposal for ECHT '90

Constanzo, W.V. (1989) The electronic text: Learning to write, read and reason with computers. Prentice Hall, Englewood Cliffs, NJ

Elm, W.C., and Woods, D.D. (1985). Getting lost: A case study in interface design, *Proceedings of the Human Factors Society*, pp. 927–931

Fiderio, J. (1988) *Hypertext and the need for authoring facilities*

Freeman, L.C. (1979) Centrality in Social networks. Conceptual clarification. *Social Networks*, 1, 215–219

French, Jr., J.R.P. (1956) A formal theory of social power. *Psychological Review*, 63, 181–94

Frisse, M. (1988a): From text to hypertext, traditional tools like outline processors already incorporate many of hypertext's lessons. *BYTE*, October, 1988

Frisse, M. (1988b): Searching information in a hypertext medical handbook. *Communications of the ACM*, 31 (7)

Furuta, R., and Stotts, P.D. (1989) Programmable browsing semantics in Trellis. *Proceedings of the HYPERTEXT '89 Conference*, Pittsburgh, PA

Garfield, E. (1980): Is information retrieval in the arts and humanities inherently different from that in science? The effect that ISI's citation index for the arts and humanities is expected to have on future scholarship. *Library Quarterly*, 50 (1), 40–57

Garfield, E. (1983): Document delivery systems in the Information Age. *Phi Kappa Phi Journal*, 63 (3), 8–10

Harary, F., Norman, R.Z. and Cartwright, D. (1965) *Structural models: An introduction to the theory of directed graphs*, New York

Hatzopoulos, M., Gouscos, D., Spiliopoulou, M., and Vassilakis, C. (1990) HYP/20 An Object Oriented Data Model for Hypermedia Systems The SAFE Project Report. University of Athens, Athens

Hoede, C. (1978) *A new status score for actors in a social network*. Twente Univ. of Technology, Dept. of Applied Mathematics (Internal report)

Hoivik, T., and Gleditsch, N.P. (1970) Structural parameters of graphs: a theoretical investigation. *Quality and Quantity*, 4, 195–209

Hubbell, C.H. (1965) An input output approach to clique identification. *Sociometry*, 28, 377–399

International Organization for Standardization, Information Processing (1979) *Text and Office Systems – Standard Generalized Markup Language (SGML)*, ISO 8879–1986(E)

International Organization for Standardization, Information Processing (1990) Working draft of Hypermedia/Time-based structuring language (HyTime). Source SC 18/WG8 – *Standard Generalized Markup Language (SGML)*, ISO/IEC JTC 1/SC 18

Jonassen, D.H. (1982) *The Technology of Text*, Principles for structuring, designing and displaying text. Educational Technology Publications, Englewood Cliffs, NJ

Katz, L. (1953) A new status index derived from sociometric data analysis. *Psychometrika*, 18, 39–43

Kibby, M.R., and Mayes, J.T. (1988) Towards intelligent hypertext. In: R. McAleese (ed.), *Hypertext 1, Theory into Practice*. Ablex, Norwood, NJ, pp. 164–172

Kibby, M., Tanner G., and Hardman, L. (1991) HYP/21 *Final Report on Hypermedia User Interfaces*. The SAFE Project Report, UK

Kommers, P.A.M. (1988), Textvision, elicitation and acquisition of conceptual knowledge by representation and multi-windowing. In: G.C. v.d. Veer and G. Mulder (eds.) *Human-Computer Interaction: Psychonomic Aspects*. Springer, Berlin, pp. 237–249

Kommers, P.A.M. (1989a) Graph computation as an orientation device in extended and cyclic hypertext networks. In: D.H. Jonassen, H. Mandl (eds.) *Designing Hypermedia for Learning;* NATO Advanced Research Workshop, Rottenburg, 3–8 July 1989. NATO ASI Series F, Vol. 67, Springer-Verlag, Berlin (1990), pp. 117–134

Kommers, P.A.M. (1989b) Hypertext as a tool for advanced learning situations. In: H. Mandl (ed.) *Interactive Learning with New Media*, Mainz, 27–28 April 1989. Internal Report published by the University of Tübingen, pp. 165–193

Kommers, P.A.M. (1991a) Virtual structures in hypermedia resources. In: H.J. Bullinger (ed.) *Proceedings of the HCI'91 International Conference*. Springer-Verlag, Berlin. ISBN: 0921-2647, pp. 1343–1351

Kommers, P.A.M. (1991b), *Hypertext and the Acquisition of Knowledge*. Doctoral Thesis, University of Twente, The Netherlands

Kommers, P.A.M. and Ferreira, A. (1992a) Hypermedia: Generic resources for exploratory learning. In: S. Dijkstra, Merrienboer, J. & Krammer H. (eds.) *Advanced Educational Technology: Instructional Models in Computer-Based Learning Environments*. NATO ASI Series F, Vol. 104. Springer-Verlag, Berlin, pp. 349–364

Kommers, P.A.M., Jonassen, D.H., Mayes, T. (eds.) (1992b) *Cognitive Tools for Learning*. NATO ASI Series F, Vol. 81. Springer, Berlin

Kommers, P.A.M. (1993) Scenarios for the development of educational hypermedia. In: *Educational & Training Technology International*, Vol. 30 (3), 234–254

Kommers, P.A.M., Grabinger, S., and Dunlap, J. (1996) *The Technology of Hypermedia Learning Environments: Instructional Design and Integration*. Lawrence Erlbaum, Hillsdale, NJ

Kwak, A. (1996), Ontwerp en Implementatie van een Instrument ter Navigatie in Hypermedia Bestanden. Dpt. of Computer Science, University of Twente, Enschede, The Netherlands.

Lesk, M. (1989) What to do when there's too much information, *Hypertext '89 Proceedings*, November, pp. 305–318

Levesque, H.J., and Brachman, R.J. (1985) A fundamental tradeoff in knowledge representation and reasoning. In: Brachman R.J. and Levesque H.J. (eds.) *Readings in knowledge representation*. Morgan Kaufmann, Los Altos, CA

Merrill, M.D., Reigeluth, C.M., and Faust, G.W. (1977) *The instructional strategy diagnostic profile training manual*, Courseware Inc., San Diego, CA

Neuwirth, C.M., and Kaufer, D.S. (1989) The role of external representation in the writing process: implications for the design of hypertext-based writing tools. In: *HYPER-TEXT '89 Proceedings*, Pittsburgh, PA

Pask, G. (1975) *Conversation, cognition and learning: A cybernetic theory and methodology*. Elsevier, Amsterdam

Peterson, J.L. (1981) *Petri Net Theory and the Modeling of Systems*. Prentice Hall, New York

Price and Schneider (1988) Evolution of an SGML application generator. In: *ACM Conference on Document Processing Systems*, pp. 51–60. Santa Fe, NM

Reigeluth, C.M., Merrill M.D., Wilson B.G., and Spiller, R.T. (1980) The elaboration theory of instruction: A model for sequencing and synthesizing instruction. *Instructional Science, 9*, 195–219

Romiszowski, A.J. (1990) The Hypertext/Hypermedia solution – but what exactly is the problem? In: D.H. Jonassen and H. Mandl (eds.) *Designing Hypermedia for Learning*. NATO ASI Series F, Vol. 67. Springer, Berlin, pp. 321–354. Reprint 1996

Salton, G., and McGill, M.J. (1983) *Introduction to modern information retrieval.* McGraw-Hill, New York

Smith, B.C. (1982) *Reflection and semantics in a procedural language,* Ph.D. thesis and technical report MIT/LCS/TR-272, MIT, Cambridge, MA

Sprenger, C.J.A., and Stokman, F.N. (1989) *GRADAP, Graph Definition and Analysis Package.* Groningen

Streitz N., and Hannemann, R. (1990) Elaborating arguments: Writing, learning and reasoning in a hypertext-based environment for authoring. In: D.H. Jonassen and H. Mandl (eds.) *Designing Hypermedia for Learning.* NATO ASI Series F, Vol. 67. Springer, Berlin. Reprint 1996

Taylor, M. (1969) Influence Structures. *Sociometry,* 32, 490–502

Travers, M. (1989) A visual representation for knowledge structures. *Proceedings of the Hypermedia '89 Conference.* Pittsburgh, November

Waterworth, J.A., and Chignell, M.H. (1989) A Manifesto for hypermedia usability research. *Hypermedia,* 1 (3)

Deliverables by the COSYS Project

COSYS Project and DELTA 2011 Deliverables; DELTA Office, DG XIII

DELTA Deliverable D/WP05.2 (1993) *Co-Authoring Workbench – Phase II,* Danish Technological Institute, Denmark

Dimopoulou, K., et al. (1990) *A proposal for the design of an object-oriented Hypermedia system* SAFE/HYP

Hardman, L. (1990): *A proposal for a collection of navigation tools for a Hypermedia Learning Environment .*The SAFE Project

Hatzopoulos, M., Gouscos, D., Spiliopoulou, M., and Vassilakis, C. (1990) HYP/15 *Second Intermediate Report on Hypermedia Databases.* University of Athens, Athens

Kibby, M. (1990) *Tailoring Hypermedia.* The SAFE Project

Kibby, M., and Hardman, L. (1990) *The minimal hypermedia database element.* DELTA-SAFE-Hyperate working paper

Kibby, M., Tanner, G., and Hardman, L. (1990) HYP/16 *Second Intermediate Report on Hypermedia User Interfaces*

Kommers, P.A.M., Jonker, E., Röst, L., Weimar, F., and Ferreira, A. (1989) *First Intermediate Report on Hypermedia Structures.* The Netherlands

Kommers, P.A.M., Ferreira, A. (1993) DELTA Deliverable D/WP03 *Work Bench Modules, Part C1, Co-Authoring*

Kommers, P.A.M., and Ferreira, A. (1993) DELTA Deliverable D/WP05.2 *Specification of Management & Administration, Procedures and Tools,* Part C, Part E, Tools, pp. E-1 – E-15., Part F

McArthur R., Busch, P., Ferreira, A., Nielsen, J., Mallia, M., v.d. Heide, R., and v.d Wal, M. (1993) DELTA Deliverable D/WP05.2, Co-Authoring Workbench – Phase II, *Chapter 3, Coauthoring environments in the applications,* pp. 4–1 – 4–23

McArthur, R., Cave, F., Ferreira, A. (1993) DELTA Deliverable D/WP05.2, Co-Authoring Workbench – Phase II, Chapter 4, *Common tools: Concepts, principles and techniques,* pp. 4–1 – 4–23

Ringsted, M. (1993) DELTA Deliverable D/WP05.*2 Specification of Management & Administration, Procedures and Tools,* Danish Technological Institute, Denmark

Ringsted, M. (1993) DELTA Deliverable D/WP03 *Workbench Modules,* Danish Technological Institute, Denmark

Röst, L.C.M., and Coenders, H. (1989) *DELTA-Safe-Hyperate working paper*

Vogel, R. de (1990) *Multimedia databases* DEEP/9

B. Word Translation Macros

```
Sub MAIN
REM Store name and save original file
Name$ = FileName$()
FileSave
Print "Putting all indices to index and search
fields"
StartOfDocument
EditFindClearFormatting
XE$ = "XE " + Chr$(34)
EditFind .Find = XE$, .Direction = 2, .Format = 1
While EditFindFound()
      CharRight 1, 0
      NotFoundQuote = 1
      While NotFoundQuote
            CharRight 1, 1
            Selected$ = Selection$()
            If Right$(Selected$, 1) = Chr$(34) Then
                  NotFoundQuote = 0
                  CharLeft 1, 1
                  Selected$ = Selection$()
            EndIf
      Wend
      If NotFoundQuote = 0 Then
            CharLeft Len(Selected$), 0
            EditFind .Find = Selected$, .Direction = 0
            Insert "{vfld 13}" + Selected$ + "{vfld}"
            InsertFootnote "K"
            Insert "3:" + Selected$
            ClosePane
            EditFind .Find = XE$, .Direction = 2,
            .Format = 1
            CharRight 1, 0
      EndIf
      EditFind .Find = XE$, .Direction = 2,
      .Format = 1
Wend
```

```
Print "Converting all double-underlined text to
strikeout"
StartOfDocument
EditFindClearFormatting
EditFindChar .Underline = 3
EditFind .Find = "", .Direction = 2, .Format = 1
While EditFindFound()
      Underline 0
      Strikeout 1
      EditFind .Find = "", .Direction = 2,
      .Format = 1
Wend

Print "Converting all bold text to index and search
fields"
StartOfDocument
EditFindClearFormatting
EditFindChar .Bold = 1
EditFind .Find = "", .Direction = 2, .Format = 1
While EditFindFound()
      Selected$ = Selection$()
      ResetChar()
      Insert "{vfld 11}" + Selected$ + "{vfld}"
      InsertFootnote "K"
      Insert "1:" + Selected$
      ClosePane
      EditFind .Find = "", .Direction = 2,
      .Format = 1
Wend

Print "Converting all italic text to index and search
fields"
StartOfDocument
EditFindClearFormatting
EditFindChar .Italic = 1
EditFind .Find = "", .Direction = 2, .Format = 1
While EditFindFound()
      Selected$ = Selection$()
      Insert "{vfld 12}" + Selected$ + "{vfld}"
      ResetChar()
      InsertFootnote "K"
      Insert "2:" + Selected$
      ClosePane
      EditFind .Find = "", .Direction = 2,
      .Format = 1
```

```
Wend

Print "Converting all headings to the same level"
StartOfDocument
fendofdoc = 0
While fendofdoc = 0
      CurrentStyle$ = StyleName$(0, 0)
      FoundHeading = 0
      If CurrentStyle$ = "heading 2" Then
           FoundHeading = 1
      End If
      If CurrentStyle$ = "heading 3" Then
           FoundHeading = 1
      End If
      If FoundHeading Then
           FormatStyle .Name = "heading 1", .Apply
      EndIf
           If CmpBookmarks("\para", "\endofdoc") =
           5 Or CmpBookmarks("\sel", "\endofdoc") =
           0 Then
           fendofdoc = 1
      End If
      ParaDown
Wend

EditFindClearFormatting
REM    Find all topics, set titles, fields, index,
       browse order
Print "Create topics, set titles etc."
StartOfDocument
fendofdoc = 0
TopicNumber = 0
While fendofdoc = 0
      CurrentStyle$ = StyleName$(0, 0)
      If CurrentStyle$ = "heading 1" Then
           ParaDown, 1
           CharLeft 1, 1
           Selected$ = Selection$()
           EditCut
           If TopicNumber > 0 Then
                Insert Chr$(12)
           End If
           Insert "{vfld 10}" + Selected$ + "{vfld}"
           Number$ = Str$(TopicNumber)
```

```
                Number$ = Right$(Number$,
                Len(Number$) - 1)
                Zeros = 6 - Len(Number$)
                TopicNumber$ = String$(Zeros, "0")
                + Number$
                InsertFootnote "#"
                Insert "T_" + TopicNumber$
                ClosePane
                InsertFootnote "$"
                Insert Selected$
                ClosePane
                InsertFootnote "+"
                Insert "T:" + TopicNumber$
                ClosePane
                InsertFootnote "K"
                Insert Selected$
                ClosePane
                REM   To make it easier to find the topic
                      number
                Hidden
                Insert "T_" + TopicNumber$
                Hidden
                TopicNumber = TopicNumber + 1
        End If
        If CmpBookmarks("\para", "\endofdoc") = 5 Or
        CmpBookmarks("\sel", "\endofdoc") = 0 Then
                fendofdoc = 1
        End If
        ParaDown
 Wend
Print "Finding all keys of references"
EditFindClearFormatting
StartOfDocument
EditFindChar .Strikeout = 1
EditFind .Find = "", .Direction = 2, .Format = 1
While EditFindFound()
        Selected$ = Selection$()
        CharRight
        ResetChar()
        Hidden
        Insert "#=#=#=#=#"
        Hidden
        StartOfDocument
```

```
            EditFindClearFormatting
            EditFindStyle .Style = "heading 1"
            EditFind .Direction = 2, .Find = Selected$,
            .Format = 1
            If EditFindFound() Then
                    EditFindClearFormatting
                    EditFindChar .Hidden
                    EditFind .Find = "", .Direction = 2,
                    .Format = 1
                    Key$ = Selection$()
            Else
                    Key$ = "T_000000"
            End If
            StartOfDocument
            EditFind .Find = "#=#=#=#=#", .Direction = 2,
            .Format = 0
            Insert Key$
            EditFindClearFormatting
            EditFindChar .Strikeout = 1
            EditFind .Find = "", .Direction = 2,
            .Format = 1
Wend

Print "Throwing out all keys hidden in text"
StartOfDocument
EditFindClearFormatting
EditFindStyle .Style = "heading 1"
EditFind .Direction = 2, .Format = 1
While EditFindFound()
            If EditFindFound() Then
                    EditFindClearFormatting
                    EditFindChar .Hidden
                    EditFind .Find = "", .Direction = 2,
                    .Format = 1
                    EditCut
            End If
            EditFindClearFormatting
            EditFindStyle .Style = "heading 1"
            EditFind .Direction = 2, .Format = 1
Wend
REM    Save translated file
FileSaveAs .Name = "D:\TEST\DEFAULT.RTF", .Format = 6
REM    Close and reopen original file
FileClose 2
```

```
FileOpen .Name = Name$
End Sub
```

A sample project file text:

```
[OPTIONS]
COMPRESS =NO
ROOT =D:\TEST
WARNING =1
SYSTEM =PC
MAKE =FULL
BATCH =TRUE
IGNORESECTION =PANEASSOC
copyright=University of Twente
title=Test of Microsoft Word conversion macro
citation=No citation

[CONFIG]
Std20Menus()
Std20Buttons()
RegisterRoutine("mvbmp2", "CopyBmp", "v=USS")
RegisterRoutine("mvmci2", "MCICommand", "USSS")
RegisterRoutine("mvftsui2", "SearchDialog", "USU")

[FILES]
Default.RTF

[KEYINDEX]
keyword=0, "Topic titles"; headings
keyword=1, "Bold"
keyword=2, "Italic"
keyword=3, "Index"
keyword=4, "Keyword list 4"

[WINDOWS]
main= "Test of conversion macro", (0, 0, 1023, 1023,
0), (0), (192,192,192)

[PANES]

[POPUPS]

[PANEASSOC]

[FTINDEX]
dtype0=mvbrkr2.dll!FBreakWords;
dtype1=mvbrkr2.dll!FBreakNumber
dtype2=mvbrkr2.dll!FBreakDate
```

```
dtype3=mvbrkr2.dll!FBreakTime
dtype4=mvbrkr2.dll!FBreakEpoch

[GROUPS]
group=T, "Topics"

[BUILDTAGS]

[SEARCHDLG]
near=8
ebox=0, "Topic titles",, 10 ; headings
ebox=0, "Bold",, 11
ebox=0, "Italic",, 12
ebox=0, "Index",, 13
ebox=0, "Index list 4",, 14

[BAGGAGE]
```

C. Glossary

Article: Any (normally textual) part of the hyperbase which is shown or displayed as one integral piece of information.

Authoring: Concerns all activities that deliver new information and ideas or new views on existing information and ideas. Text is a definitive format for expressing new ideas, and is also versatile enough to describe other media like scripts and story boards for video and movie fragments, audio sequences, and interaction procedures. In case of authoring hypermedia the task of authoring goes further than writing *what* is to be presented to the user; the major effort is to define the *transitions* between the information elements (items), so that the user can adapt the information sequence to his/her actual task to be solved, personal interests, prior knowledge, and individual style of learning. The various transitions that are evoked as the user browses can be anticipated by 'linking' items in a meaningful way, so that the user will be made aware of the availability of more detailed information (zooming effect) when clicking a part of the information in an item.

Browsing: The typical way to navigate through hypermedia. The user can choose among different (object) areas in the current presentation on the screen. Ideally, the screen presentation prompts the user where to find the hotspots (the click-able areas), which brings them to other items.

CALS: Computer-aided Acquisition and Logistics Support. For a more elaborate definition see page 61 and beyond in this book.

Concept: A mental or cognitive representation of an object, idea or feeling. Concepts are essential for thinking, imagery, remembering, and problem solving. Besides the declarative aspects of concepts, they can be considered as mental procedures triggering other (associated) concepts from prior knowledge. One concept may exist in different 'mental contexts'. Concepts need other concepts to be explained and restored in human memory. Hypermedia relations enable authors to embed concepts in one or more semantic context(s).

Concept Map: A representation in a spatial form of the relationships between concepts showing semantic closeness, relational associations, structural status, etc.

DTD: Document Type Definition. This is the part of a SGML document in which the structure of the document is described.

Editor: A person who modifies existing texts.

First Author: A person who creates texts from scratch.

GML: Generalized Mark-up Language.

Hyper Editor: A tool with special functions to add (semantic) information, such as anchors and their properties, in order to create hypermedia efficiently.

Hypermedia: The family of information processing applications that have hypertext and/or multimedia capabilities. Hypermedia are like hypertext, but contain other items too like sounds, pictures, video, smells, etc.; with links between these items that can be triggered.

Hyperbase: The database behind the hypermedia program containing all the texts, sounds, pictures, video, smells, etc.

Hypermedia Design: Refers to the product planning and the functional description of its behavior to the final user. Publications on paper media are submissive to the manipulations of the user. Hypermedia are *de facto* interactive, and have the potential to respond to the user in a more active way. The design of hypermedia has to specify the types of initiatives in interaction with the user that we would finally expect. Prototypes of hypermedia are useful to elicit new ideas from product planners. In the context of hypermedia production we may expect new initiatives from traditional publishers in the next five years.

Hypertext: Texts stored in a (computer) system with (predetermined) triggerable links from texts to other texts.

HyTime and **SMSL:** HyTime is a new ISO standard for hypermedia and multimedia data. HyTime is used as the basis of the ISO Standard Multimedia Scripting Language or SMSL.

Item: A self-contained information element which will not be fragmented in smaller parts when presented to the user. It can be the content of a window (text, table, picture, or moving video).

Lemma: The title, keyword, heading, or name (of an article) as it is used by publishers of dictionaries and encyclopedias.

Linking: Linking of items is a crucial activity in authoring hypermedia as it anticipates the interaction with the user. Creating a link means assigning a relation between an element in an item and another item. In most cases it means that the author defines a hotspot and adds the identity of it by giving the name of another item. The effect of the linking procedure is that the user can activate (e.g., by clicking with the mouse) a created hotspot, and the hypermedia system will present a new item which carries more information about the element in the clicked hotspot.

Main Editor: A person who co-ordinates a group of editors, and who has the ultimate right to add, change, and delete parts of the developing document. (S)he has also the right and responsibility to assign database access privileges to the members of the editorial team.

Media-editors: Applications for creating drawings, text, music, etc.

MHEG: The Multimedia and Hypermedia Expert Group is currently working on a new standard for describing multimedia material. It will be a standard describing how to envelope data and the content type. It will not describe how the enveloped data itself is formatted, although SGML is noted as one of the preferred formats.

ODA and **HyperODA:** Office Document Architecture. HyperODA is an extension to ODA to provide services for hypertext and hypermedia within the ODA.

Production: Refers to the physical preparation of all the information to be brought together for a hypermedia publication, as well as its layout and rendering in a medium that can be delivered to the user. In case of hypermedia, the production is more complex than making a book. While the step from manuscript to printed book is mainly a question of correcting, making the layout, and printing, hypermedia require the addition of interaction procedures so that the user is assisted to browse between the items in many ways. The step of digitizing analogue data, mastering, and final reproduction on optical media like CD-ROM(XA) will be delegated to special companies in the electronics industry.

RTF: This is the acronym for Rich Text Format, which is a Microsoft standard text formatting format. This format supports paragraph styles, colors, headers, footers, other typographical formatting, and embedded or linked pictures, drawings, tables, and formulas. An RTF file only contains ASCII characters so it can be read as text, and does not have to be handled as a binary file. RTF is a typographically oriented format. Although RTF can be used to semantically label paragraphs, it will only work on a paragraph level and not on a word or character level.

Second Author: A person who modifies existing texts.

SGML: Standardized Generalized Mark-up Language. A standard format that is becoming more and more popular as more hypertext packages accept or prefer input in this format. As a result, more SGML WYSIWYG word processors and extensions to word processors are becoming available. This format has been pioneered by IBM with their Generalized Mark-up Language or GML format. This format was later extended and accepted as the ISO 8879-1986 standard. SGML is a semantically oriented format. Character sequences called tags are used to tag parts of a text as being different types of information such as title, heading, paragraph, reference, list, etc. There are also some typographical tags such as bold and italic, but these should be used sparingly, as they makes it more difficult to connect a certain typographical format to specific tagged text parts.

T$_E$X: Tau Epsilon Xi. An elegant mark-up language developed by Donald Knuth. T$_E$X is very powerful for mathematical formulas. It can be used on several platforms and it is in the public domain. It is much like RTF and there are several extensions of it such as L^{A}T$_E$X.

WYSIWYG: What You See Is What You Get. This acronym is used for word processors that display the text exactly as it will be printed on paper. Thus text that will be printed bold will also be displayed bold on the computer display.

D. First Demonstrator Case Description

Introduction

This a description of the behavior of a program developed by the University of Twente called HyperNet, in this case for handling a medical encyclopedia. The description is accompanied by graphics, representing stages the program passes through while demonstrating all its relevant features.

Before describing the features, it is convenient to recall the methods used for representing (parts of) conceptual structures. At the highest level there are three ways of representing conceptual structures:

1. There is the textual representation of a concept, in which other concepts (if any) related to it are emphasized by means of different colors.
2. There is the network representation of a set of concepts, the members of which might be interrelated.
3. There is a view in which concepts are presented in a three-dimensional way.

The first approach is the most straightforward one and is very much like the basic hypertext system. The second one resembles the TextVision method (Kommers 1991a, 1991b) for presenting conceptual structures, while the third one is a new and highly experimental representation. Since the concepts of hypertext are widely and heavily discussed, we will not emphasize the problems that are specific for a hypertext system. When using the second approach, however, problems arise in deciding which tools to offer to the user to accommodate him or her while searching in very large structures. The tools offered to the user are described next.

Top View

The appearance of the top view is very much like TextVision with respect to the representation of concepts and their relations. However, there is quite a difference between this program and TextVision. Within TextVision the number of concepts that can be managed is strictly limited. In HyperNet, this is not the case, as it is designed to work with encyclopedia-sized documents. In this context a problem arises: What part of the structure should be offered to the user? Or, to state it more from the user's point of view, what must be offered to the user to let him or her select a part of the structure? To be more precise, the problem is how to facilitate efficient browsing through a very large structure and how to select a part to be viewed.

Zooming

The user should be able to get an overall view of the structure but also, if he or she decides, to get a local view. This leads to the introduction of zooming, which offers the user the possibility of seeing the structure from a distance (so the user only sees the most important concepts and their indirect relations), but also, by zooming in, that of looking from a closer distance. This enables the user to get details if desired.

Browsing

The user should be able to select other concepts than those currently on his or her screen. At any time it must be possible to select one or more concepts, either from those on the screen, or from a list of concepts. A new network is built around the chosen concepts. This, in combination with the zooming, makes it very easy to get around in the whole structure.

Pruning

The last structural problem in selecting part of the structure is the question of pruning: What happens if the structure selected is larger than the screen capacity (number of concepts it can display)? This problem is dealt with in two ways. The screen capacity is set to a constant value, which the user can change up to a maximum. The concepts to be presented are ordered by descending centrality and only those with the largest centrality are shown. The other concepts are latent and appear if the screen capacity is increased.

Inside View

The inside view is basically different from the top-view approach. The desired effect is that the user stands in a town on a certain concept with a view to a chosen other concept. (S)he can see a street, along which several other concepts are arranged. The concepts that are more indirect from the concept the user is standing on are further away along the street.

Example

In the next part an exhaustive example is presented, accompanied by screens which the program shows at the stages it reaches. You will find that some options (like the save or load state options) are not dealt with. But these options are very straightforward and do not need further explanation. The system starts by presenting the structurally most important concepts of the network (the nodes with the greatest centrality) and their relations (Figure 74). Note that some lines are thick and some are thin. The thinner a line is, the more intermediate steps have to be taken to go from one node to another. The user might be interested in concepts related to drugs, selects the concept drugs, and zoom halfway (Figure 74). The user then sees the concepts that are relevant with respect to drugs (Figure 75).

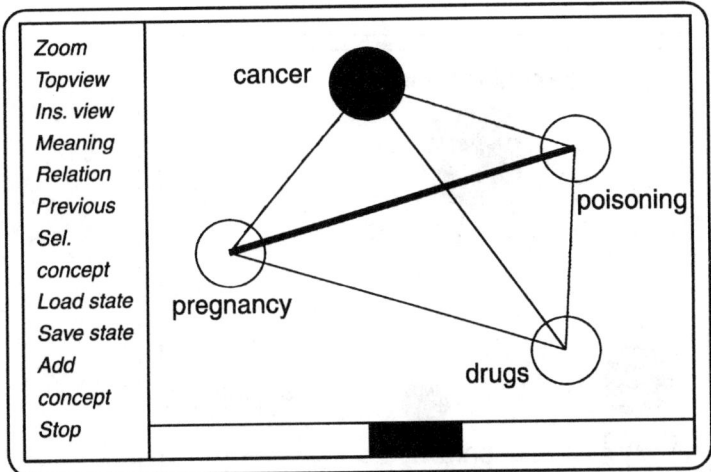

Figure 74. The most central concepts of the entire medical encyclopedia

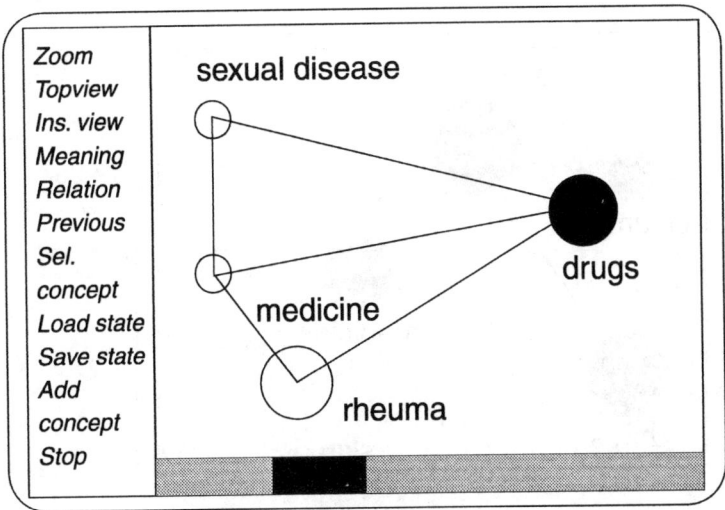

Figure 75. Concepts relevant to drugs

From there he sees a concept that interests him much in combination with drugs, namely sexual disease. The user would like to see what the combination of these concepts will bring at a very low level, so (s)he chooses the closest zooming factor on these. This brings Figure 76, which shows quite detailed information.

The user didn't want this and checks whether there is more to be presented. (S)he chooses more concepts to be shown, by using the scrollbar at the bottom of the screen. (S)he then sees Figure 77.

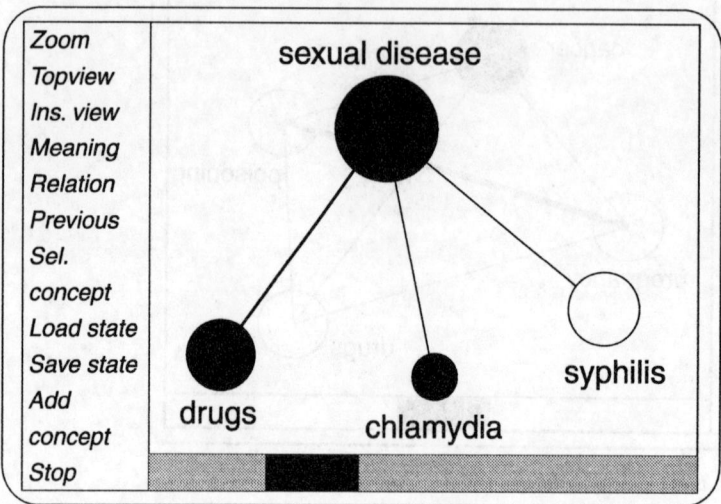

Figure 76. Detailed information

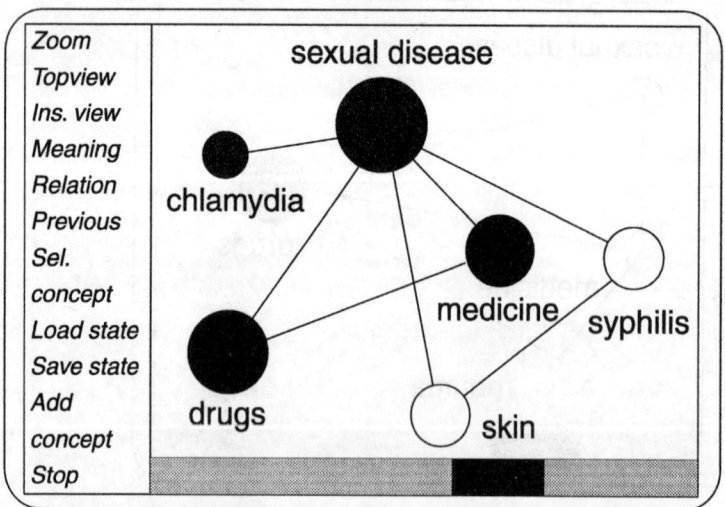

Figure 77. More concepts shown

Now the user wants to see what happens if AIDS is added to the network. (S)he chooses "add concept" from the menu and types AIDS. This brings Figure 78.

From there (s)he wants to see what other concepts are important when (s)he looks from drugs to AIDS. (S)he chooses the inside view with these concepts and gets Figure 79.

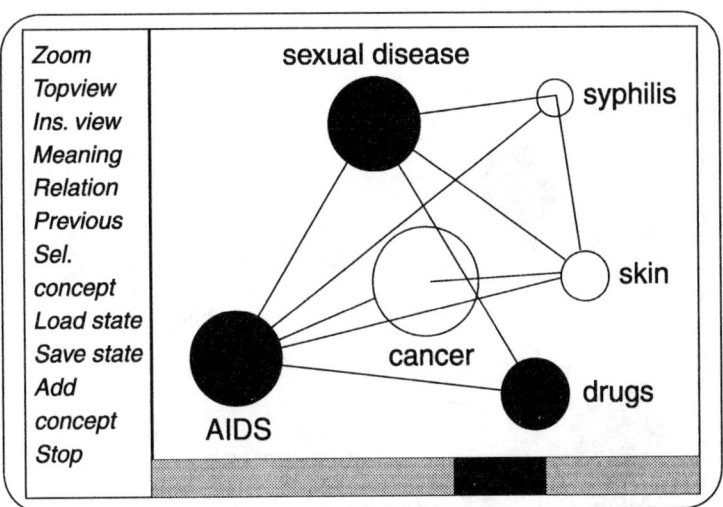

Figure 78. AIDS

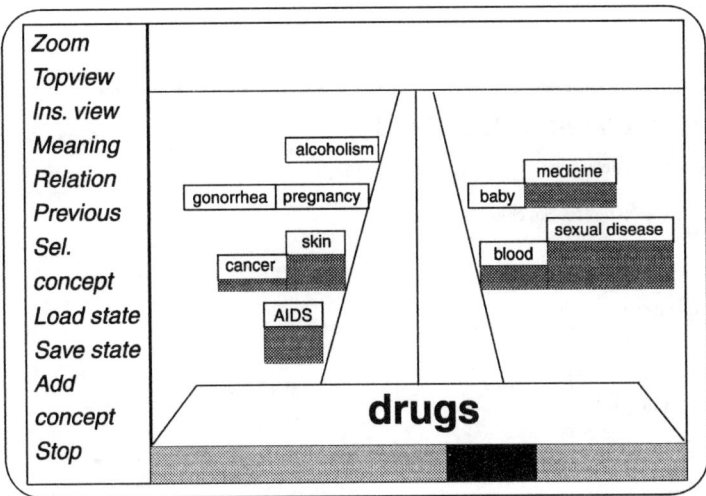

Figure 79. Inside view: Looking from drugs to AIDS

From this inside-view presentation (s)he notices the concepts blood and pregnancy, which (s)he finds of great interest. (S)he therefore chooses these three concepts and lets them show in top view (Figure 80).

The user might have already heard about blood having some relation with AIDS. (S)he therefore wants to see the text belonging to AIDS, but only those parts that also deal with blood. (S)he chooses relation from the menu and sees Figure 81.

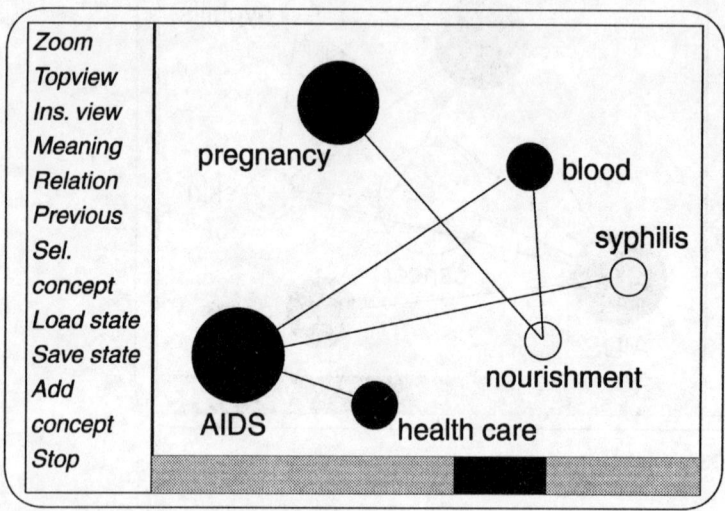

Figure 80. AIDS, blood and pregnancy

AIDS related with BLOOD

(abbr. of acquired immune deficiency

...... blood vessel-like cells in the skin

...... blood analysis

..... blood and sperm are infectious ......

Figure 81. Relations

If this was what (s)he wanted to know, (s)he can select a new network about a totally different subject. (S)he uses select concept and types eye. (S)he then gets the network presented in Figure 82.

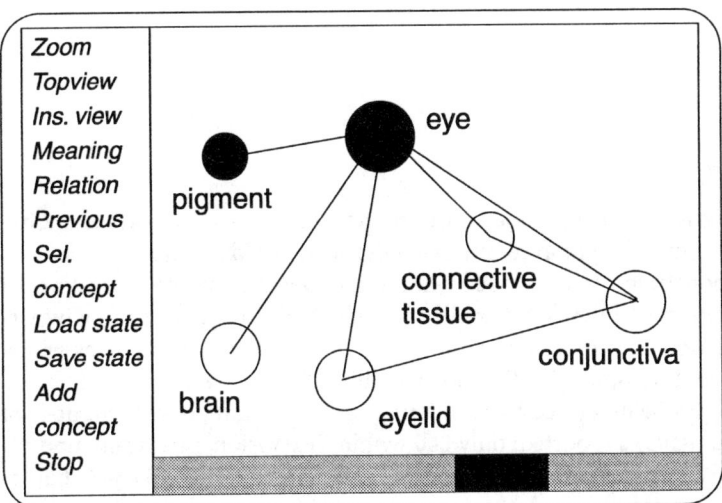

Figure 82. New network centered around 'eye'

E. Second Demonstrator Case Description

Introduction

This appendix is included for the reader to get some idea how a hypertext/hypermedia program, with graph computation included, could function.

This demonstrator is developed within the Department of Education of Twente University as a hypertext application which will be extended to a hypermedia application. It is more or less a further development on the ideas which where used for developing TextVision. The difference between TextVision and this program can be described by comparing the maximum possible number of articles (documents) supported: only 200 within TextVision, practically unlimited within this demonstrator (2 147 483 647 articles with 2 147 483 647 characters each).

An article is considered to be information (data) grouped under a keyword (or heading).

There are different ways to find information. It is possible to search for keywords, or just browse through the articles. To prevent the user from getting lost, there is the possibility to ask for a graphical overview in which the most important references within or to an article or set of articles can be viewed. In this way the most important references between articles can be viewed without having to read or view the articles.

General information

Windows are used for presenting information. The windows have a number of parts, and in different windows different parts will be shown. In Figure 83 a window with different parts, some of them marked, is shown.

There can be more than one window on the screen. Selecting and topping a window can be done by clicking in a part of the window to be selected and topped.

Besides normal movable windows there are dialogue windows. These windows can have different forms. Some dialogue windows must be dealt with by the user before anything else can be done. Some dialogue windows are movable while others are not. In dialogue windows different fields may be present: text entry fields, selection or list fields, buttons, title bar, close box, and/or size box. Two examples of dialogue windows are shown in Figure 84.

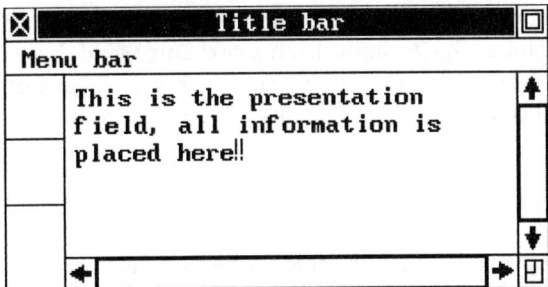

Figure 83: Basis window for reading reference material

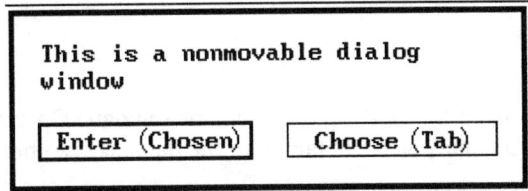

Figure 84: Response window

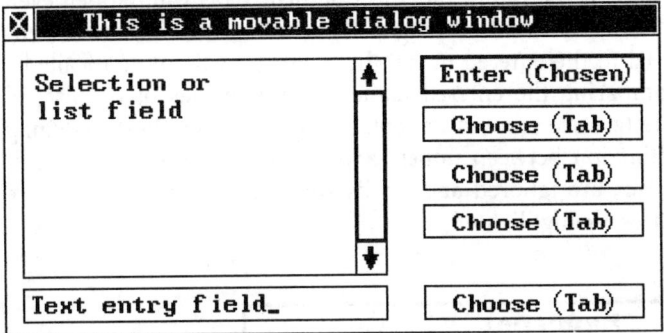

Figure 85: Text entry fields, selection or list fields

A dialogue window can contain a text entry field. When the dialogue window is activated, all keyboard input is redirected to its text entry field, all entered characters appear in this field, and the backspace key is supported.

Buttons can be activated by clicking on them with the mouse or by using the keyboard. One of the buttons will have a thick border, this one may be activated by using the enter or return key. By pressing the tab key with or without pressing the shift key, another button may be selected. The selected button will get a thick border. If the text (or icon) within a button is gray, the button is inactive and cannot be activated.

A selection or list field is a special kind of presentation field. In selection or list field a list is shown, sometimes due to input from a text entry field, but it could also be a list of files in a directory. The difference is that whereas one or more items in a selection field can be selected, no items can be selected in a list field.

Use

The demonstrator starts by showing its start-up screen, which contains a copyright notice, and a number of buttons: Texts, Pictures, Sounds, Overviews, Databases, and Quit.

Clicking on the different buttons give different actions, which are described in the next paragraphs.

Opening Texts

After choosing the button Texts from the start-up dialogue, the dialogue Open Texts will be shown. Using this dialogue, texts contained in the database can be selected and opened.

The name of an article can be typed into the text entry field. When the list of possible names is shortened until it is less than or equal to the maximum amount of entries that can be stored in a special memory buffer (50 to 100 entries), the list will be displayed in the selection field. This will happen even when the user is not yet done with typing in the whole name. If there are entries which are equal to the entered name, these entries will automatically be selected. When comparing the entered name and the entries of the list, all characters except letters are ignored or replaced by the letters best matching them, with no distinction between upper- and lower-case letters. So spaces, diacritical marks, etc., are ignored and words such as *däs*, *Das* and *das* are equal. Selected entries are highlighted.

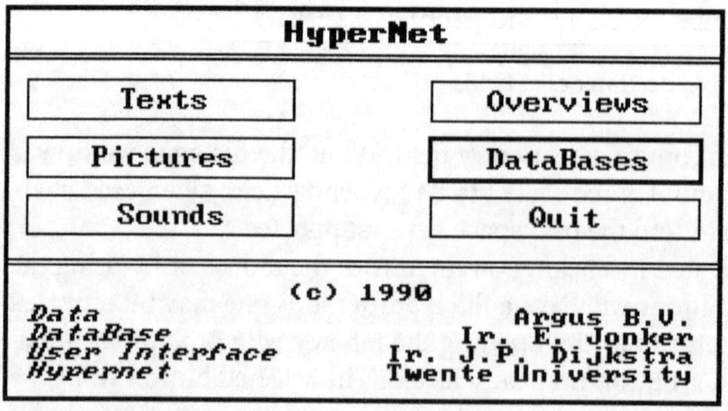

Figure 86. Start-up screen

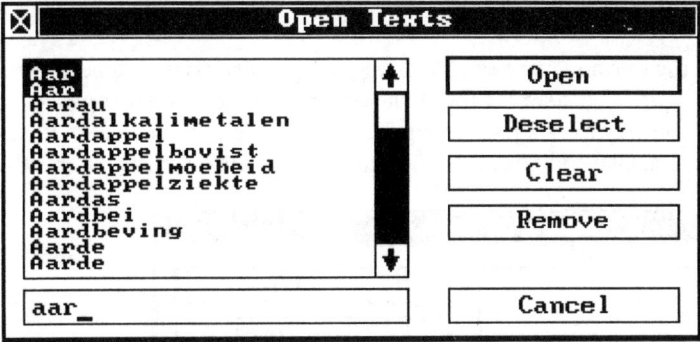

Figure 87. Open text dialogue

In Figure 87, the selection field is field with a number of entries and a name is being entered into the text entry field. (In this figure the selected entries are displayed inverse, white on black.)

When entries have appeared in the selection field, the user can follow two approaches. First, the user can continue to type the full name of the wanted article or select entries in the selection field. There may be more entries in the selection field than can be shown at once. In this second case the user can use the slide bar to scroll through the whole list, while selecting entries. Selecting and deselecting can be done by clicking on an entry. A list of entries can be selected and/or deselected by dragging from the first entry to the last entry wanted. Selecting twice is equal to deselecting.

Opening Pictures

After choosing the button Pictures the dialogue Open Pictures will be shown. Using this dialogue pictures contained in the database can be selected and opened in the same way as when choosing Texts.

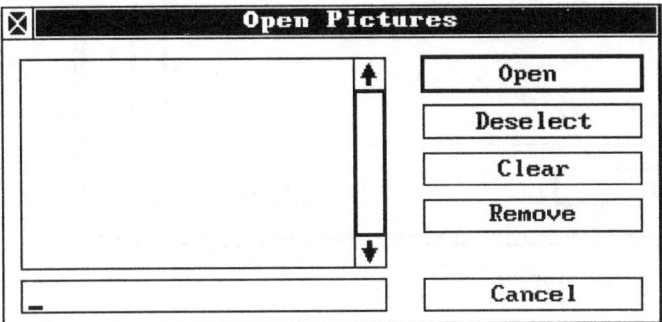

Figure 88. Open pictures dialogue

Opening an Overview

After choosing the button Overview, the dialogue Open Overview will be shown. Using this dialogue, overviews of the database can be created and opened. It works in the same way as when choosing Texts, with the difference that all selected articles are displayed in one overview, not in separate overviews.

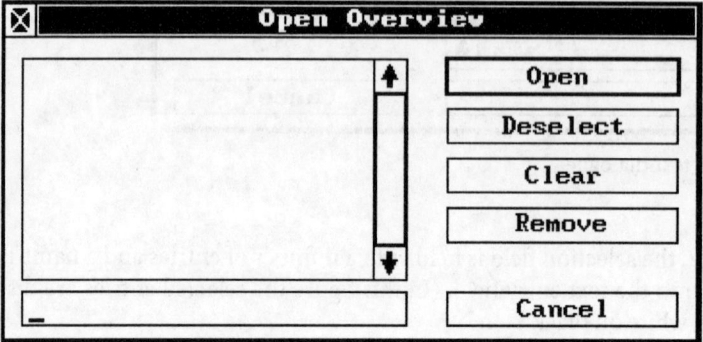

Figure 89. Open overview dialogue

Selecting a Database

After choosing the button Database the dialogue Select a Database will be shown. This button is only available if there is more than one database available to choose from. In this dialogue one of the available databases must be selected to work with in order to use the program.

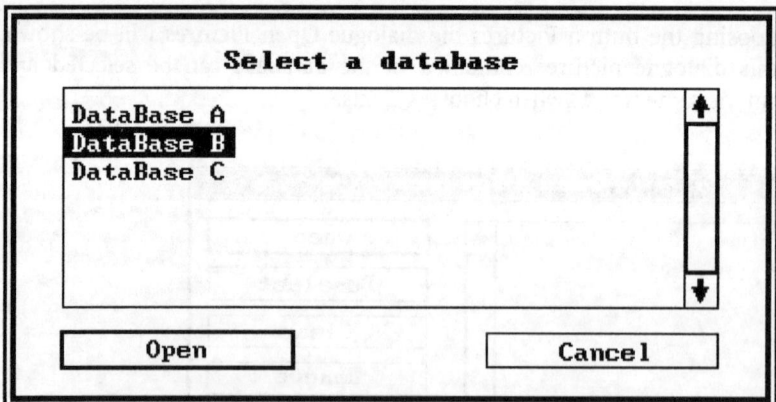

Figure 90. Select a database dialogue

After choosing the database the user can continue. If another database was already in use, all windows opened using that database will be closed and deleted after choosing another database.

Opening an Article from a Text

In the text some words have a colored background. These works are marked. The color of the background will be a light shade of cyan or yellow (In this black and white user's guide the background will be black instead of those colors). If the mouse cursor is moved over the marked words, it changes shape from an arrow to a hand, if the marked word is a reference to another article. By double clicking, the article referred to is opened. The two background colors are used to show the difference between references added by the author (cyan) and references added by the computer (yellow). In general the cyan references will be more important than the yellow ones. Sometimes, however, an article referred to by the author is not in the list of articles in the database. In that case the cursor does not change its shape when over a cyan reference; the reference cannot be opened.

Opening an Overview from a Text

By clicking on a marked word (or words) with the right mouse button, the overview related to that word is created and opened.

Icons

In a text window there is a vertical palette or button bar with five icons, from top to bottom, 'Open Overview', 'Add to TextVision database', 'References to text exist', 'References to pictures exist', and 'References to sounds exist' (Figure 91). These icons are shortcuts for menu items with those names.

Figure 91. Palette in a text or picture window

Hotspots

Hotspots can be present in a picture. A hotspot is a part within the picture which has a reference associated with it. Hotspots can be detected by using the mouse: The cursor will change from an arrow to a hand when above a hotspot. By double clicking in a hotspot the article referred to is opened.

Overviews

One of the special features is the ability to visualize references between articles in what will be called an overview. An overview is determined according to the references stored with the articles. If an article has more references to/from it, it is supposed (by the program) to be more important. A higher importance improves the chances for an article to be shown in an overview.

There are two possible ways to determine and present an overview: According to indegree or outdegree. According to indegree implies that the references *to* the selected article(s) are presented in the overview. According to outdegree implies that the references *from* the selected article(s) are presented in the overview. If the overview is presented according to indegree, the icon with the ingoing arrows is presented. If it is presented according to outdegree, the icon with the outgoing arrows is presented.

When determining an overview according to indegree, the importance of an article is determined by the number of direct and indirect references made *to* that article. When determining an overview according to outdegree, it is just the opposite, the importance of an article is determined by the number of direct and indirect references made *from* that article.

Overview Windows

An overview window differs somewhat from text and picture windows. It has a title bar, close box, zoom box, palette, size box, and presentation field. But the palette contains different icons of a different size and it also has its own menu bar with a menu (Figure 92).

In the presentation field a small overview is drawn. An overview is composed of nodes drawn as circles and links drawn as lines between the circles. A node is associated with an article and a link is associated with a reference. Direct references are drawn as normal lines, indirect references (references which go via a node not shown) are drawn as dotted lines. If the window is zoomed, the names of the nodes appear beneath the nodes.

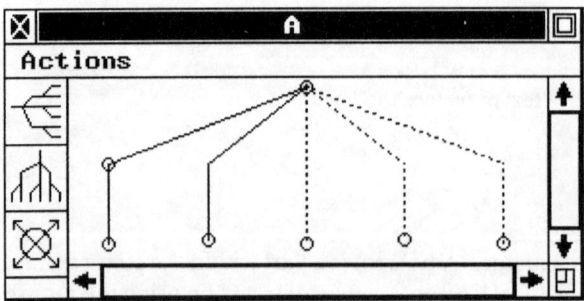

Figure 92. An overview window with an overview presented according to outdegree

Selecting and Deselecting Nodes

Selecting and deselecting a node can be done by moving the mouse cursor above the node to be selected or deselected (the cursor changes to a hand) and then clicking. The border of the node will change color: If it is selected it will becomes red, if deselected black. The name of the node will also change color, yellow if selected, invisible or light cyan if deselected. The name is invisible if scaling is on (which it is by default) and the node is not selected (Figure 93). If the node is selected the name appears (Figure 94).

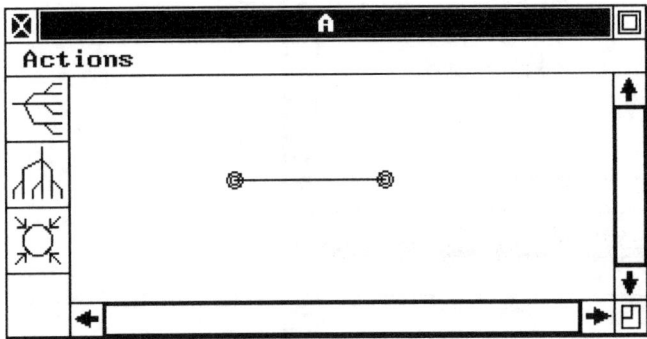

Figure 93: Selecting and deselecting a node

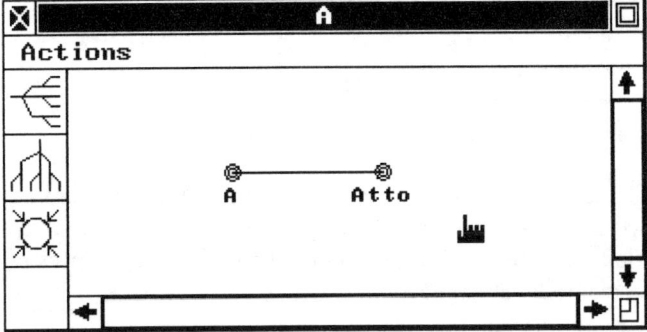

Figure 94: After selecting a node

Dragging a Node

By dragging a node in an overview, the appearance of that overview can be changed. If the shift key is held down during dragging, all selected nodes are dragged. There is a special feature for overview windows: Not only is it possible to drag nodes within an overview, but it is also possible to drag nodes from one overview to another. If nodes are dragged from one overview to another a copy of the nodes is placed in the other overview and the original nodes will stay at their starting position. (When dragging within a window no copy is made and the original nodes will move.) After dragging nodes to another window the overview for that other window will be updated.

Dragging a node from one overview to another is demonstrated in the display sequence in Figure 95. The node E is dragged from overview E to overview A.

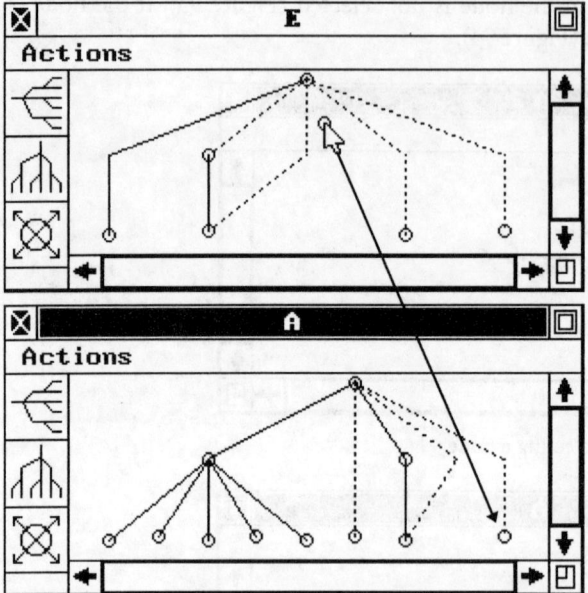

Figure 95. Dragging a concept node from one network to another

After placing the node E in the overview of A the old overview A is reconfigured. Figure 96 clearly shows a different overview A. Opening an article from an overview is possible by (left) double clicking in a node. If the shift key is pressed while clicking, all selected nodes are opened.

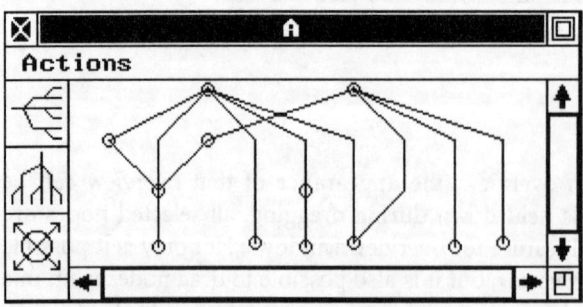

Figure 96. Opening an article from an overview

Opening an Overview from Another Overview

Opening an overview from another overview is possible by right clicking in a node of the other overview. If the shift key is pressed while clicking, all selected nodes are used when determining the new overview.

Overview Icons

There are three icons visible in the vertical palette or button bar of an overview window. The bottom icon has two forms, depending on the way the overview is displayed (Figure 97).

Figure 97. Palette in overview window

The icons in the palette are shortcuts for the menu items Draw horizontally, Draw vertically, Show by outdegree, or Show by indegree.

Menus

In the overview the menu bar contains a menu with several items (Figure 98). Most of these items are self-explanatory.

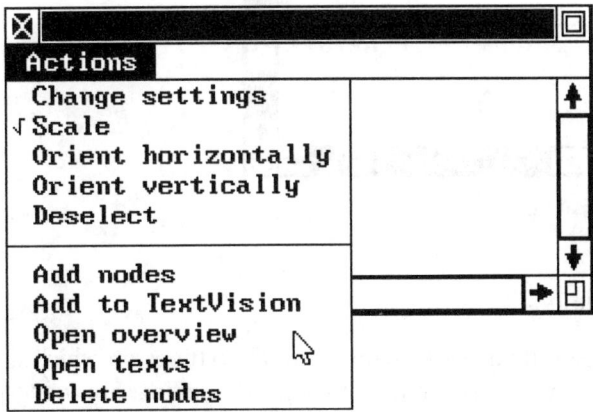

Figure 98. Menu bar of overview window

However, a few items do need a bit of explanation. The first item, Add to TextVision, is a special option to make it possible for someone to extract a subset from a database for use with TextVision (the earlier two-dimensional version of TextVision-3D, which is explained in Appendix F).

The second item is Scale. If scaling is on, for an overview, the nodes in the overview are displayed very small. If scaling is off for an overview the nodes are drawn with their names sized in proportion to their degree value. Also, the links will have arrows to indicate the directions of the references. If scaling is on, a mark is displayed before the scaling choice in the menu.

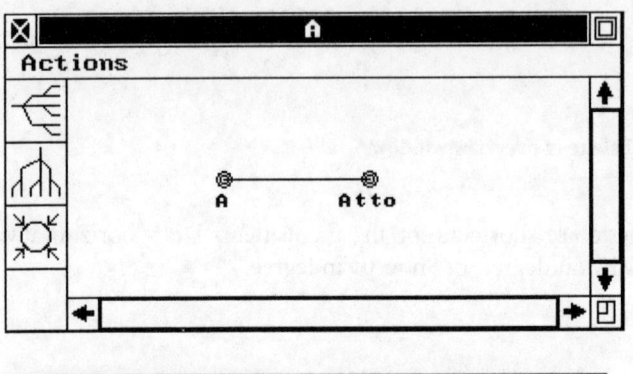

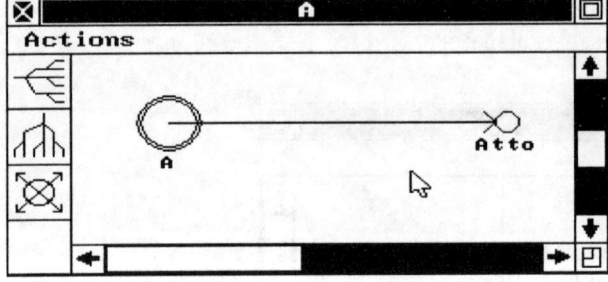

Figure 99. Scaling off and scaling on

Dialogue Change Settings

The third item is Change setting. These settings are the settings on which the calculation and presentation of the overviews is based. The settings are changed in the dialogue presented after selecting this item (Figure 100). The dialogue is composed of three buttons, two sets of radio buttons, and six slides. The slides are not used to move a presentation field, but to give visual feedback on a number of settings. A setting is set at its minimum when the slide box is at the left end of the slide and at its maximum when the slide box is at the right end.

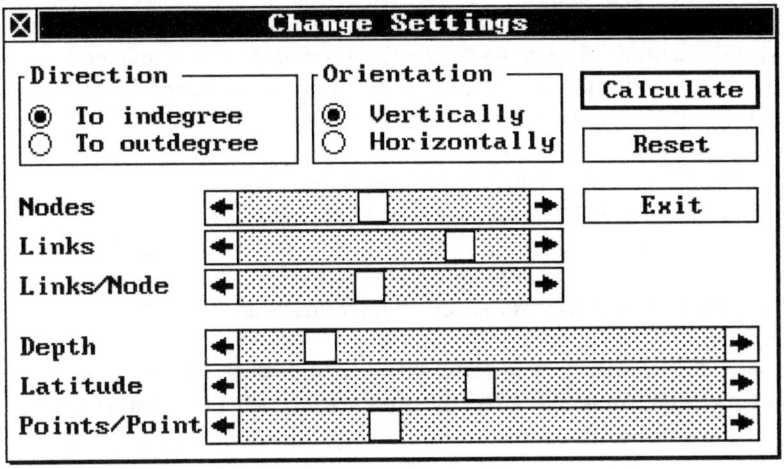

Figure 100. Dialogue for changing settings

- The settings only have an effect on the overview from which the dialogue was opened.
- The settings often have some effect on each other; in the following descriptions of the settings some but not all of the possible effects are mentioned.
- The calculate button uses the new values set to refresh the overview in the same window and closes the dialogue.
- The reset button resets the values to the values the dialogue had when it was opened.
- The exit button does the same as the reset button and then closes the dialogue without reconfiguring the overview.
- The direction radio buttons have the same function as the icons 'present to indegree and outdegree' in the overview window.
- The orientation radio buttons have the same functions as the icons with the same names. The radio button Orient horizontally does the same as the upper icon in the palette of the overview window, the radio button Orient vertically the same as the middle icon in the palette.
- The nodes slide is used to set the maximum total number of nodes that may be displayed in an overview.

With the lines slide the maximum total number of lines in an overview can be varied. With the lines per node slide the maximum number of links displayed to/from each node in an overview can be set. The depth slide is used to set the search depth. If the depth is set to its minimal value, then the search is only done to articles directly referred to/from. If the depth is set to a greater value, the search will be deeper for important articles, and articles which are referred to indirectly are also searched. Articles are deemed more important when they have more references to/from them.

With the latitude slide the latitude can be set. The latitude can vary between zero and one. Latitude is coupled to Depth. A smaller latitude makes articles which are directly referred to relatively more important than articles indirectly referred to/from. If the latitude is greater the relative difference in importance gets smaller. A small latitude gives a very local overview, a big latitude gives a more global overview value, depending on the depth.

The points per point slide is like the slide Lines/Point but with the difference that if during the determination of the overview a reference is found from one article to another, this reference is only added to the list of references from this point if the article is not referred to from another article and the list of references is not yet filled.

All these different slides and radio buttons have different impacts on the overview presented. Some only affect the presentation, others the content.

F. TextVision-3D

Why TextVision-3D? The differences with the older TextVision version are color support, 3D display emulation, and a user interface more following the Apple user-interface guidelines. It was hoped that these differences would make it possible to display more data in a user-friendly way than was possible in the older two-dimensional version of TextVision.

As with most Macintosh applications, after starting up an introductory message is displayed (Figure 101). After this a dialogue box is displayed asking for the name of the user (Figure 102). This dialogue is used to keep track of which users are logged and deter-mining their privileges.

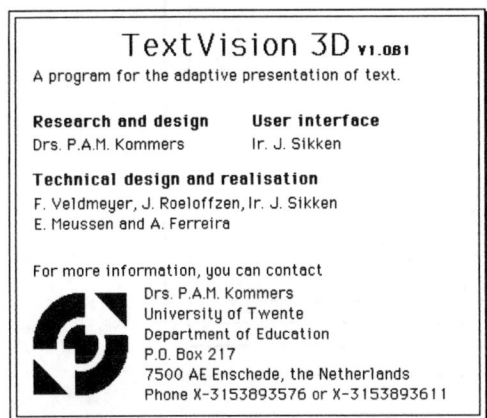

Figure 101. The introductory message

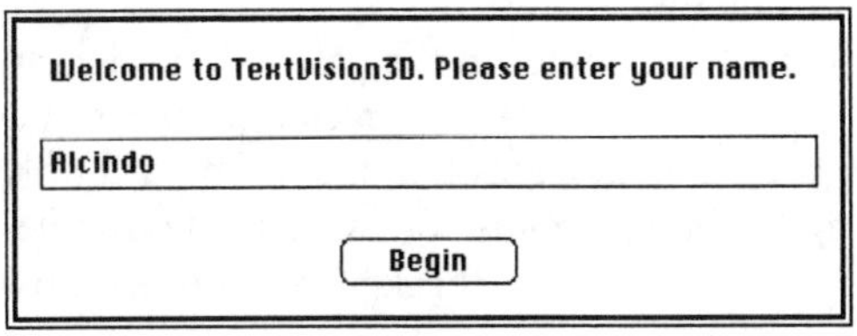

Figure 102. User name dialogue

Depending on the privileges of the user, the user has a different menu bar. If the user has full privileges, the user will also have a print menu, otherwise this menu will be absent (Figure 103).

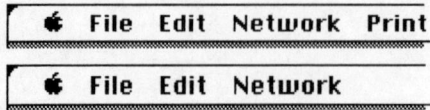

Figure 103. The full and reduced menu bars

After entering the name and dismissing the dialogue box, the privileges of the user are decided and a window is opened. This window is the network window in which a network can be build.

The network window consists of two parts, a part for the palette on the left and a part for the network (Figure 104).

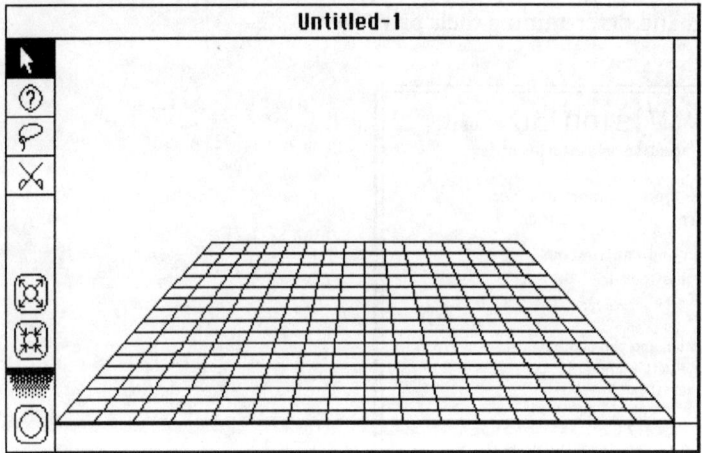

Figure 104. The network window

In the palette there are a number of icons. With these icons a number of modes and functions can be actuated. Here a number of the most used function can be found without having to resort to a menu.

By clicking on one of the four cursor rectangles in the palette a mode and cursor are selected (Figure 105). By clicking once in a rectangle the background of the rectangle becomes gray. This indicates that this mode will only support one action before reverting to the normal mode (arrow). By double-clicking on a cursor rectangle the rectangle inverts (background black), now the mode will not change as long as legal actions are tried.

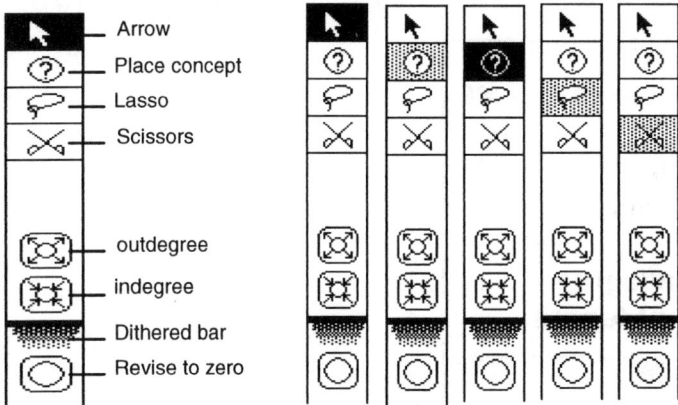

Figure 105. The palette and some of its states

In the palette a dithered or colored bar can be found. When the computer is in a black and white mode a dithered bar will be displayed. If the computer uses more than 15 colors a colored bar is displayed. The colors or dithering of the borders of the globes are drawn using the same rule. Which dithering or color is used depends on the centrality of the concept represented by the globe. A greater centrality gives blacker or redder borders, a smaller centrality gives a whiter or bluer border. The bar is there just to help the user.

Depending on the version there are two or three buttons in the palette. The two buttons which are always used have four arrows pointing outward from or inward to a circle. By clicking on the button with the arrows pointing inward the indegree is calculated. And by clicking on the button with the arrows pointing outward the outdegree is calculated. The third button has no arrows, only a circle, and can be used to display a network with all concepts of the same degree.

The network menu is the menu with all the special functions of TextVision-3D (Figure 106). It should be noted that a few changes have been made in this menu compared to the original TextVision (2D version 4.0) network menu. The menu items Remove Concept and Confirm Concept have been removed and Rotate has been added. Remove Concept was removed because it did not adhere to the Apple desktop interface guidelines. By using Clear in the edit menu, the se-lected objects, concepts, text, or relations can be removed. Confirm concept was removed because the difference between concepts made from within a text window and concepts made from within the network window has been removed for now. Rotate is added for the possibility of rotating the whole or part of the network.

There are three special cursors and modes in TextVision-3D (Figure 107): the place concept cursor, the lasso, and the scissors. Besides these special cursors the arrow, I-beam, and clock are also used (Figure 107).

```
┌─────────────────────────────────┐
│ Network                         │
├─────────────────────────────────┤
│ New                       ⌘T    │
│ Edit name concept...      ⌘E    │
│ ································· │
│ Add relation              ⌘+    │
│ Delete relation           ⌘−    │
│ ································· │
│ ✓Revise to indegree             │
│ Revise to outdegree             │
│ ································· │
│ Rotate                          │
└─────────────────────────────────┘
```

Figure 106. The network menu

Figure 107. The different cursors

Some explanation about the different menu items, cursors, and cursor modes is needed, because of the difference between working with TextVision and TextVision-3D.

Adding New Concepts

Selecting the New concept item in the network menu changes the cursor mode into the New Concept or Place Concept mode. Changing to this mode will make the cursor change into a (?) when in the network window. This is quite different to TextVision where immediately a new concept is placed in a arbitrary place in the network window after asking for the name of the concept. The user moves this cursor to the place where a new globe is wanted and clicks. Then a dialogue window appears where the name of the concept can be entered (Figure 108). The length of the name is limited to 63 characters. The user can cancel, if a new concept is not wanted. In the other case the user can click on the OK button or use the return key to add and place the new concept. If the name is already in use, a warning is issued and another name has to be entered (Figure 109).

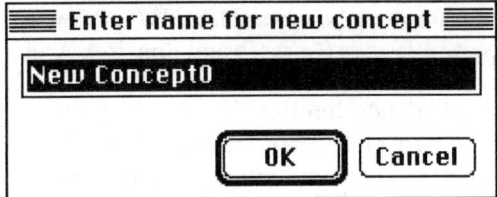

Figure 108. Concept name dialogue

Figure 109. 'Name in Use' dialogue

Figure 110. Newly placed globe

If needed the name of the concept can be changed by selecting the Edit name of concept item in the network menu (Figure 111). This calls up a dialogue box with the name of the selected concept within it. The name can only be changed to one not already in use.

We will now construct a network about the Netherlands Antilles. These islands are an autonomous part of the Kingdom of the Netherlands. The autonomy is arrange by the Statute, a sort of super constitution arranging basic rights of all parts of the Kingdom of the Netherlands. One of the rights of the Islands is to become independent. This is something which Surinam, previously also a part of the Kingdom of the Netherlands, has already done.

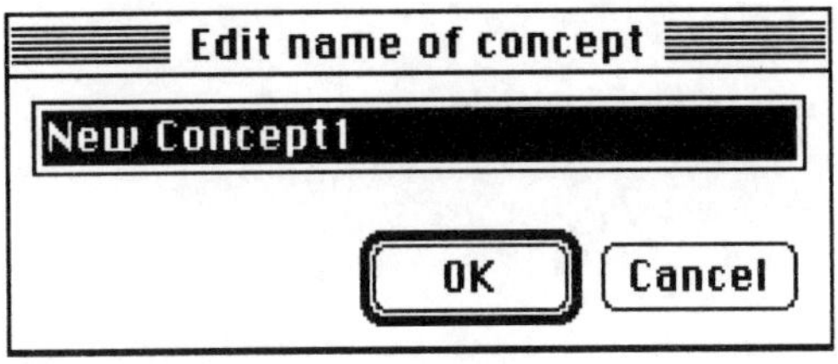

Figure 111. Edit name dialogue

The islands are split in two groups, the three Windward Islands (St. Maarten, St. Eustatius, and Saba) and the Leeward Islands (Curaçao and Bonaire). Aruba is also included, even though it is no longer a part of the Netherlands Antilles. It still is a part the Kingdom of the Netherlands, but has what is called a Status Aparte, a separate status. Aruba is a part of Leeward Islands. Most of these items, and the references among them, can be found in our final network. See Figure 112.

Adding Relations

Selecting the Add Relation item from the network menu changes the cursor mode into the Add Relation mode. Changing to this mode will make the cursor change into a lasso 𝒫 when in the network window. The lasso mode is used for connecting globes together, thus adding relations between concepts. The lasso is placed on the globe to which a pipe is to be added. Then the lasso is dragged to the globe the pipe is to be connected to. When dragging, a thick black line between the source-globe and the lasso provides feedback to the user. When the lasso moves over a globe the globe inverts so that the user will always know which globe the pipe is going to be connected to. By releasing the mouse button when the lasso is on a globe, a pipe is added to that globe. If there already was a pipe between the two globes, no pipe is added. If the lasso in the palette was inverted (black background) and a pipe is added, the cursor stays a lasso; in all other cases the cursor will become an arrow.

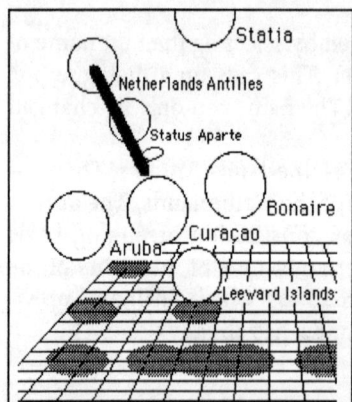

Figure 112. Dragging from the source node to the target node

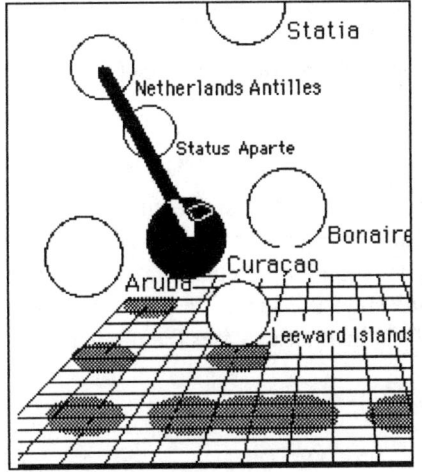

Figure 113. Above the target node: During dragging a node is inverted when the cursor is above it

Figure 114. Releasing the mouse button stops dragging and creates a relation

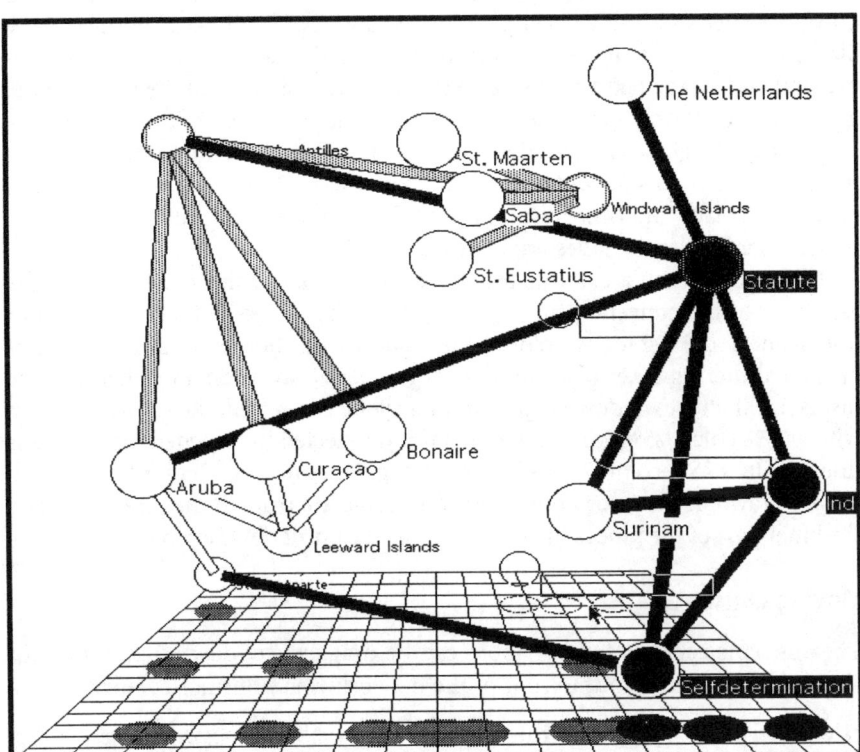

Figure 115. A possible network with multiple nodes and relations

Deleting Relations

Choosing the Delete relation item from the network menu will delete any rela-
tion(s) selected in a text window.

Relations can also be deleted by using the scissors (✂). The scissors
mode can be enabled by clicking on the scissors pictogram in the palette. By
clicking on a pipe it is deleted. When clicking on a globe, the globe with all connected pipes are deleted. If the wrong globe or pipe is deleted don't worry, it is
always undoable. After an action the mode stays the same if a pipe or globe is
snipped and the lasso in the palette was black; in all other cases the mode reverts
to normal and the cursor to an arrow.

Selecting Concepts and Relations

Because the arrow is primarily used for selecting and dragging, some notes may
be useful about the appearance of the globes and pipes when selected. This is
different for the pipes and the globes and also for computers using a color or
black and white display. First, globes in black and white: A globe has a thin black
outside border and inside it a larger dithered border. The dithered border can be
black, white, or gray, depending on the centrality of the concept the globe represents. When the text window is neither opened nor selected the center of the
globe is white. If only the globe is selected the center is black. If the text window
is open and the globe is selected, the center has a 75% black dithering; in the last
possible case, unselected but opened, the center has a 25% black dithering. Pipes
drawn on a black and white display are black when selected or dithered the same
as the inner border the pipes originate from.

Globes drawn on a color display have a border in a color depending on the
centrality of the concept represented by the globe. If the globe is selected, but
not opened, the center is colored the same as the border. If the concept is
opened, dithering takes place in roughly the same way as on a black and white
display: If the text window is open and the globe is selected, the center is drawn
with a 75% color, 25% white dithering; if it unselected but opened, the center is
drawn with a 25% color, 75% white dithering. Pipes drawn in color have a thick
border drawn in the color of the globe they originate from. If the pipe is selected
the inner part of the pipe is the same color as the border of the pipe.

Moving Concepts

The concepts represented by globes can be dragged up, down, left, right, but
also to the back and to the front of the network when normal cursor mode is
selected. This is when the arrow cursor (↖) is visible. Dragging the globes up,
down, left and right is quite trivial, and can be done in much the same way as the

for Finder. Dragging the globes forward or backward is less trivial. This was solved by using the grid, as shown in Figure 116 drawn at the bottom of the network window. Shadows of the globes in the network are visible on this grid. To drag a globe to the back just drag its shadow. If the mouse is moved vertically up or down, the globes follow the gridlines!

Nodes are dragged to make the network clearer to oneself and others. Whereas two-dimensional versions of the program can only order a network in two dimensions this three-dimensional version makes it possible to order the nodes in three dimensions. This makes it possible to move secondary nodes to a secondary level, tertiary nodes to a tertiary level, etc.

In Figure 117, the individual islands are in the foreground, Netherlands Antilles and Leeward and Windward Islands are on a secondary level, and Independence, Status Aparte, and Statute, Autonomy are on a tertiary level.

Revising to Indegree

The Revise to indegree item in the network menu will compute the centrality of the network according to the indegree computation. Often the cursor will change to a watch ( ). When the computer is busy with a calculation for a longer time, the watch is displayed so the user will know something time-consuming is happening.

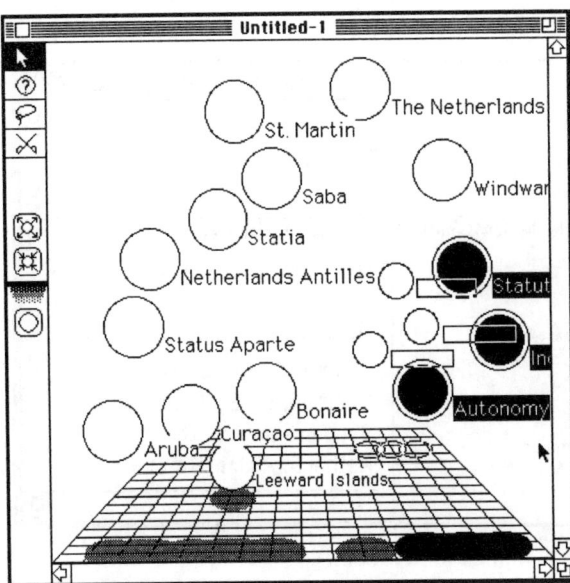

Figure 116. Dragging some nodes from front to back

Revising to Outdegree

The Revise to outdegree item in the network menu will compute the centrality of the network according to the outdegree computation.

Text Windows

The text window pertaining to the text associated with a concept can be opened by double-clicking on the globe representing the concept. The text window contains three parts: The subterm view, the superterm view with the concepts referring to this concept, and the text view with the text of the concept (Figure 117).

The upper part contains subterms Saba, St. Eustatius and St. Maarten. The middle part contains a superterm the Netherlands Antilles. The bottom part contains the associated text.

Subterm View

In the upper view in the text window is the view with the concepts this concept refers to. In the network window these are drawn as pipes in the same color as the globe representing this concept. A relation can be removed by clicking on the name of the soubrette and thereafter selecting Remove relation from the network menu. (beware–selected superterms in the superterm view will also be deleted). Also, by double-clicking on a subterm the text window of a subterm can be opened.

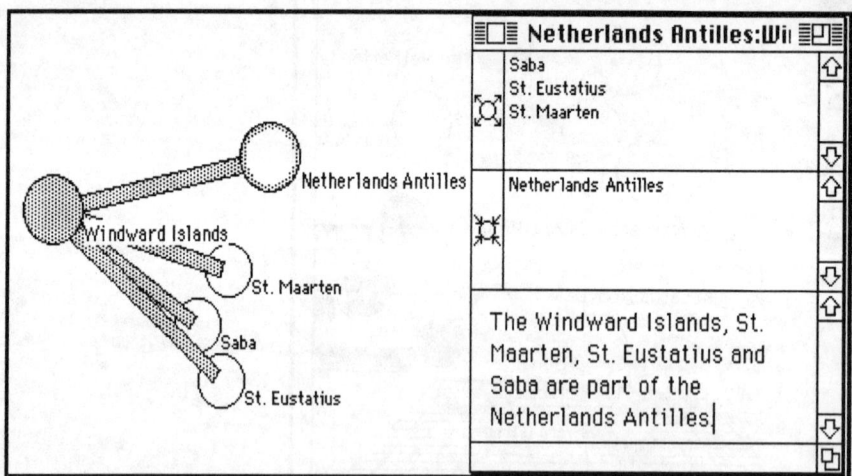

Figure 117. A text window (right) with network window

Superterm View

In the superterm view, the middle view, all superterms (concepts whose relations refer to this concept) are listed. It works like the subterm view.

Text View

In the bottom view of the text window, all text related to the concept represented by the globe can be found. Such actions as cut, paste, copy, clear are all possible. Parts of the text can be selected with the mouse. By using add relation in the network menu a new concept can be added with a name as the selected text. Again, a name cannot be longer than 63 characters.

Rotating the Network

Rotate is a new menu item. Selecting it calls the rotate dialogue (Figure 118). With this dialogue the user can rotate the network or a selected part of it.

The angle of rotation of the network can be adjusted in several ways. The angle can be typed, or the mouse can be used to push with the mouse button on the arrows placed around the three axes in the dialogue (Figure 119).

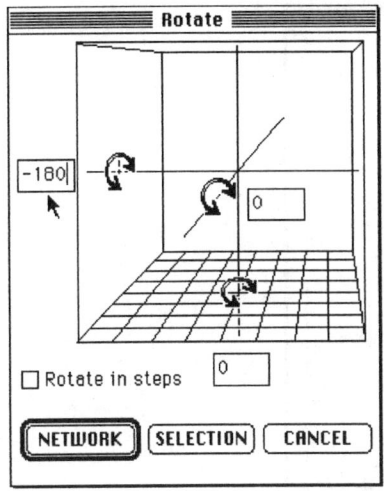

Figure 118. The 'rotate' dialogue

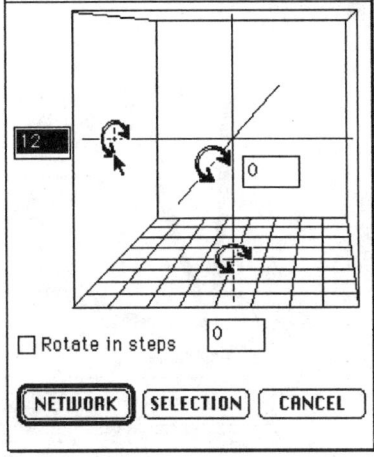

Figure 119. Pushing an arrow

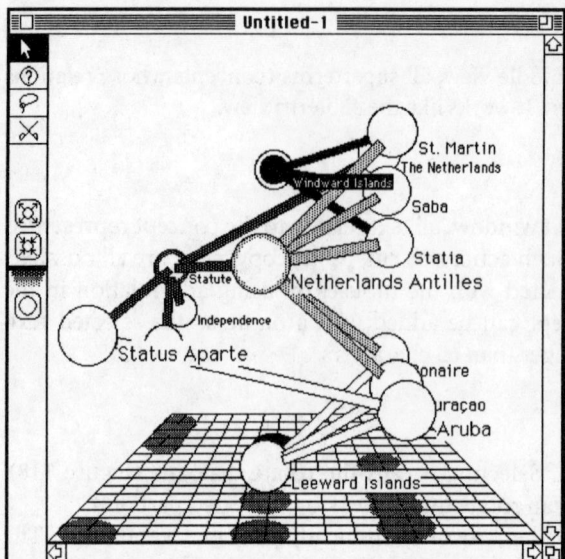

Figure 120. A view of the rotation process: The geographical concepts are on the right and the structural concepts are on the left

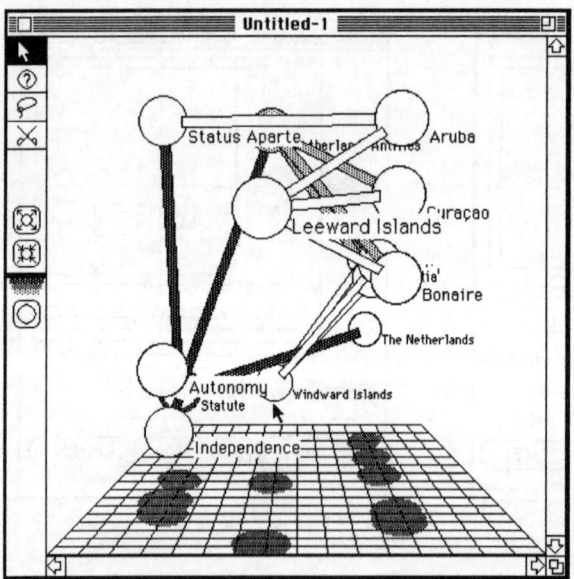

Figure 121. Rotating 90 degrees from the bottom to the front: Leeward Island concepts appear on a vertical line

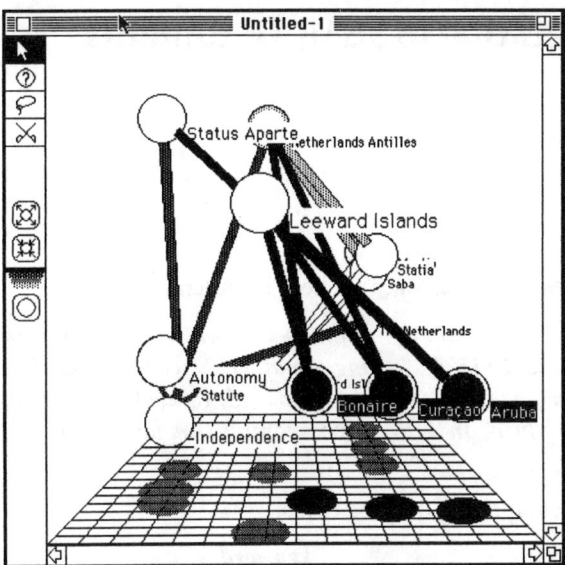

Figure 122. Rotating

In Figure 122 the Windward Islands are somewhat hidden, and the concepts related to the Leeward Islands are visible. The Leewards have now been rotated so that they are on a horizontal line. The rotation angles will never be bigger than 360 degrees nor smaller than minus 360 degrees. If the Rotate in steps button is checked the network is rotated in a number of steps.

By selecting the 'Network' button the whole network is rotated. If the 'Selection' button is selected only the selected concepts are rotated.

G. Prolog Interpretation of SGML Documents

Traditional typesetting codes (Italic passages are kept in Dutch).

@Y369@-Amalrik@BR (Fr.: >Amaury<), naam van twee koningen van Jeruzalem: >Amalrik I <(1135\1^1174), koning vanaf 1162, wist tijdelijk (tot 1171) zijn protectoraat over Egypte te vestigen; >Amalrik II <(1144\1^1205), werd in 1194 koning van Cyprus, in 1197 tevens koning van Jeruzalem. Hij zetelde in Accoa.

SGML-based encoded text, comprising the next fields:

<tw>:	*trefwoord*	*keyword*
<bt>:	*betekenisveld*	*explanation field*
<c>:	*italic*	*italic*
<vn>:	*voornaam*	*forename*
<a>:	*paragraaf (alleen sluitcode)*	*paragraph delimiter*

<tw>Amalrik</tw> <bt>(Fr.: <c>Amaury</c>), naam van twee koningen van Jeruzalem:<vn>Amalrik I</vn> (1135*t-1174), koning vanaf 1162, wist tijdelijk (tot 1171) zijn protectoraat over Egypte te vestigen; vn>Amalrik II</vn> (1144*t-1205), werd in 1194 koning van Cyprus, in 1197 tevens koning van Jeruzalem. Hij zetelde in Acco.</a></bt>

The next article has been taken from a currently available Dutch dictionary, encoded in GML.

<TW>:	*TrefWoord*	keyword
<A>:	*Afbreekpunt*	hyphenation dot
<K>:	*Klemtoon*	accent or stress (mark)
<USTW>:	*UitSpraak TrefWoord*	pronunciation keyword
<HKTW>:	*HerKomst TrefWoord*	origin of keyword
<VV>:	*VerVoeging*	declination
<TS>:	*Toegelaten Spelling*	allowed spelling
<BT> :	*BeTekenis*	meaning
<SY> :	*Synoniem*	synonym

<TW>re<A>va<A>lo<A>ri<A>se<A>ren</TW>
<USTW>*a-<K>zee*a-</USTW>
<HKTW>*aZFr</HKTW> <VV>revaloriseerde, h. gerevaloriseerd</VV>
<TS>revalorizeren</TS>

<BT>opnieuw waarde of geldigheid geven; <SY>herwaarderen</SY>;
andere waarde aan de munt geven</BT>

option :	The given symbol or combination of symbols may or may not occur.
seq :	The given predicate may appear one or several times.
option_seq :	The given predicate may appear zero or several times.

```
/* article/2 */
article([end_of_file|_],[ ]) :- ! .
article(In,Out) :-
option('#',In,Between) ,
/* optional # before */
'C'('<TW>',Between,Between1) ,
option('<VC>',Between1,Between2) ,
! , rest_article(Between2,Out) .
/* rest_article/2 */
rest_article(In, Out) :-
( key_word(In,Out)
; abbreviation(In,Out)
; allowed_spelling(In,Out) ) , ! .


/* key_word/2 */
key_word(In,Out) :-
key_word_extension(In,Between) , ! ,
option('</VC>',Between,Between1) ,
'C'('</TW>',Between1,Between2) ,
option(punctuation_mark(Between2,
Between3)) ,
option(number(Between3,Between4)) ,
gramm(Between4,Between5) ,
option(punctuation_mark(Between5,
Between6)) ,
option_seq(same_sp,Between6,Between7),
option_seq(synonym,Between7,Between8) ,
option(verkl_vorm(Between8,Between9)) ,
option(vrwl_vorm(Between9,Between10)) ,
option(punctuation_mark(Between10,
Between11)) , ! ,
meaning_key_word(Between11,
Between12) ,
option(derived(Between12,Out)) , ! .


/* punctuation_mark/2 */
punctuation_mark(In,Out) :-
'C'(@(Y),In,Out) ,
characters(Y,Inh) ,
punctuation_mark(Inh) .
```

```
/* means_key_word/2 */
means_key_word(In,Out) :-
( seq(nbr,In,Out)
; 'C'('<BT>',In,Between) ,
meaning(Between,Out) ) , ! .
/* abbreviation/2 */
abbreviation(In,Out) :-
'C'('<AF>',In,Between) , ! ,
tw(Between,Between1) ,
'C'('</AF>',Between1,Between2) ,
option('</VC>',Between2,Between3) ,
'C'('</TW>',Between3,Between4) ,
option(number(Between4,Between5)) ,

option('<TWAK>',tw,'</TWAK>',
Between5,Between6) ,
gramm(Between6,Between7) , ! ,
'C'('<BT>',Between7,Between8) ,
rest_abbreviation(Between8,Out) , ! .

/* rest_abbreviation/2 */
rest_abbreviation(In,Out) :-
nba_short(In,Between) , ! ,
option_seq(bt_nba_short,Between,Out) , ! .
rest_abbreviation(In,Out) :-
means_short(In,Between) ,
'C'('</BT>',Between,Out) , ! .

/* allowed_spelling/2 */
allowed_spelling(In,Out) :-
'C'('<TWTS>',In,Between) ,
tw(Between,Between1) ,
'C'('</TWTS>',Between1,Between2) ,
'C'('</TW>',Between2,Between3) , ! ,
gramm(Between3,Between4) ,
option_seq(synonym,Between4,Between5),
option_seq(vrwl_kwts,Between5,Between6,
'C'('<BT>',Between6,Between7) , ! ,
seq(chr_gtl_br,Between7,Between8) ,
preferred_sp(Between8,Between9) ,
'C'('</BT>',Between9,Out) , ! .
```

```
/* tw/2 */
tw(In,Out) :-
seq(chr_a_k,In,Between) ,
option(replace_bar(Between,Out)) , ! .
/* gramm/2 */
gramm(In,Out) :-
option_seq(hyp_var,In,Between) ,
option_seq(klemt_var,Between,Between1) ,
option_seq(accepted,Between1,Between2) ,

option('<USTW>',seq(chr_cur_k),'</UST
W>',Between2,Between3),
option_seq(accepted,Between3,Between4),
option_seq(origin,Between4,Between5) , ! ,
 kind(Between5,Between6) ,
option('<VGTW>',seq(character),'</VGT
W>',Between6,Between7) ,
option('<RTW>',seq(character),'</RTW>',
Between7,Out) , ! .


/* kind/2 */
kind(In,Out) :-
( verb(In,Out)
; words_kw(In,Out)
; gender(In,Out) ) , ! .


/* nba_short/2 */
nba_short(In,Out) :-
'C'('<NBA>',In,Between) ,
character(Between,Between1) ,
'C'('</NBA>',Between1,Between2) ,
means_short(Between2,Between3) ,
'C'('</BT>',Between3,Out) , ! .


/* means_short/2 */
bet_short(In,Out) :-
option(subject(In,Between)) ,
option_seq(chr_gtl_br,Between,Between1) ,
seq(oaf,Between1,Between2) , ! ,
option(origin_means(Between2,Between3),

option('<BAF>',seq(chr_gtl_br_cur_ref),'<
/BAF>',Between3,Between4) ,
option_seq(chr_gtl_br,Between4,Between5,
option(example,Between5,Between6) ,
option(ref_kw_of_means(Between6,Out)) !


/* oaf/2 */
oaf(In,Out) :-
'C'('<OAF>',In,Between) ,
```

```
seq(chr_gtl_br_rom_ref,Between,Between1
) 'C'('</OAF>',Between1,Between2) ,
option(punctuation_mark(Between2,Out))


/* punctuation_mark/1 */
punctuation_mark(";").
punctuation_mark(",").
punctuation_mark(":").
punctuation_mark("; ").
punctuation_mark(", ").
punctuation_mark(": ").


/* bt_nba_short/2 */
bt_nba_short(In,Out) :-
'C'('<BT>',In,Between) ,
nba_short(Between,Out) , ! .


/* replace_bar/2 */
replace_bar(In,Out) :-
'C'('<SA>',In,Between) ,
alf_wissel(Between,Between1) ,
'C'('</SA>',Between1,Out) , ! .


/* key_word_extension/2 */
key_word_extension(In,Out) :-
seq(chr_a_k_u,In,Between) ,
option(replace_bar(Between,Out)) , ! .


/* origin/2 */
origin(In,Out) :-
'C'('<HKTW>',In,Between) ,
seq(chr_rom,Between,Between1) ,
'C'('</HKTW>',Between1,Out) , ! .


/* verb/2 */
verb(In,Out) :-
'C'('<VV>',In,Between) ,
seq(chr_cur_k,Between,Between1) ,
'C'('</VV>',Between1,Between2) ,
option_seq(accepted,Between2,Out) , ! .


/* words_kw/2 */
words_kw(In,Out) :-
'C'('<WSTW>',In,Between) ,
seq(chr_ref,Between,Between1) ,
'C'('</WSTW>',Between1,Between2) ,
option(character,Between2,Out) , ! .


/* gender/2 */
gender(In,Out) :-
```

option('<GTW>',seq(chr_rom),'</GTW>',I
n,Between), option('<MVTW>',
cont_gender, '</MVTW>',Between,Out) , ! .

/* cont_gender/2 */
cont_gender(In,Out) :-
seq(chr_cur_k_hkb,In,Between) ,
option('<USMV>',seq(character),
'</USMV>',Between,Out) , ! .

/* ref_kw_of_means/2 */
ref_kw_of_means(In,Out) :-
'C'('<VTW>',In,Between) , ! ,
ref(Between,Between1) ,
'C'('</VTW>',Between1,Out) , ! .
ref_kw_of_means(In,Out) :-
'C'('<VWB>',In,Between) , ! ,
ref(Between,Between1) ,
italic_means(Between1,Between2) ,
'C'(@(Y),Between2,Between3) ,
characters(Y,Contents) ,
list(List,Contents) ,
last(List,Last) ,
Last = 41 , /* ')' */
'C'('</VWB>',Between3,Out) ,
! .

/* chr_ref/2 */
chr_ref(In,Out) :-
(character(In,Out)
; ref_kw_of_means(In,Out)) , ! .

/* last/2 */
last([Element],Element) :- ! .
last([_|Rest],Element) :-
last(Rest,Element) , ! .

/* ref/2 */
ref(In,Out) :-
'C'('<CU>',In,Between) , ! ,
reference(Between,Between1) ,
'C'('</CU>',Between1,Between2) ,
('C'(@(Y),Between2,Out) , ! ,
characters(Y,Contents) ,
Contents = " (" ; Between2 = Out) , ! .
ref(In,Out) :-
'C'('<SY>',In,Between) , ! ,
reference(Between,Between1) ,
'C'('</SY>',Between1,Between2) ,
('C'(@(Y),Between2,Out) , ! ,

characters(Y,Contents) ,
Contents = " (";
Between2 = Out) , ! .
ref(In,Out) :-
reference(In,Out) , ! .

/* reference/2 */
reference(In,Out) :-
option(superior(In,Between)) ,
seq(character,Between,Between1) ,
option(special(Between1,Between2)) ,
option(replace_bar(Between2,Out)) , ! .

/* italic_means/2 */
italic_means(In,Out) :-
'C'('<CU>',In,Between) ,
character(Between,Between1) ,
'C'('</CU>',Between1,Out) , ! .

/* superior/2 */
superior(In,Out) :-
'C'('<SU>',In,Between) ,
character(Between,Between1) ,
'C'('</SU>',Between1,Out) , ! .

/* character/2 */
character(In,Out) :-
'C'(@(_),In,Out) , ! .

/* alf_wissel/2 */
alf_wissel(In,Out) :-
'C'(@(Y),In,Out) ,
characters(Y,Contents) ,
list([H|List],Contents) ,
length(List,Size) , ! ,
Size=2 , H= 42 , /* '*' */ ! .

/* italic/2 */
italic(In,Out) :-
'C'('<CU>',In,Between) ,
seq(chr_gtl_br,Between,Between1) ,
'C'('</CU>',Between1,Out) , ! .

/* roman/2 */
roman(In,Out) :-
'C'('<ROM>',In,Between) ,
seq(character,Between,Between1) ,
'C'('</ROM>',Between1,Out) , ! .
roman(In,Out) :-
'C'('</CU>',In,Between) ,

```
seq(character,Between,Between1) ,
'C'('<CU>',Between1,Out) , ! .

/* preferred_sp/2 */
preferred_sp(In,Out) :-
'C'('<VS>',In,Between) ,
option(superior(Between,Between1)) ,
seq(character,Between1,Between2) ,
option(replace_bar(Between2,Between3)) ,
'C'('</VS>',Between3,Out) , ! .

/* number/2 */
number(In,Out) :-
'C'('<NRTW>',In,Between) ,
character(Between,Between1) ,
'C'('</NRTW>',Between1,Out) , ! .

/* verkl_vorm/2 */
verkl_vorm(In,Out) :-
'C'('<TWVK>',In,Between) ,
key_word_extension(Between,Between1) ,
'C'('</TWVK>',Between1,Between2),
! , gramm(Between2,Out) , ! .

/* vrwl_vorm/2 */
vrwl_vorm(In,Out) :-
'C'('<TWVR>',In,Between) ,
key_word_extension(Between,Between1) ,
'C'('</TWVR>',Between1,Between2) , ! ,
gramm(Between2,Out) , ! .

/* vrwl_kwts/2 */
vrwl_kwts(In,Out) :-
'C'('<TWVR>',In,Between) ,
( 'C'('<TWTS>',Between,Between1) ,
key_word_extension(Between1,Between2) ,
'C'('</TWTS>',Between2,Between3) ;
key_word_extension(Between,Between3) ) ,
'C'('</TWVR>',Between3,Between4) , ! ,
gramm(Between4,Out) , ! .

/* meaning/2 */
meaning(In,Out) :-
( bt_nba_seq(In,Out,eerste)
; seq(contents,In,Between) ,
'C'('</BT>',Between,Out) ) , ! .

/* derived/2 */
derived(In,Out) :-
'C'('<TWA>',In,Between) ,
```

```
tw(Between,Between1) ,
'C'('</TWA>',Between1,Between2) , ! ,
gramm(Between2,Out) , ! .

/* hyp_var/2 */
hyp_var(In,Out) :-
'C'('<TWAV>',In,Between) ,
tw(Between,Between1) ,
'C'('</TWAV>',Between1,Out) , ! .

/* klemt_var/2 */
klemt_var(In,Out) :-
'C'('<TWKV>',In,Between) ,
key_word_extension(Between,Between1) ,
'C'('</TWKV>',Between1,Out) , ! .

/* accepted/2 */
accepted(In,Out) :-
'C'('<TS>',In,Between) ,
seq(chr_a_k,Between,Between1) ,
'C'('</TS>',Between1,Out) , ! .

/* same_sp/2 */
same_sp(In,Out) :-
'C'('<TWGS>',In,Between) ,
key_word_extension(Between,Between1) ,
'C'('</TWGS>',Between1,Between2) ,
gramm(Between2,Out) , ! .

/* synonym/2 */
synonym(In,Out) :-
'C'('<TWSY>',In,Between) ,
inh_kwsy(Between,Between1) ,
'C'('</TWSY>',Between1,Between2) ,
gramm(Between2,Out) , ! .

/* inh_kwsy/2 */
inh_kwsy(In,Out) :-
( key_word_extension(In,Out)
; klemt_var(In,Out) ) , ! .

/* gramm_means/2 */
gramm_means(In,Out) :-
option(pron_means(In,Between)) ,
option(origin_means(Between,Between1)) ,
kind_means(Between1,Between2) ,
option(subject(Between2,Between3)) ,
option('<RB>',seq(character),'</RB>',
Between3,Out) , ! .
```

```
/* kind_means/2 */
kind_means(In,Out) :-
( verb(In,Out)
; words_means(In,Out)
; gender_means(In,Out) ) , ! .


/* pron_means/2 */
pron_means(In,Out) :-
'C'('<USB>',In,Between) ,
seq(chr_k,Between,Between1) ,
'C'('</USB>',Between1,Out) , ! .


/* origin_means/2 */
origin_means(In,Out) :-
'C'('<HKB>',In,Between) ,
'C'('@(Y),Between,Between1) ,
characters(Y,Contents) ,
list(List,Contents) ,
length(List,Size) , ! ,
Size < 4 , 'C'('</HKB>',Between1,Out), ! .
/* words_means/2 */
words_means(In,Out) :-
'C'('<WSB>',In,Between) ,
seq(character,Between,Between1) ,
'C'('</WSB>',Between1,Out) , ! .


/* gender_means/2 */
gender_means(In,Out) :-
option('<GB>',seq(character),'</GB>',
In,Between) ,
option('<MVB>',seq(chr_cur_k_hkb),
'</MVB>',Between,Out) , ! .


/* bt_nba_seq/2 */
bt_nba_seq(In,Out,Keer) :-
( Keer = eerste ,
/* alleen de eerste keer wordt <BT> */
Keer1 = volgende , /* overgeslage*/
In = Between ;
'C'('<BT>',In,Between) ,
Keer1 = Keer ) , ! ,
'C'('<NBA>',Between,Between1) ,
character(Between1,Between2) ,
'C'('</NBA>',Between2,Between3) ,
seq(contents,Between3,Between4) ,
'C'('</BT>',Between4,Between5) , ! ,
( bt_nba_seq(Between5,Out,Keer1) ;
Between5 = Out ) .


/* synonym/2 */
```

```
synonym(In,Out) :-
'C'('<SY>',In,Between) ,
inh_sy(Between,Between1) ,
'C'('</SY>',Between1,Out) , ! .


/* inh_sy/2 */
inh_sy(In,Out) :-
( italic(In,Out)
; refijzing(In,Out)
; seq(chr_gtl_br,In,Out) ) , ! .


/* refijzing/2 */
refijzing(In,Out) :-
option(superior(In,Between)) ,
seq(character,Between,Between1) ,
means_gedeelte(Between1,Out) , ! .


/* means_gedeelte/2 */
means_gedeelte(In,Out) :-
( italic_means(In,Between),
'C'('@(Y),Between,Out) ,
characters(Y,Contents) ,
list(List,Contents) ,
last(List,Last) ,
Last = [41] /* ')' */
; In = Out ) , ! .


/* inferior/2 */
inferior(In,Out) :-
'C'('<IN>',In,Between) ,
character(Between,Between1) ,
'C'('</IN>',Between1,Out) , ! .


/* example/2 */
example(In,Out) :-
vb(In,Between) ,
option(character(Between,Between1)) ,
option(origin_means(Between1,Between2))
,
option(subject(Between2,Between3)) ,
option(regio(Between3,Between4)) ,
option(character(Between4,Between5)) ,
option(italic(Between5,Between6)) ,
means_vb_opt(Between6,Out) , ! .


/* vb/2 */
vb(In,Out) :-
'C'('<VB>',In,Between) ,
seq(chr_i_rom_stw_ref,Between,Between1)
,
```

```
'C'('</VB>',Between1,Out) , ! .

/* means_vb_opt/2 */
means_vb_opt(In,Out) :-
( seq(nbv,In,Out)
; 'C'('<BV>',In,Between) ,
option(origin_means(Between,Between1)) ,
option(words_means(Between1,Between2))
,
seq(inh_bv,Between2,Between3) ,
'C'('</BV>',Between3,Out)
; In = Out ) , ! .

/* nbv/2 */
nbv(In,Out) :-
'C'('<NBV>',In,Between) ,
character(Between,Between1) ,
'C'('</NBV>',Between1,Between2) ,
! ,
'C'('<BV>',Between2,Between3) ,
option(origin_means(Between3,Between4))
,
option(words_means(Between4,Between5))
,
seq(inh_bv,Between5,Between6) ,
'C'('</BV>',Between6,Out) , ! .

/* special/2 */
special(In,Out) :-
'C'('<BZ>',In,Between) ,
character(Between,Between1) ,
'C'('</BZ>',Between1,Out) , ! .

/* same_sp/2 */
same_sp(In,Out) :-
'C'('<GE>',In,Between) ,
option(superior(Between,Between1)) ,
seq(character,Between1,Between2) ,
option(replace_bar(Between2,Between3)) ,
'C'('</GE>',Between3,Out) , ! .

/* regio/2 */
regio(In,Out) :-
'C'('<RB>',In,Between) ,
seq(character,Between,Between1) ,
'C'('</RB>',Between1,Out) , ! .

/* subject/2 */
subject(In,Out) :-
'C'('<VGB>',In,Between) ,
```

```
seq(chr_rom,Between,Between1) ,
'C'('</VGB>',Between1,Out) , ! .

/* sub_kw/2 */
sub_kw(In,Out) :-
'C'('<STW>',In,Between) ,
inh_sub_kw(Between,Between1) ,
'C'('</STW>',Between1,Out) , ! .

/* inh_sub_kw/2 */
inh_sub_kw(In,Out) :-
( seq(chr_a_k,In,Out)
; 'C'('<AF>',In,Between) ,
seq(chr_k,Between,Between1) ,
'C'('</AF>',Between1,Out) ) , ! .

/* chr_gtl_br/2 */
chr_gtl_br(In,Out) :-
( character(In,Between) ,
option(exponent(Between,Out))
; breuk(In,Out) ) , ! .

/* chr_gtl_br_rom_ref/2 */
chr_gtl_br_rom_ref(In,Out) :-
( character(In,Between) ,
option(exponent(Between,Out))
; breuk(In,Out)
; roman(In,Out)
; ref_kw_of_means(In,Out) ) , ! .

/* chr_gtl_br_cur_ref/2 */
chr_gtl_br_cur_ref(In,Out) :-
( character(In,Between) ,
option(exponent(Between,Out))
; breuk(In,Out)
; italic(In,Out)
; ref_kw_of_means(In,Out) ) , ! .

/* exponent/2 */
exponent(In,Out) :-
'C'('<EP>',In,Between) ,
option(negatief(Between,Between1)) ,
character(Between1,Between2) ,
'C'('</EP>',Between2,Out) , ! .

/* breuk/2 */
breuk(In,Out) :-
'C'('<BR2>',In,Between) ,
character(Between,Between1) ,
'C'('<BRN2>',Between1,Between2) ,
```

```
character(Between2,Between3) ,
'C'('</BR2>',Between3,Out) , ! .

/* chr_k/2 */
chr_k(In,Out) :-
( character(In,Out)
; 'C'('<K>',In,Out) ) , ! .

/* chr_a_k/2 */
chr_a_k(In,Out) :-
( character(In,Out)
; 'C'('<A>',In,Out)
; 'C'('<K>',In,Out) ) , ! .

/* chr_a_k_u/2 */
chr_a_k_u(In,Out) :-
( character(In,Out)
; 'C'('<A>',In,Out)
; 'C'('<K>',In,Out)
; 'C'('<U>',In,Out) ) , ! .

/* chr_i_rom_stw_ref/2 */
chr_i_rom_stw_ref(In,Out) :-
( character(In,Out)
; roman(In,Out)
; sub_kw(In,Out)
; ref_kw_of_means(In,Out)
; 'C'('<I>',In,Out) ) , ! .

/* chr_rom/2 */
chr_rom(In,Out) :-
( character(In,Out)
; roman(In,Out) ) , ! .

/* chr_cur_k/2 */
chr_cur_k(In,Out) :-
( character(In,Out)
; italic(In,Out)
; 'C'('<K>',In,Out) ) , ! .

/* chr_cur_k_hkb/2 */
chr_cur_k_hkb(In,Out) :-
( character(In,Out)
; italic(In,Out)
;          roman(In,Out)
; 'C'('<K>',In,Out)
; origin_means(In,Out) ) , ! .

/* negatief/2 */
negatief(In,Out) :-
alf_wissel(In,Out) , ! .

/* nbr/2 */
nbr(In,Out) :-
'C'('<NBR>',In,Between) ,
character(Between,Between1) ,
'C'('</NBR>',Between1,Between2) , ! ,
gramm(Between2,Between3) ,
'C'('<BT>',Between3,Between4) , ! ,
meaning(Between4,Out) , ! .

/* contents/2 */
contents(In,Out) :-
'C'('</BT>',In,Out) , ! , fail.

contents(In,Out) :-
( chr_gtl_br(In,Out) , ! ;
italic(In,Out) , ! ;
synonym(In,Out) , ! ;
ref_kw_of_means(In,Out) , ! ;
example(In,Out), ! ;
'C'('<I>',In,Out) , ! ;
special(In,Out) , ! ;
same_sp(In,Out) , ! ;
          regio(In,Out) , ! ;
subject(In,Out) , ! ;
inferior(In,Out) , ! ;
sub_kw(In,Out) , ! ) .

/* inh_bv/2 */
inh_bv(In,Out) :-
( chr_gtl_br(In,Out) , ! ;
italic(In,Out) , ! ;
subject(In,Out) , ! ;
synonym(In,Out) , ! ;
special(In,Out) , ! ;
regio(In,Out) , ! ;
'C'('<I>',In,Out) , ! ;
ref_kw_of_means(In,Out) , ! ;
vb(In,Out) , ! ;
pron_means(In,Out) , ! ) .
```

H. SGML ↔ RTF Conversion

CPART.G

```
#header <<#include "charptr.h">>
<<
#include "charptr.c"          /* needed for $i-
reference */
int st;                       /* styledefinition-
                                 boolean */

main()
{
      ANTLR(rainbow(), stdin);     /* function call
                                      to "PCCTS" */
                                   printf("\n");
}
>>
```

F.G

```
#header <<
      #include "int.h"

#define STACKSIZE 10
>>

<<
int stack[STACKSIZE][STACKSIZE];
int sp;            /* this one represents the
                      bracketlevel */
int lokalsp;       /* this one represents the
                      i-th TAG on same level */

void
initstack(
) {
      int i;
```

```
        for (i = 0; i < STACKSIZE; i++)
            stack[i][0] = 0;
}
void
printstack(
){
     int x, y = 0;

     for (x = 0; x < STACKSIZE; x++) {
         y = 0;
         while (stack[x][y] != 0){
             printf("pos[%d][%d]=%d\n", x, y,
                                   stack[x][y]);
             y++;
         }
     }
}
void
push(
 int value
){
     stack[sp][lokalsp++] = value; /* put new
     state on stack */
     stack[sp][lokalsp] = 0;      /* mark top of
                                   stack with 0 */
}
void
pop(
){
     stack[sp--][0] = 0;          /* remove top of
                                   stack */
}
void
printSGMLclose(
){
     int i = 0;

     while (i <lokalsp) {
         switch(stack[sp][i])
         {
         case Bold : printf("</BOLD>");
         break;
         case Ital : printf("</ITALICS>");
```

```
                break;
                case Underl : printf("</UNDERLINED>");
                break;
                default : printf("NYI\n");
                }
        i++;
        }
}

main(
){
        initstack();
        ANTLR(document(), stdin);
        printstack();
        printf("\n");
}
>>

#token "\n"              <<zzline++; zzskip();>>
#token "\t"              <<printf("%s",
                         zzlextext);zzskip();>>
#token B_OPEN            "\{"
#token B_CLOSE           "\}"
#token RTFversion        "\\rtf[0-9]{(\ |\;)}"
#token Bold                "\\b{(\ |\;)}"
#token Ital                "\\i{(\ |\;)}"
#token Underl              "\\ul{(\ |\;)}"
#token Plain               "[A-Za-z\ ]+"
                           <<printf("%s",
                           zzlextext);>>

document :  <<sp = 0;>>
            B_OPEN <<sp++;>> docheader textpart
            B_CLOSE ;

docheader : RTFversion;

textpart : (
            (
             B_OPEN <<sp++;>>
             escapecodes textpart
             B_CLOSE << printSGMLclose();
                   pop();>>
             )
             |
            normaltext)* ;
```

```
escapecodes :      << lokalsp = 0; >>
                   (
                   (Bold << push(Bold);
                        printf("<BOLD>");>>) |
                   (Ital << push(Ital);
                        printf("<ITALICS>");>>) |
                   (Underl << push(Underl);
                        printf("<UNDERLINED>"); >> )
                   )+;

normaltext :       Plain ;
```

GRAMMAR.G

This file contains the grammar of a Rainbow-SGML document. It is very similar to the Rainbow DTD.

```
rainbow :   << st=0;>>
            "<RAINBOW>" {fileinfo} styinfo doc
            "</RAINBOW>" ;

fileinfo :  Fihdr {origin} dtdver Big ;
origin :    Origin quotedterm[0] ;
dtdver :    Dtdver quotedterm[0] ;
styinfo :   <<st=1;>> "<STYINFO>" (paratype)+
            (clftype)* "</STYINFO>"
            <<st=0;>> ;

doc :       "<DOC>" << printf("{\\rtf1\\ansi ");>>
            {head}
            ( ( ( para | illus | table | clf |
            idxterm )+ (struclvl)*)
            |
            (struclvl)+)
            "</DOC>" <<printf("}");>> ;

idxterm:    "<IDXTERM>" "</IDXTERM>" ;
escaped :   "\&\#168\;" | "\&\#169\;" | "\&\#199\;"
            | "\&\#200\;" |
            \&ldblquote\;" |
            "\&rdblquote\;" |
            ( "\&lquote\;" <<printf("`");>> ) |
            ( "\&rquote\;" <<printf("'");>> ) |
            ( "\&tab\;" <<printf("\t");>>) |
            "\&bsol\;" |
            "\&endash\;" |
            "\&emdash\;" |
```

```
                "\&bullet\;" |
                "\&lcub\;" |
                "\&rcub\;" |
                "\ \;" ;

paratype :    Parathdr (plfatt|clfatt)* name Big ;

clftype :     "<CLFTYPE" (clfatt)* name ">" ;

head :        Head { Paratype quotedterm[0] } Big
              {sysattrs} (para|paracont)+
              "</HEAD>" ;

para :        ParaPara quotedterm[0]
              (plfatt|clfatt)*
              { Id quotedterm[0] }
              { Continue quotedterm[0] }
              { Precret quotedterm[0] }
        Big
        {sysattrs} paracont { "</PARA>" };

name :                     Name quotedterm[0] ;
quotedterm[int i]:         Eql Quote CDATA <<if ((i==1)&&
                           (st==0)) printf("%s", $3);>>
                                              Quote ;
/* quotedterm gets a (boolean) parameter; if it's 1,
the CDTA string has to
be printed */

plfatt:       (Lindent quotedterm[0] ) |
              (Rindent quotedterm[0] ) |
              (Findent quotedterm[0] )|
              (Justif Eql Quote justpos Quote ) |
              (Linespc quotedterm[0] ) |
              (Spacebef quotedterm[0] ) |
              (Spaceaft quotedterm[0] ) |
              (Keepwith Eql Quote (Next | Prev )
              Quote )|
              (Tabstop quotedterm[0] ) |
              (Keeptog Eql Quote boolean Quote )|
              (Pgbrkbef Eql Quote boolean Eql Quote )|
              (Colbrkbef Eql Quote boolean Quote )|
              (Border quotedterm[0] );

justpos :    "LEFTJUST" |
             "CENTERJUST" |
             "RIGHTJUST" |
```

```
                "FULLJUST" |
                "INJUST" |
                "OUTJUST" ;
clfatt :        (Charset quotedterm[0] ) |
                (Fontfam quotedterm[1] <<printf("}");
                >> ) |
                (Fontsize quotedterm[1] <<printf("}");
                >> ) |
                (Fontweight Eql Quote
                      (Medium <<printf("\\m");>> | Bold <<
                      if (st==0)
                            printf("\\b");>>)
                      Quote ) |
                (Fontslant Eql Quote
                      ( Roman <<printf("\\i0");>> |
                       Ital <<if (st==0) printf("\\i");
                       >> ) Quote ) |
                Scoreloc Eql Quote CDATA
                <<printf("\\ul");>> Quote ) |
                (Scoretype Eql Quote (Single
                <<printf("\\ul");>>
                      | Double <<
                      printf("\\uldb");>>
                      | Dotted << printf("\\uld");>>
                      ) Quote ) |
                (VertOff quotedterm[0] ) |
                (Foregnd quotedterm[0] ) |
                (Backgnd quotedterm[0] ) |
                (Lowcase Eql Quote
                      (SmallCaps <<printf("\\scaps");>> |
                      FullCaps <<printf("\\caps");
                      >> ) Quote ) |
                (Changebar quotedterm[0] ) |
                (Outline Eql Quote boolean Quote ) |
                (Hidden Eql boolean <<printf("\\v");>>) ;

boolean :       CDATA ;

struclvl:       "<STRUCLVL>" {sysattrs} head
                      para|illus|table|anchor)*
                      (struclvl)*
                "</STRUCLVL>" ;

paracont:       "<PARACONT>" <<printf("\\par ");>>
```

```
                  (pcont | namedclf | clf | idxterm)*
                  {"</PARACONT>"} ;

illus :           "<ILLUS" { "ID=" "\"" CDATA "\""
                  }"\>" {sysattrs} (graphic | eqn)
                  {"</ILLUS>" };

graphic :         Graphic    Filename quotedterm[0]
                             Format quotedterm[0] Big;

eqn :             "<EQN FORMAT=" "\"" CDATA "\"" ">"
                  {sysattrs} {eqncont}        {"</EQN>" } ;
pcont :               (CDATA << printf("%s", $1);>>) |
                  escaped |
                  anchor | xref | autogen | graphic |
                  eqn |              note ;

eqncont :   ""<eqncont>" CDATA "</eqncont>";

namedclf :   "<NAMEDCLF" name { "ID=" "\"" CDATA "\"" }
             ">"
             {sysattrs} (pcont|clf)+ "</NAMEDCLF>" ;

clf :        Clfhdr <<printf("{");>>
             (clfatt )*
             { Id quotedterm[0] } Big <<printf(" ");>>
             {sysattrs} (pcont)* "</CLF>"
             <<printf("}");>> ;

note :       "<NOTE>" {sysattrs} (para | illus |
             table )*
             "</NOTE>" ;

anchor :     Anchor Id quotedterm[0] Big
             { (CDATA | clf)* "</ANCHOR>"} ;

xref :       "<XREF" "REFID=" "\"" CDATA "\"" ">"
             (CDATA | clf)+
             "</XREF>" ;

autogen :    "<AUTOGEN>" {sysattrs} CDATA
             "</AUTOGEN>" ;

datafld :    "<DATAFLD" "TYPE=" "\"" CDATA "\"" ">"
             CDATA "</DATAFLD>" ;

textfld :    "<TEXTFLD" "TYPE=" "\"" CDATA "\"" ">"
             (CDATA|clf)+
             "</TEXTFLD>" ;
```

```
sysattrs :  "<SYSATTRS>" (sysattr)* {
            "</SYSATTRS>" } ;

sysattr :   "<SYSATTR" "ATTRNAME=" "\"" CDATA "\""
            ">" "</SYSATTR>" ;
table :     "<table" { "ID=" "\" "CDATA "\"" }
                    ">"
            (tgroup|colspec|tbody|thead|spanspec)+
            {"</table>" };

tgroup :    Tgroup Cols quotedterm[0] Big
            (colspec)* (spanspec)* {thead} tbody
            "</tgroup>" ;

colspec :   Colspec    {Colnum quotedterm[0] }
                       {Colname quotedterm[0] }
                       {Colwidth quotedterm[0] }
                       {Align quotedterm[0] } Big;

spanspec :  Spanspec   Namest quotedterm[0]
                       Nameend quotedterm[0]
                       Spanname quotedterm[0]
                       {Align quotedterm[0] } Big ;

thead :     "    <thead>" (row)+ "</thead>" ;

tbody:               "<tbody>" (row|para|CDATA)+
                     "</tbody>" ;

row :       Rowstart (entry)+ Rowend ;

entry :              Entry        {Colname quotedterm[0] }
                              {Spanname quotedterm[0] } Big
            (pcont | para | clf | illus | idxterm)*
            "</entry>" ;
```

TOKENDEF.G

This file contains the tokendefinitions for all tokens that can be used in an SGML
document. Some of the tokens have an action attached (action == C-function)

```
#lexclass START
#token "\n"        <<zzline++; zzskip();>>
#token Fihdr       "<FILEINFO" <<zzmode(INFO);>>
#token ParaPara    "<PARA\ PARATYPE"
                   <<zzmode(LEVELFORMAT);>>
#token Parathdr    "<PARATYPE" <<zzmode(LEVELFORMAT);>>
#token Anchor      "<ANCHOR"   <<zzmode(LEVELFORMAT);>>
#token Clfhdr      "<CLF"<<zzmode(LEVELFORMAT);>>
```

```
#token Colspec     "<colspec"  <<zzmode(LEVELFORMAT);>>
#token Entry       "<entry"    <<zzmode(LEVELFORMAT);>>
#token Spanspec    "<spanspec"<<zzmode(LEVELFORMAT);>>
#token Graphic     "<GRAPHIC"  <<zzmode(LEVELFORMAT);>>
#token Tgroup      "<tgroup"   <<zzmode(LEVELFORMAT);>>
#token Head        "<HEAD"     <<zzmode(LEVELFORMAT);>>
#token Rowend      "</row>"
#token Rowstart    "<row>"
#token CDATA       "[A-Za-z\[\]\.\,\-\;\:0-9\
                   \/\(\)\*\~\"\_\|\']+"

#lexclass INFO
#token "\n"              <<zzskip();zzline++;>>
#token "\ "             <<zzskip();>>
#token Quote            "\""
#token Origin           "ORIGIN"
#token Dtdver           "DTDVER"
#token Eql              "\="
#token CDATA            "[A-Za-z \[ \] \- \.0-
                        9i\,\/\~\_\|\']+"
#token Big "\>"         <<zzmode(START);>>

#lexclass LEVELFORMAT
#token "\n"              <<zzskip();zzline ++;>>
#token "\ "             <<zzskip();>>
#token Backgnd           "BACKGROUND"
#token Bold             "Bold"
#token Border            "BORDER"
#token Changebar        "CHANGE\-BAR"
#token Charset          "CHARSET"
#token Colbrkbef        "COL\-BRK\-BEFORE"

#token Colnum            "colnum"
#token Colname           "colname"
#token Align             "align"
#token Colwidth          "colwidth"
#token Nameend           "nameend"
#token Namest            "namest"
#token Spanname          "spanname"
#token Cols              "COLS"

#token Continue          "CONTINUE"
#token Dotted            "Dotted"
#token Double            "Double"
#token Eql               "\="
#token Filename          "FILENAME"
```

```
#token Findent            "FIRST\-INDENT"
#token Fontfam            "FONT\-FAMILY"
                          <<printf("{\\v %s ",
                          zzlextext);>>
#token Fontsize           "FONT\-SIZE"<<printf("{\\v %s
                          ", zzlextext);>>
#token Fontslant          "FONT\-SLANT"
#token Fontweight         "FONT\-WEIGHT"
#token Foregnd            "FOREGROUND"
#token Format             "FORMAT"
#token FullCaps           "FullCaps"
#token Hidden             "HIDDEN"
#token Id                 "ID"
#token Ital               "Ital"
#token Justif             "JUSTIFICATION"
#token Keeptog            "KEEP\-TOGETHER"
#token Keepwith           "KEEP\-WITH"
#token Lindent            "LEFT\-INDENT"
#token Linespc            "LINE\-SPACING"
#token Lowcase            "LOWERCASE\-DISPLAY"
#token Medium             "Medium"
#token Name               "NAME"
#token Next               "Next"
#token Outline            "OUTLINE"
#token Paratype           "PARATYPE"
#token Pgbrkbef           "PG\-BRK\-BEFORE"
#token Precret            "PRECED\-HARD\-RETURNS"
#token Prev               "Prev"
#token Quote              "\""
#token Rindent            "RIGHT\-INDENT"
#token Roman              "Roman"
#token Scoreloc           "SCORE\-LOCATION"
#token Scoretype          "SCORE\-TYPE"
#token SmallCaps          "SmallCaps"
#token Spaceaft           "SPACE\-AFTER"
#token Spacebef           "SPACE\-BEFORE"
#token Tabstop            "TAB\-STOPS"
#token VertOff            "VERTICAL\-OFFSET"
#token CDATA              "[A-Za-z \[ \] \,\- \. 0-
                          9\/\~\_\|\']+"

#token Big                "\>"  <<zzmode(START);>>

#lexclass START
```

I. Interesting FTP and WWW Sites

FTP Sites

Below is a selection of prominent FTP sites who may be helpful to you in providing update information on the newest tools for electronic document management. Using search engines like Alta Vista, Lycos etc. however may bring you many other ones.

FTP.MICROSOFT.COM	The Microsoft FTP site, patches and extensions for Microsoft products such as MS-DOS, Windows, Windows Help compiler, Video for Windows, drivers, etc., can be found here.
FTP.CICA.INDIANA.EDU	The CICA site where a large repository of Windows applications, drivers, tools, examples and documentation, freeware and shareware is kept. The well-known CICA-CDs are composed of a selection of this site.
FTP-OS2.CDROM.COM	Also known as HOBBES, the site where OS/2 stuff can be found. It is like the CICA site but for OS/2.
WUARCHIVE.WUSTL.EDU	MS-Windows and MS-DOS site, Simtel mirror.
OAK.OAKLAND.EDU	MS-Windows and MS-DOS site, Simtel mirror.
RTFM.MIT.EDU.	One of the sites with the WWW Beginners Index and the WWW FAQ (Frequently Asked Questions).
FTP.LAW.CORNELL.EDU	The home site of the WWW client Cello (in the directory /pub/LII/Cello).

FTP.NCSA.UIUC.EDU	The home site of the WWW client Mosaic (Windows version in /PC/Mosaic).
FTP.IFI.UIO.NO	An SGML site.
FTP.EBT.COM	Electronic Book Technology company site; Producer of Dynatext.

WWW Sites

HTTP://INFO.CERN.CH/hypertext/WWW/Tools/Filters.html
WWW tools

HTTP://ONEWORLD.WA.COM/htmldev/devpage/dev-page.html
WWW tools

HTTP://WWW.NCSA.UIUC.EDU/SDG/Software/Mosaic/MetaIndex.html
NCSA Info Resource Meta-Index

HTTP://LIFE.ANU.EDU.AU/education/hypermedia.html
Hypermedia and the Internet

HTTP://WCL-RS.BHAM.AC.UK/~djh/index.html
Games FAQ

HTTP://WWW.CS.COLORADO.EDU/home/mcbryan/wwww.htmlsome
WWW Worm (comparable to
Veronica for Gopher or Archie
for FTP)

About the Authors

The authors were all members of the HyPresS Research Project from 1988 until 1993, and also of the DELTA SAFE and DELTA COSYS Projects, funded by the European Commission at the same period.

The project leader at Twente University was Piet Kommers. Alcindo Ferreira was the software engineer who built the software packages for document manipulation, but who was also in charge of working out the delivery reports for the European Commission. Alex Kwak made his contribution to the projects and this book as the final work for his Master's degree in Computer Science. He de-veloped a navigational support system for hypermedia and his contributions have been brought together in Chapter 16.

Dr. Piet Kommers is Lecturer and Researcher in the Faculty of Educational Science and Technology at Twente University in the Netherlands. His specialities are hypermedia, knowledge representation and concept mapping. He was Director and Scientific Editor of NATO's Advanced Research Workshop on 'Cognitive Tools for Learning' in 1991 (NATO ASI Series F, Vol. 81, Springer 1992). Based upon Graph Theory and SGML meta-information he defined document management procedures for the design and the maintenance of technical documentation and CD-ROM based encyclopedias for learning. His dissertation, 'Hyper-text and the Acquisition of Knowledge', addressed the evoked learning effects while studying via hypertext. He is main editor of *Cognitive Tools for Learning* (Springer 1992), *Hypermedia Learning Environments; Instructional Design and Integration* (Lawrence Erlbaum 1996), and *Media and Telematic Technologies for Education in East European Countries* (Twente University Press, 1997). He was also Visiting Professor and Consultant in East China Normal University at Shanghai, the Glushkov Institute for Cybernetics at Kiev, Colorado University at Denver, and Jordan University at Amman.

Contact address:
Dr. P.A.M. Kommers; University of Twente, Faculty of Educational Technology Box 217, 7500 AE Enschede, The Netherlands
Office: Tel.   +31 53 4893576 or +31 53 4893611, Fax   +31 53 4894580
         E-mail: kommers@edte.utwente.nl

Alcinda F. Ferreira, B.Sc., is computer engineer and hypermedia specialist. While contributing to the projects SAFE and COSYS he developed quite a number of programs for navigation in large documents. TextVision-3D is one of them. It allows students and teachers to negotiate about concept structures and complex relations in knowledge. Ferreira participated in many scientific events as a system designer and a computer consultant. His recent specialty is communication technology in relation to ISDN and Internet services. He can be reached via ferreira@edte.utwente.nl

Alex Kwak is computer scientist in the fields of databases, user interface design, and software engineering in general. He was successful in the implementation and didactic management of computer programming courses in the Faculty of Educational Science and Technology. Alex contributed to this book by writing Chapter 16 on rule-based navigation in hypermedia.

Figures and Tables

Figure 1. The traditional publishing process 6
Figure 2. Extended production process for conventional materials................ 6
Figure 3. The hypermedia publishing process, based on new material 7
Figure 4. Steps to take... 9
Figure 5. Hypermedia production... 12
Figure 6. Two initiative streams for authoring hypermedia......................... 13
Figure 7. Publisher-driven hypermedia project.. 14
Figure 8. Project initiated by publisher and electronic company 15
Figure 9. Postponed acceptance model 16
Figure 10. Corporate-driven publishing.. 17
Figure 11. Technology supported migration.. 17
Figure 12. Re-exploitation of corporate information resources 18
Figure 13. Overview of a large publishing corporation................................ 28
Figure 14. Organization diagram of management structure 29
Figure 15. Organization diagram of production management 30
Figure 16. Administration of the pick-and-mix process.............................. 32
Figure 17. Financial administration.. 34
Figure 18. Function and process 38
Figure 19. Data exchange 39
Figure 20. Work flow diagram 43
Figure 21. SGML document structure... 47
Figure 22. WWW Servers on the Internet 53
Figure 23. The MHEG composite object can be a MHEG document or a part of it 57
Figure 24. Three phases... 74
Figure 25. Differential streams for hypertext applications........................... 77
Figure 26. The stack as a mechanism for nested brackets 90
Figure 27. Compiling, importing, indexing, direct storage 92
Figure 28. Entry roads for DynaText resources 93
Figure 29a. Simple outline of a document.. 107
Figure 29b. Document outline with heading levels 1 and 2 107
Figure 29c. Dragging headings in the outline view 108
Figure 30. Implicit and explicit information.. 115
Figure 31. Adding explicit information 116
Figure 32. Stages in the document life cycle.. 118
Figure 33. Products and formats 118
Figure 34. An embedded control and a custom control 120
Figure 35. The index list dialogue 123
Figure 36. The full search dialogue 123
Figure 37. DynaText scheme... 127
Figure 38. Upgrading paths for plain text 131
Figure 39. Level of hypermedia relations 145
Figure 40. Browsing 145
Figure 41. A sample concept map 146

Figure 42. Strongly connected (directed) sub-graphs.. 147
Figure 43. Blocks in the graph.. 148
Figure 44. Three cliques in a graph... 148
Figure 45. Basic structures... 150
Figure 46. Example of recursions.. 159
Figure 47. On a line.. 167
Figure 48. In a circle 167
Figure 49. Evenly distributed 167
Figure 50. The standard graph 169
Figure 51. First part of the first phase: Assignment of levels 169
Figure 52. Second part of first phase: Addition of dummy nodes................................ 170
Figure 53. Second phase: minimizing the number of crossings 170
Figure 54. Third phase: Parents (where possible) centered above siblings and
            straightened lines.. 170
Figure 55. The final graph. The dummy nodes get a radius of one and
            the direction arrows are drawn in again 171
Figure 56a. The 3D concept space.. 173
Figure 56b. A sample 3D network display.. 173
Figure 57. Grid 174
Figure 58. The simplified structure of hypertext system used.................................... 181
Figure 59. Nothing selected in the navigation strategy dialogue................................. 182
Figure 60. Outcome of Figure 59... 182
Figure 61. First strategy selected in navigation strategy settings dialogue................... 183
Figure 62. Outcome of Figure 61... 183
Figure 63. Distribution of number of nodes with certain weights................................ 185
Figure 64. Finding a relation between nodes 1 and 2.. 186
Figure 65. 'Find Relation' dialogue with instruction to find the relation between
            coughing and sneeze, one way only and with a maximal depth of two 187
Figure 66. Outcome of Figure 65... 187
Figure 67. 'Find Relation' dialogue with instruction to find
            the backwards relation between coughing and sneeze,
            one way only and with a maximal depth of 2 188
Figure 68. Outcome of Figure 67... 188
Figure 69. 'Find Relation' dialogue with instruction to find the relation between
            coughing and sneeze, both ways and with a maximal depth of two.............. 189
Figure 70. Outcome of Figure 69... 189
Figure 71. Paper document flow 194
Figure 72. New document flow, added steps in bold 195
Figure 73. Structure of references.. 197
Figure 74. The most central concepts of the entire medical encyclopedia.................... 225
Figure 75. Concepts relevant to drugs.. 225
Figure 76. Detailed information... 226
Figure 77. More concepts shown.. 226
Figure 78. AIDS... 227
Figure 79. Inside view: Looking from drugs to AIDS... 227
Figure 80. AIDS, blood and pregnancy 228
Figure 81. Relations.. 228
Figure 82. New network centered around 'eye' 229
Figure 83: Basis window for reading reference material 231
Figure 84: Response window 231
Figure 85: Text entry fields, selection or list fields.. 231
Figure 86. Start-up screen.. 232
Figure 87. Open text dialogue... 233

Figure 88. Open pictures dialogue..233
Figure 89. Open overview dialogue...234
Figure 90. Select a database dialogue...234
Figure 92. An overview window with an overview presented
            according to outdegree..236
Figure 93: Selecting and deselecting a node..237
Figure 94: After selecting a node..237
Figure 95. Dragging a concept node from one network to another...............238
Figure 96. Opening an article from an overview..238
Figure 98. Menu bar of overview window..239
Figure 99. Scaling off and scaling on..240
Figure 100. Dialogue for changing settings..241
Figure 101. The introductory message..243
Figure 102. User name dialogue...243
Figure 103. The full and reduced menu bars..244
Figure 104. The network window...244
Figure 105. The palette and some of its states...245
Figure 106. The network menu...246
Figure 107. The different cursors...246
Figure 108. Concept name dialogue...247
Figure 109. 'Name in Use' dialogue...247
Figure 110. Newly placed globe..247
Figure 111. Edit name dialogue..247
Figure 112. Dragging from the source node to the target node.....................248
Figure 114. Releasing the mouse button stops dragging and creates a relation..............249
Figure 113. Above the target node: During dragging a node is inverted
            when the cursor is above it..249
Figure 115. A possible network with multiple nodes and relations...............249
Figure 116. Dragging some nodes from front to back.....................................251
Figure 117. A text window (right) with network window...............................252
Figure 118. The 'rotate' dialogue...253
Figure 119. Pushing an arrow...253
Figure 120. A view of the rotation process: The geographical concepts
            are on the right and the structural concepts are on the left..........254
Figure 121. Rotating 90 degrees from the bottom to the front:
            Leeward Island concepts appear on a vertical line......................254
Figure 122. Rotating...255

Table 1.   Fourteen stages in hypermedia production.......................................19
Table 2.   Tabular and outline author and editor plan....................................111
Table 3.   Hoede's status to in- and outdegree..161
Table 4.   Structural measures for concept nodes in a graph..........................163
Table 5.   Graph Connections...169

Index

A

adjacency **157**; 161
    matrix **158**; 159
administrative system 26
annotation 101
Anthonisse 162
Apple Quick Time 95
ASCII 64; 119
ASN.1 55
author 7; **67**; 102
    second 7
author and editor plans 109
authoring 3; 98
    action 67
    hypermedia 13
    phase 72
    process 67; 71
    step 67

B

Bakker 150; 166
Bavelas 163
betweenness **157**; 160
bills 26
bitmaps 133
block 147
BMP 65
Borland Paradox 92; 100
Brachman 153; 166
bridge 147
browsing 124; 162
BRS-Search 101

C

CALS 46; **58**; 205; 219
Cartwright 146
Castelli 149
categories 176
CD-ROM 120; 201

CDT **69**; 70
centrality 160; 164; 165
CGM 58
citation indexing 156
CITED 26
client server 92
clique 147
coaching 176; 204
Colazzo 142; 149
compiling 91
Component Display Theory **69**
Computer Graphics Metafile (CGM) 58
Computer-aided Acquisition and Logistics Support (CALS) 46; 205; 219
Computer-aided Acquisition and Logistics Support (CALS) **58**
concept map
    displaying 167
        3D 171
connectivity 162
considerations
    macro 69
    micro 69
contextual awareness 142
Continuous Acquisition and Life cycle Support (CALS) **58**
copyrights 24
cutpoint 147
cyclic relations 149

D

database 67
DELTA V; 142
    HYPERATE 143
design considerations 69
designing instructional texts 68
directed graph 144; 149
distance **157**; 160
DLL 65
DocToHelp 63; 133
Document Template Definition 117
Documentary Information Systems 119

DTD 76; 82; 87; 117; **219**
DynaText 91; 101; 119; 127

E

editor 71; 102
Elaboration Theory 70
electronic publishers 26
Elm & Woods 144
embedded resources 95
ET **70**
explicit information 115
expressiveness 166
extrinsic weight 156

F

Faust 69
Fiderio 152
flow control 75
FolioViews 101
Freeman 157; 160
French 158
Frisse 142; 153; 155; 165
full text search 121
Furuta 148

G

Garfield 156
genealogical research 197
Gleditsch 157
GML 13
     -tag, (S) 72
GRADAP **158**; 161
graph theory 142; 165

H

Hamming distance 154
Harary 146
Hardman 143
HelpWizard 133
hierarchy 164
Hintzman 153; 154
history list 124
Hoede 150; 158; 160; 166; 176
Hoede's Status **160**; 161; 162; 163; 164
Hoivik 157
hotspot 61; 64; 96; 124; 143
HTML 52
Hubbell 158; 161
Hubbell's Status 162

hyperbase 75
     existing 75
     use 75
hypergraph 145
HyperGraphics 96; 133
Hyperlearning
     session 7
hypermedia 3; 5; 6; 7; 8; 76
     authoring 13
     database 75
          application 75
     enterprise 8
     exploitation 12
     product 7
     production **3**; 6; 7; 8; 9; 12
     publisher 3
     resource 7
     system 5; 7; 8; 13; 72; 176
Hypermedia/Time-based Structuring
Language (HyTime) **51**
HyperODA 221
hypertext 76; 180; 220
     development 72
     instructional 204
     system 67; 71; 73
HyTime 51; 220

I

IBM OS/2 Help 101
Implicit information 115
importing 92
importing material 67
incremental information growth 193
indegree 251
indexing 91
influence 160
information
     semantic
          explicit 78
          implicit 78
     tagged 93
     types 93
     typographical 62; 77
InStEd 128
instructional
     material 204
interactivity 6
intrinsic weight 156

K

Katz 158; 160
Katz' Index 160
Katz' Status 162
Kaufer 150
keyword lists 122
Kibby 143; 154
Kommers 165

L

L^AT_EX 222
Levesque 153; 166
ligature expansion 122
Linking 220
Lotus AmiPro 62; 79; 100
Lotus Notes 100

M

Macro Mind Director 68
magazine 194
maintenance information 201
managing hypermedia documents 98
managing material 98
material
    preparing
        text 76
Mayes 154
McHill 156
MegaDoc 100
Merrill 69
metafiles 133
MHEG **55**; 221
Mic 149
Microsoft Access 92
Microsoft Encarta 127
Microsoft Help 62; 63; 64; 76; 91; 92; 94; 101;
120; 124; 133
Microsoft Multimedia Viewer 62; 63; 64; 92;
101; 120; 124
    publishing tool kit 120
Microsoft Video for Windows 95
Microsoft Word 62; **63**; 79; 81; 95; 100; 106;
120
MIDI 68
MINERVA 154
multimedia 13
Multimedia and Hypermedia Expert Group
(MHEG) 221
Musical Instruments Digital Interface
(MIDI) 68

N

navigating 204
navigation 176; 177
navigation engine 180
Nelson 152
Neuwirth 150
newspaper 194; 201
Norman 146
N-P complete 165
n-sequency 158; 159; 161

O

Object Link Embedding 96
OCR **78**; 116; 196
    applications 78
Office Document Architecture (ODA) 221
Open System Interconnection (OSI) 58
Optical Character Recognition 116
OSI 58
outdegree 252
outlining tool 105; 106
OWL Guide 101; 119

P

Pask 164
PDES 58
permeability 162
Peterson 147
Petri net 165; 204
    graph 147
Pick and Mix system 26
popular formats 45
procedures 25
producing
    hypermedia 9
product catalogue 205
Product Data Exchange using STEP (PDES)
58
production planning 98
PROLOG 177; 180
Publish and Subscribe 96
publisher 7; 13

R

reference works 202
references
    automatic **82**
Reigeluth 69

resources
    embedded 95
    linked 95; **96**
    picture 95
    video 95
reusing 25
revising 24; 102; 105
Rich Text Format (RTF) 76; 221
rights 24
RoboHelp 63; 133
Rowe 168
royalties 24; 26
RTF 58; 62; 63; 64; 76; 80; 82; 87; 91; 95; 101; 117; 133; 134; **221**
RTF-reader 86
rubric 73
rubrics 176
navigational 177
RUSH 162; 163

S

sales 24
Salton's algorithm 156
scenario 3; 6
search categories 121
search query operators 121
second author 71; 72; 73; 221
semantic information 46
SGML 46; 51; 52; 55; 58; 75; 78; 80; 81; 82; 87; 91; 101; **221**
    DTD 62
    -editor 75
    tags 62
Smith 153
software houses 26
Standard for The Exchange of Product model data (STEP) 58
Standard Multimedia Scripting Languages (SMSL) 220
Status Index 160; 161; 163; 164
STEP 58
stop words 122

Stotts 148
styles
    paragraph 78
Sugiyama 168
Sybase 100

T

Tanimoto similarity 154
target
    age 68
    education 68
    interest 68
taxonomy 149
Taylor 158; 161
technical documentation 201
$T_{E}X$ 58; 78; **222**
text
    structured **79**
    tagged 80
    unstructured **79**
TextVision 172
TextVision 3D 174
Textvision3D **243**
title delivery 193
Topics 101
tractability 166
Travers 143
typographical information 46

V

versioning 101; 105

W

Waterworth 143
Windows95 105
word stemming 122
WordPerfect 62; **64**; 79; 100
WWW 52
WYSIWYG **61**; 64; 65; **222**

Springer
and the
environment

At Springer we firmly believe that an
international science publisher has a
special obligation to the environment,
and our corporate policies consistently
reflect this conviction.
We also expect our business partners –
paper mills, printers, packaging
manufacturers, etc. – to commit
themselves to using materials and
production processes that do not harm
the environment. The paper in this
book is made from low- or no-chlorine
pulp and is acid free, in conformance
with international standards for paper
permanency.

Printing: Mercedesdruck, Berlin
Binding: Buchbinderei Lüderitz & Bauer, Berlin